Just environments

'A timely and well-edited interdisciplinary anthology . . . The survey essay on rights, justice and ecology will be especially valuable for orienting novices to the fundamental concepts in these fields. There is a dearth of good material in environmental studies that integrates the perspectives of philosophy, geography and the social sciences. This volume is a welcome exception.'

Dale Jamieson, *University of Colorado at Boulder*

'Written by philosophers, academics in other disciplines and members of environmental institutes, it covers both the philosophical and factual aspects of our environmental predicament, and should be of interest to students and scholars in a wide range of disciplines.'

Nigel Dower, *University of Aberdeen*

Can we do what we want with other species? What happens when conflicting international interests get involved in global environmental management? What do we owe future generations? *Just Environments* is a multidisciplinary examination of these issues and of the social, political and historical contexts within which they are discussed. It is the first book to consider such a wide range of issues from a variety of perspectives that includes philosophy, politics and ecology.

The organization of the book is exceptionally clear. Part I explores the ethical, sociopolitical, ecological and geographical principles and contexts that frame environmental debates. The remaining parts examine three key themes in greater detail: our obligations to future generations (Part II), our relations with the developing world (Part III) and our treatment of non-human species (Part IV). Each part in turn divides into three chapters which approach their common theme from three distinct perspectives: one chapter argues from the position of moral philosophy, another identifies the social and political factors that influence current practice, and the third examines the geographical, ecological and other scientific considerations that are crucial for any informed debate in these areas.

Written by acknowledged authorities in their respective fields, at a level accessible to students from various backgrounds, *Just Environments* will be particularly useful for students on environmental studies courses. It will also appeal to students of ethics, international relations, ecology, geography and population studies.

David E. Cooper is Professor of Philosophy at the University of Durham. **Joy A. Palmer** is Reader in Education and Director of the Centre for Research on Environmental Thinking and Awareness at the University of Durham. Both have published widely; they are the editors of *The Environment in Question* (Routledge, 1992).

Just environments

Intergenerational, international and interspecies issues

Edited by David E. Cooper
and Joy A. Palmer

London and New York

First published 1995
by Routledge
11 New Fetter Lane, London EC4P 4EE

Simultaneously published in the USA and Canada
by Routledge
29 West 35th Street, New York, NY 10001

Typeset in Times by LaserScript, Mitcham, Surrey
Printed and bound in Great Britain by
Mackays of Chatham PLC, Chatham, Kent

British Library Cataloguing in Publication Data
A catalogue record for this book is available from the British Library.

Library of Congress Cataloging in Publication Data
Just environments: intergenerational, international, and interspecies issues/edited by
   David E. Cooper and Joy A. Palmer.
   p. cm.
   Includes bibliographical references and index.
   1. Environmental sciences.   2. Human ecology.   I. Cooper, David Edward.
   II. Palmer, Joy.
   GE105.J87   1995
   304.2–dc20   94–23953
                                                                         CIP

ISBN 0–415–10335–5 (hbk)
ISBN 0–415–10336–3 (pbk)

Contents

Illustrations

Contributors

Brenda Almond is Professor of Moral and Social Philosophy at the University of Hull.

James P. Barber is Professor of Politics and Master of Hatfield College at the University of Durham.

Holly B. Brough has been a researcher at the Worldwatch Institute, Washington, D.C.

John I. Clarke is Emeritus Professor of Geography at the University of Durham and Chairman of the Population and Environment Committee of the International Union for the Scientific Study of Population

David E. Cooper is Professor of Philosophy at the University of Durham.

Anna K. Dickson is Lecturer in Politics at the University of Durham.

Alan T. Durning directs the Northwest Environment Watch, Seattle, Washington.

Barry S. Gower is Pro-Vice-Chancellor and Senior Lecturer in Philosophy at the University of Durham.

Andrew Johnson is a partner in the White Horse Press.

Steven Luper-Foy is Professor of Philosophy at Trinity University, San Antonio, Texas.

Joy A. Palmer is Reader in Education and Director of the Centre for Research on Environmental Thinking and Awareness at the University of Durham.

Robert Prosser is Lecturer in Recreation and Tourism Studies in the Centre for Urban and Regional Studies at the University of Birmingham.

I. G. Simmons is Professor of Geography at the University of Durham.

Léon Tabah is Chairman of CICRED, and former Head of the Population Division, United Nations.

Preface

There are issues concerning the proper treatment of human beings and other living creatures which, while never entirely ignored, have taken on much greater prominence through the recent explosion of interest in the impact of human practices on the environment. While these issues are not sharply distinct, they can be conveniently grouped under the headings of 'intergenerational', 'international' and 'interspecies' issues. What are our responsibilities to the generations which will follow our own, and how should they be discharged? What are our obligations in the West to less developed nations, and how might they be met? Should we concern ourselves, for reasons other than self-interest, with the impact of our way of life upon animals and the wider living world?

It is issues such as these which are addressed in this book, the contributions to which – after a trio of 'framework' chapters – are grouped into the three areas just indicated. The three 'framework' chapters provide overviews of the different perspectives from which issues in all those areas may be approached, and in each of the other parts those perspectives are represented. The questions illustrated above are normative questions: in a broad sense of the term, they are questions about *justice*. There are, therefore, chapters of a philosophical kind, exercises in 'applied ethics', on each of the issues. Informed answers to our questions, however, must clearly rely upon an understanding of the social and political realities which provide the contexts in which policies, however morally enlightened, must try to operate. Each part, therefore, contains a chapter examining those realities. Nor are informed answers possible without an understanding of the kind provided by environmental scientists, agriculture and population experts, and geographers of current and potential developments in the effects of our policies and practices upon the environment. Accordingly, there is a chapter in each part written by a specialist in one or more of these areas.

Just Environments is especially designed for courses in environmental studies which attempt to integrate the various perspectives – moral, political, ecological, and so on – which it is necessary to consider if informed and balanced judgements on our treatment of the natural world and of each other are to be reached. Appropriate chapters will, as this implies, also be of interest to students of applied ethics, international politics, ecology, population studies and geography.

Joy A. Palmer
David E. Cooper

Part I
The framework

1 Rights and justice in the environment debate

Brenda Almond

'Environment' is a term that may be as specific or as general as we care to make it. A city street in a teeming capital city in the northern hemisphere, a no-go area for police, ruled by mobsters and drug syndicates, is an environment of sorts – for some individual human beings the only environment they have experienced.

Even so, there is a sense in which this is a chosen or contingent environment, an environment under human control. For if, socially and economically, it is hard to escape, it is not *physically* so. A resident of this community, given the means, may step into an aeroplane – a sealed micro-environment, itself situated some distance from the surface of the earth – and thus be transferred to some other region, polar or tropical, urban or rural, at some other point on the face of the planet.

Modern technology, in facilitating travel in this way, has given human beings, perhaps for only a moment in history, the illusion that environment is essentially a matter of choice. So far, however, our ventures *beyond* the confines of the earth, our exploration of space, have merely confirmed that environmental choice is in a broader sense confined and constrained. This planet represents the only realistic locus for human existence. In a more general sense, then, 'environment' is the context which provides the conditions for the existence of the human *species*, together with other living creatures and the vegetation on which they depend for sustenance. The science of ecology has brought understanding of the intimate web of connections of humans, animals, plants, earth, water. It has increasingly led us to see ourselves as neither independent nor self-sufficient, but as systems within systems. Knowledge of the extent of these systems in either direction seems to be limited only by the present scope of our microscopes and telescopes.

There is, too, a developing historical perspective. We see our species, the various human groups, as having until a very recent point in the planet's history lived in balance with other species and with planetary conditions. It is true that there were issues of conservation and preservation in the past – recognition of the threat of species loss through uncontrolled exploitation such as led to the virtual wiping out of the bison population in North America, concern about over-cultivation of the land even in ancient and medieval times, pessimistic assessments of the polluting potential of large cities from the seventeenth century on, and the Malthusian perception around the beginning of the nineteenth century that population and food-supply need to be kept in balance (Malthus 1970). Nevertheless, nature has in the past been extremely resilient in coping with the worst that human beings could do. Today, in contrast, we see that natural balance as having been dramatically distorted in the last few micro-seconds of planetary time by scientific and technological advance which has led to an unprecedented explosion of populations in some parts of the world, to the rapid depletion of irreplaceable resources including important species, and to a threat to the *outer* environment of the earth itself, its protective ozone layer. Moreover, the attempts to harness powers which are intrinsically beyond the control of humans within their limited life-span has generated toxic (particularly nuclear) wastes which will remain with this generation and its successors further into the future than the records of humanity's past (see Meadows *et al.* 1972).

To apply a term like 'justice' to these multiple contexts may not always seem appropriate, for many ethical issues are embedded here. There is a sense, however, in which the concept of justice plays a distinctively useful role in relation to certain key environmental issues, for it provides something firmer and more tangible than broader ethical concepts such as value or goodness – although admittedly these are terms which play a part in the wider picture (Almond 1987). However, justice, unlike some broader terms, brings with it implicit reference to rights, needs, desert – concepts underlying discussion of environmental issues. It would be a mistake, then, to see justice as narrowly confined to issues of punishment and reward, and, more broadly conceived, it provides an alternative to other ethical theories often invoked here, for example, utilitarianism – the idea that the morally right course of action is that which produces the most satisfactory outcome, whether in terms of pleasure, happiness or preference-satisfaction – or virtue ethics, which links what is morally right to the promotion of flourishing. But before turning to the question of the role of justice, it would be useful to consider very briefly the relevance of these other approaches to the environmental debate.

THE UTILITARIAN ALTERNATIVE

Utilitarianism is prominent in philosophical discussion of environmental issues as the ethical position of a number of influential environmental philosophers. Of these, Peter Singer (1993) is typical in applying the theory both to relations between human beings (contemporary issues of poverty and inequality, the impending problem of the heritage we leave for future generations) and to relations between humans and animals (for example, conservation of species, vegetarianism, animal experimentation). As far as the latter area is concerned, Singer's utilitarianism had led him to argue for care, concern and a general raising of standards in the treatment of animals by human beings. However, when we turn away from the world of theory to the world of practice, it seems that a very different kind of utilitarianism holds sway. This is an essentially shallow approach which takes a much narrower view of what interests are to be taken into account, and, because it tends to adopt a short-term perspective, it has very different consequences for policy. It is this unfettered and unqualified form of utilitarianism – perhaps better described as narrow cost–benefit calculation, since it is hardly a philosophical view – that lies behind the uncontrolled exploitation of some of the opportunities provided by technological development. Examples of the practical outcome of this unreflective approach include:

1 *factory farming* – in the drive to produce better and cheaper bacon or veal, or higher egg-producing hens, animals (now classified as 'agricultural products') have been subjected to production-line techniques which ignore their natural condition and instincts. It is this kind of uncritical cost-saving that has led to the introduction through the food-chain of new threats of disease or the transmission of harmful chemicals, as every animal residue is utilized and refed to animals tricked into cannibalism in a distorted imitation of the closed cycles of ecology;
2 *genetic experiments, including the breeding of animals for disease* – the 'oncomouse', a mouse with a genetic susceptibility to cancer, bred as a suitable subject for cancer research, is just one example of an attempt to supplant nature's evolutionary preference for the more survival-*enhancing* traits, with the scientific pursuit of survival-*inimical* traits where this will advance our own (human) interests;
3 *more general environmental hazards* – included here are a number of well-publicized problems such as the production of toxic wastes, the depletion of important resources, erosion and desertification of vast tracts of land, damage to the ozone layer, the greenhouse effect, pollution of rivers – in short, a variety of changes with large-scale environmental impact.

Very often, in these cases a greater good is being sacrificed for purely short-term gains – or even the good (*profit*) of some for the good (*health*) of others, so that they cannot in the long run be defended on grounds of utility, since this requires an overall balance of good effects over bad. This is a point made strongly by philosophical utilitarians such as Singer, who oppose many of these practices. But while it is true that a more reflective and philosophical form of utilitarianism can avoid *these* consequences, there are other problems of a more theoretical nature that its philosophical defenders must confront. Briefly, these amount to, first, difficulties in dealing with certain specific categories of cases, and second, a more fundamental difficulty in giving a satisfactory account of justice.

The special categories of cases that pose problems for utilitarianism are, first, nations whose standard of living is currently vastly lower than that taken for granted in the affluent countries of the developed world. Utilitarianism seems to require some equalization of the situation, but implications of that for the inhabitants of rich nations are problematic, particularly if asymmetry in population growth is taken into account. That is to say, if the population of potential donor countries declines, while the population of countries which might qualify for help continues to expand, the steady state needed to make realistic utilitarian calculations is lacking. Second, there is the case of future generations, problematic not only because of the sheer impossibility of knowing what their wishes or preferences are likely to be, or even whether such generations will exist and in what numbers, but also because, if their preferences were to rank equally alongside our own, the calculations demanded by the theory would be overwhelmed by the infinite number of preferences that would need to be taken into account.

Finally, although leading defenders of animal rights like Singer are utilitarians, it is hard to see that utilitarianism itself entails consideration for animals – this despite the tradition initiated by Jeremy Bentham when he famously advanced the claims of animals for moral consideration by saying that 'The question is not, Can they *reason*? nor, Can they *talk*? but, *Can they suffer*?' (1960: ch. 17, sec. 1). That is to say, the judgement that animals are included in our moral universe – that their happiness and welfare *matter* – cannot itself be made on utilitarian grounds. The question of *who* or *what* should be included is in the end a line-drawing exercise and may in the end be a matter of arbitrary decision. Even leading advocates of animal rights hesitate as to whether a virus must be protected and preserved, while the conscientious philosophical vegetarian, searching for criteria, may sometimes be found hesitating in the borderland inhabited by prawns and scallops. A distinction proposed by Robin Attfield (1991: 154) between moral *significance* and moral *standing* might suggest a way out of this difficulty – his suggestion is that we can allot moral *standing* to lesser creatures, but still decide to sacrifice them for beings of greater moral *significance*. This has the advantage of fitting with intuition and common sense, but does not necessarily provide a way out of their difficulties for utilitarians. Utilitarian theory makes central the notion of equal consideration of interests, and cannot therefore easily accommodate this concept of differential worth. To value some more than others is to import a notion of value from some quite different source.

Of most relevance to the present discussion, however, is the debate that centres round the question of whether utilitarianism necessarily involves a willingness to countenance the sacrifice of the few for the many, and hence *in*justice. John Rawls (1981: 315) writes:

> The conception of justice in classical utilitarianism conflicts . . . with the conception of justice as reciprocity. For on the utilitarian view justice is assimilated to benevolence and the latter in turn to the most effective design of institutions to promote the general welfare. Justice is a kind of efficiency.

Rawls goes on to cite Bentham's contemptuous rejection of the notion of justice:

> justice, in the only sense in which it has a meaning, is an imaginary personage, feigned for the convenience of discourse, whose dictates are the dictates of utility, applied to certain particular cases. Justice, then, is nothing more than an imaginary instrument, employed to forward on certain occasions, and by certain means, the purposes of benevolence.

However, Bentham's successor and disciple in utilitarian theory, John Stuart Mill, had a higher regard for the notion, which he believed could in fact be *derived* from utility. Mill's view was that: 'Justice is a name for certain classes of moral rules, which concern the essentials of human well-being more clearly, and are therefore of more absolute obligation than any other rules for the guidance of life' (Mill 1954: ch. 5). There is a form of utilitarianism, then, which would seek to reconcile the claims of justice and utility; meanwhile, utilitarianism, even in its classic form, cannot in any event be written off as wholly irrelevant to the environmental debate: to value life but not to value happiness – even human happiness – would strike most people as perverse, although a few extreme environmentalists do this. For everyone else, the immediate question is: what of apparent environmental value may be sacrificed for the sake of the comfort of some members of the current human population? There is, however, a more fundamental question to be asked as well: what in fact *is* it for humans to be happy? The theory known as virtue ethics addresses this second question directly in the notion of flourishing.

VIRTUE ETHICS

The idea of flourishing, which is an essential aspect of virtue ethics, is in many ways more useful to environmental concerns than the cruder measure of utility. It is a notion familiar from Greek philosophy, particularly that of Aristotle, although Plato had already suggested a model of this kind when he equated justice with health, and immorality with disease. The theory begins by noting that every kind of object has an end or function that in a sense defines it – a knife is for cutting, a seat for sitting on, and so on. With animate creatures, or even with plants, this end may be more complex and open to debate. In the case of humans, Aristotle identified it with what is most uniquely distinctive of human beings – the exercise of their rational faculty. For an object or a creature to flourish, then, is for it to be fulfilling its essential function *well*. More broadly, flourishing may be taken as a matter of well-being or health in general, and the flourishing of animals and plants is easily graspable by analogy (see Pence 1991).

This theory can be applied, too, to generate obligations beyond the present generation to the people of the future, for the well-being of our descendants can be seen as essential to our own flourishing. Something of this thought is captured in Solon's saying – 'Call no man happy until he is dead.' It is a remark we would do well to ponder as we reassess the value that we could attach to our *own* lives and projects – our raising of children, our cultural products, our political achievements – if we were to have no posterity.

Some would argue that virtue ethics with its concern for flourishing is too inward-looking, in that it encourages a focus on the self and an egotistical preoccupation with its improvement; it is also generally taken to be concerned with individuals, whereas environmentalism is concerned with species and with the natural world. However, a selfish concern with only one's own flourishing is far from an essential aspect of virtue ethics, and it would be a very reasonable step to progress from that to concern for other individuals and their flourishing; it would be natural to move on from there to concern with the flourishing of species and indeed of the biosystem itself. Hence there are no a priori considerations that prevent the incorporation of a broadly conceived and extended virtue ethics *within* the justice framework, and there is certainly no incompatibility in their practical implications. The Greek conception of the scope of virtue was in any case extensive and overlapped with justice. Aristotle quotes with approval a Greek proverb: 'In justice is summed up the whole of virtue' (1976: 173).

THE JUSTICE APPROACH

Justice, together with its central concept of rights, essentially looks outwards from individual persons, setting bounds to the ways in which they may interact. Historically, it is connected with the notion of balance and harmony – terms which are central to environmental thought, but which have until recently been seen as applying only to relations between human beings in a social or political setting. Within this social context, the necessity for harmonization arises from conflicts of interest. John Rawls draws together these apparently antithetical notions of harmony and conflict when he writes of 'the usual sense of justice in which it means essentially the elimination of arbitrary distinctions and the establishment within the structure of a practice of a proper share, balance, or equilibrium between competing claims' (Rawls 1981: 293).

It is these elements that constitute the liberal notion of justice, to which the idea of rights is central. The modern liberal theory of justice is related to political theories that ground the obligation to obey the laws of a state or community on contract and the consent of the governed. The idea of rational choice is fundamental to such theories. But if reason and a capacity to choose are essential conditions for rights and hence for access to justice, this will place this theory, too, at risk as far as the three categories so far considered are concerned. To begin with, it would seem to exclude other species from the liberal's moral universe, and also to confine the application of the theory to the human beings currently alive. Consent, too, is a notion applicable only within the limits of a *particular* community or political system, and, increasingly, people have been looking beyond the boundaries of their own society to extend such notions to a more internationalist conception of justice. People see themselves as having some responsibility for strangers starving, or dying from treatable disease, in distant lands, although they may disagree as to whether the morally relevant requirement in this case is indeed justice or merely compassion.

They are also more inclined to admit marginal cases to the moral community. The higher apes, for example, are currently the focus of a campaign to have them treated more on a par with their human cousins, but the interests, too, of dogs, cats and horses are taken seriously by many who have learned to appreciate their human-like qualities and intelligence. And while animal experimentation is defended by some, few would any longer defend the complete failure to acknowledge *any* moral parameters characteristic of some of the pioneer vivisectors of earlier times, who, fascinated by new discoveries about the circulation of the blood, nailed down dogs by their paws in preparation for living demonstrations of those findings, dismissing protest as sentimental and ill-informed. It does not seem unduly anthropomorphic to use a term like 'injustice' to describe this situation. 'Injustice' suggests that the humans concerned have gone beyond what is morally due to these other creatures, that they have, even if only meta-phorically, violated their rights. Joseph Raz is not the only writer in the liberal tradition who sees the liberal theory of justice as capable of being extended to animals, and possibly further, although recognizing that this means making interests rather than consent the ground of obligation. He writes: 'Rights ground requirements for action in the interest of other beings' (Raz 1986: 180).

On whatever basis, then, there are some who would go beyond defending the rights and interests of non-human animals and other individual entities, claiming that justice may also be involved in our relationship to the inanimate world around us, even indeed to the biosphere. This need not involve arguing for a *direct* responsibility to the planet. Since its preservation in an efficient state is essential for the future life of man, a duty to the planet as a whole may be formulated *indirectly* as a duty to future people, our descendants and successors. Here, too, a new ethical factor is involved. Our ancestors could do little irrever-sible harm to the environment and hence could not have analogous obligations. It seems that we, on the other hand, can set into motion chains of causation that, once initiated, cannot be halted. This generates an altogether new kind of obli-gation to the future.

But here views diverge. There are those, like the Australian philosophers John Passmore (1980) and H. J. McCloskey (1983), who have argued that relationships of duty between individual persons, the liberal concept of justice, are sufficient to generate all the environmental responsibilities we may have. And there are those, on the other hand, who follow the call of the American conservationist Aldo Leopold and his successors for a new and wholly environmental ethic – not human-centred, but eco- or bio-centred. But before considering whether a liberal approach based on justice and rights is too limited to meet these wider needs, and whether some extension of ethics is indeed needed to cope with current environ-mental concerns, it would be useful to look more closely at the basic idea of justice and related concepts such as equality and rights.

Justice has been a favoured theme of philosophers from Plato to Rawls. In the *Republic*, Plato (1974) discussed a variety of possible views of justice before offering the substantial theory which forms the main subject of the dialogue. Through Thrasymachus, in Book I, he set out and dismissed the idea, to be variously developed in modern times by Marx, and contemporary post-modernists such as Derrida and Foucault, that justice is simply the interest of the stronger. Through Glaucon in Book II, he presented the case for the view that it is nothing more than social convention – a compact, tacit or explicit, between rational egoists, who recognize that living in a community governed by behaviour-regulating laws offers the best way to achieve their own personal goals. Again, this view has a continuous history – the distinction between tacit and explicit consent features in Locke's political theory and the idea of contract was basic to the theories of Hobbes, Rousseau and Hume. Contemporary eco-nomic and philosophical discussion of games theory and the Prisoners' Dilemma is essentially a continuation of this debate (see Hollis 1987).

As noted above, justice as social convention tends to restrict its scope by locality: the rights people enjoy apply only within a particular society and under a particular system of laws. Legal positivists accept this, saying that the justice dispensed by courts of law is measured by legal rather than moral criteria – it is a matter of what the law in fact is in a particular community. However, it is possible to take a wider, indeed universal view, in which rights and justice are seen as having supra-national status and as transcending the barriers of particular times and places – in Eugene Kamenka's words, 'as the alleged idea, ideal or principle that determines impartially and rationally the nature and limits of all rights and duties, all benefits and entitlements, in society' (Kamenka 1979: 2). In this sense, your right to life may be unjustly violated by me, even if local conditions, and particularly local laws, impose no sanctions on me. For while what is just may rightly be enforced by law, it is not necessarily the case that only or everything enforced by law is just. This idea that there is another court of appeal, a higher or transcendent notion of justice, was expressed in the notion of natural law that also originated with the Greeks: Antigone's famous appeal in Sophocles' play to 'immutable and unwritten laws of Heaven' is often quoted as a poetic expression of an important ethical conception. Aristotle, however, sets the notion out more formally:

> There are two sorts of political justice, one natural and the other legal. The natural is that which has the same validity everywhere and does not depend upon acceptance; the legal is that which in the first place can take one form or another indifferently, but which, once laid down, is decisive.
>
> (Aristotle 1976: 189)

The idea of a natural or universal law to be contrasted with the actual (positive) laws of states was subsequently an important element in Stoic thought and, reflected in Roman law and in the Christian tradition, was developed further in modern times. Locke declared that natural law is a test of the justice of positive law; and the conception of rights to life, liberty and property adumbrated by Locke eventually led to the flowering of the contemporary notion of human rights. There is, then, an influential tradition linking the idea of natural law and justice to that of universally shared rights. Within this conception, just as within the narrower framework of justice within particular social or political systems, two kinds of justice can be identified, not necessarily exclusive of each other, and each, in its different way, capable of being subsumed under the principle 'To each his due'. Variously named by different writers, these are: (1) formal justice and (2) social or distributive justice.

FORMAL JUSTICE

The formal sense of justice constitutes perhaps the commonest conception of justice. It is to be found embedded in the traditional precepts of justice cited in Roman times: *honeste vivere, neminem laedere, suum cuique tribuere* – live an upright life, hurt no one, and give others their due, and is the notion of justice as reciprocity that is enshrined in legal systems. It is a retaliative or retributive sense of justice – justice as summed up also in the Judaic system of law in the phrase 'an eye for an eye' (*lex talionis*).

Implicit within it is a principle of formal equality which requires that like cases be treated alike. This implies first that justice be administered according to rules rather than the shifting and arbitrary whims of despots or private individuals. Second, it means that there should be no discrimination between people on irrelevant grounds, but that each individual person is deserving of equal respect. These two aspects are captured in the two main formulations of Kant's Categorical Imperative: as the principle that one should be able to universalize the maxim of one's actions, and as the requirement to treat other people never only as means to other people's ends, but always as ends in themselves (Kant 1948). This belief in the right of everyone to equal concern and respect has been described by Raz as the definitive belief of political liberalism (Raz 1986: 229). Applying the notion to the specific case of legal punishment, Igor Primoratz describes it as 'the application of law in an impartial, objective manner, with no regard to individual or group interest' (1989: 36). Metaphorically, it is the principle that justice must be blind – that discrimination is morally offensive, and that justice must not pay attention to such irrelevant differences between people as, for example, race, class, wealth or influence.

Notions such as desert and entitlement play a role here. For what is due to people, whether positive or negative, punishment or reward, may be what they have deserved or earned in some way, or it may be what belongs to them through gift, inheritance, etc. These concepts are often referred to in the language of rights, and it is widely held that claims of justice made on the basis of rights are and should be enforceable by authorities established for that purpose. The idea of an enforcing power is accepted from both ends of the political spectrum: it was seen as a necessary guarantee of justice both by Hobbes, who advocated the rule of an absolute sovereign, and by Mill, who defended individual liberty. Antony Flew sums up the point as follows: 'the implication of this logical truth, that justice refers to rights and entitlements, is that the claims of justice, unlike some other moral claims, may properly be enforced by the public power' (Flew 1991: 199). Hence justice conceived of in this way gives rise to a system of publicly declared laws, supported by sanctions or punishments, and to the social institutions – lawcourts, prisons, and a supporting bureaucracy – which are essential to them.

Nevertheless, the requirement of formal justice is simply that the state should operate as a kind of umpire, guarding citizens against interference in their liberties and protecting their contracts. The rights it protects are negative only, to non-interference. Adam Smith acknowledged the limits of this conception when he wrote that 'Mere justice is . . . but a negative virtue and only hinders us from hurting our neighbour' (quoted in Flew 1991: 199). For the idea that justice might require us also to *help* our neighbour in some more positive or generous way, it is necessary to turn to the idea of distributive justice, which may be put forward as an economic or social conception, sometimes called 'social justice'.

DISTRIBUTIVE JUSTICE

Distributive justice is broader in scope than formal justice in that it is concerned with the allocation of goods and benefits. Within the conception of formal justice, the principle of reciprocity means that the punishment of offenders and the settlement of legal claims are to be dealt with on the principle of treating like cases alike. Within the area of distributive justice the focus shifts to what *are* appropriate criteria for different treatment, particularly in relation to the allocation of goods and benefits. There is a requirement that benefits be seen to be fairly received – hence it includes the idea of a just price, or a fair wage.

The judgement as to whether a distribution of benefits is fair can be made from two different standpoints: distribution may be deemed fair first because the *process* or *procedure* for the handing out of social goods by government or private individuals is judged fair, or second, because the resulting *outcome* is considered fair, whatever the process. In the first case, the question is, On what principles should the distribution take place? In the second case, Who, and how many, should have how much? What would a fair distribution look like? Would it encompass striking inequalities? These questions, too, have been widely discussed by philosophers in the past. It was in connection with this sense of justice that Hume said that in a situation of plenty, there would be no need for justice – it is a virtue needed only to provide principles for the distribution of resources which are scarce or in limited supply (Hume 1985: I.II.ii). Justice in this sense, then, is linked with the notion of fairness or equity. Criteria proposed for a fair or just distribution of goods and benefits include:

1   that they should be distributed absolutely equally;
2   that they should be distributed according to need;
3   that they should be distributed in proportion to merit or desert (due return).

Utilitarianism provides another principle of distribution which may or may not take these factors into account, according to whether it judges their use to be beneficial in the long run. But since its goal is to achieve the distribution that gives the maximum overall satisfaction, it appears to be consistent with a few people losing out altogether if this raises overall utility – a situation most would agree to be a departure from justice. From this point of view, Rawls's alternative principle of distribution, the 'difference principle', also known as the *maximin* principle, which forms an important part of his account of justice, may seem to offer a criterion which has the advantage of combining a concern for welfare with a greater regard for justice. This is because the difference principle takes the welfare of the least advantaged person as its yardstick. According to Rawls's principle, inequalities are justified only if they work to the advantage of all, in particular the most disadvantaged, under conditions of fair competition. Full discussion of Rawls's theory would be out of place here: it suffices for present purposes simply to note that, like utilitarianism, it seeks to allocate social goods on the basis of the most acceptable end-result, and is thus open to some of the general objections to allocation on an outcome basis that will be discussed below.

Arithmetical or perfect equality

As we have seen, the idea that justice involves equality is perfectly suited to the idea of formal or commutative justice. It is what is required of judges in the imposing of punishments or settling of compensation claims; it is the justice governing contracts and exchange. Perfect equality, in other words, is applicable to legal rights. Within the area of distributive justice, however, where what is at issue is the distribution of material goods rather than of legal rights and privileges, it becomes a principle of more doubtful validity. Flew (1991: 200) describes the advocates of this kind of equality as Procrusteans – 'people who strive to ensure that their sort of egalitarianism is achieved by social engineering exercises of state power', while Passmore (1979: 48) suggests that only tyranny can produce this sort of equality since, left to themselves, people have a natural tendency to become unequal. Behind these objections lies the perception that, while equality provides a popular slogan, it is often misinterpreted. In particular, it is hard to defend a concept of equality that denies that there are differences between people, still more between humans and other creatures. Nor is it easy to defend a demand that all should be *treated* alike. For this is to ignore differences in needs – a person who is sick needs different treatment from one who is well, an infant's educational needs are different from those of an adult, and so on. It is considerations such as these that lead to need itself being proposed as a criterion for just distribution.

Need

At first sight, then, need seems to supply a more plausible basis for the allocation of goods than blind equality. Need, however, can be a variable concept. Julian Le Grand (1991) rejects it altogether for this reason, arguing that it is too vague a concept to be used as a principle of distribution. It may be possible to meet this objection, however, by specifying a level of *basic* needs at which it would be more appropriate to apply this kind of conception of equality. 'Hard' measures such as infant mortality rates and life expectancy may be used to identify societies as needy, thus avoiding the accusation of vagueness. Given a sufficiently firm conception of absolute poverty, a more secure ethical case exists for insisting that there is a basic minimum of food, shelter and the conditions essential for physical subsistence that all human beings should have, and that it is wrong, if human action can prevent it, that some should be left at a level of existence which is entirely governed by the threat of disease, malnutrition and early mortality. This may be what Amy Gutman has in mind when she writes:

> With reference to what we consider essential social goods, to say that people deserve those goods and that they have a right to them may be two sides of the same moral argument: In both cases we are referring to our basic moral intuition that people deserve certain goods (consistent, of course, with other people's deserts) in virtue of being moral and rational beings.
>
> (Gutman 1980: 167)

At any level above that of basic needs, however, critics are right to argue that a judgement of justice must take account of background conditions and the reasons for people's different situations. That is to say, the prodigal son is not necessarily entitled to live at the same level as the one who has devoted his life to hard work, and there is no obligation on others to see that those who have neglected their talents have the same standard of living as those who have lived wisely and sacrificed short-term pleasures for longer-term goals.

What the criterion of need and the criterion of arithmetical equality have in common is that they make justice a matter of outcome rather than process, and, while there is a case to be made for equality where basic needs are concerned, there is no reason to extend the demand for equality of treatment more generally from the area of formal justice to that of social justice. As Hayek puts it: 'there is no obvious reason why the joint efforts of the members of any group to ensure the maintenance of law and order and to organize the provision of certain services should give the members a claim to a particular share in the wealth of this group' (Hayek 1960: 101). In contrast to these two criteria, the third criterion – that of proportionality – does not offend against Hayek's principle, for it does not entail an egalitarian outcome, but is restricted in scope to specifying grounds for differential rewards. In other words, it focuses on just *procedures* rather than just *outcomes*.

Merit or desert – proportionate justice

The criterion of merit or desert is what is encompassed by Aristotle's notion of proportionate justice, summed up in the formula that it is as unjust to treat unequals equally as it is to treat equals unequally. In the area of formal justice this criterion provides the principle of impartiality: that only relevant differences are to count. In the area of distributive justice, since it makes what you get depend on what you have done or otherwise deserve, it is unlikely to produce actual or arithmetical equality as its outcome. Some social philosophers consider that a merit criterion is unfair because merit and achievement result from skills and virtues that are a matter of genetic endowment. Joel Feinberg writes: 'Native skills and inherited aptitudes will not be appropriate desert bases since they are forms of merit ruled out by the fair opportunity requirement' (Feinberg 1973: 328). This is to say that social goods should be allocated only on the basis of criteria we have all had a fair opportunity to acquire. Since we cannot alter our *character* – our genetic endowment – Feinberg holds that it is unfair to make it the subject of reward or punishment. The implication is that, whether people are resourceful or passive, trustworthy or unreliable, lazy or hard-working, this should make no difference to the rewards they enjoy in society. Feinberg points to the difficulty of separating out causal factors, and sees it as a further defect of the merit criterion that it might justify rewarding capitalists and entrepreneurs for their imagination and enterprise.

Rawls writes in similar vein:

Within the limits allowed by the background arrangements, distributive shares are decided by the outcome of the natural lottery; and this outcome is arbitrary from a moral perspective. There is no more reason to permit the distribution of income and wealth to be settled by the distribution of natural assets than by historical and social fortune. . . . Even the willingness to make an effort, to try, and so to be deserving in the ordinary sense is itself dependent on happy family and social circumstances.

(Rawls 1972: 73–4)

Although Rawls draws back from the brink of the implication that equality or justice requires the abolition of the family, his remarks are none the less surprising because of the sense of personal identity they imply. Implicit in such a position is the essentially incoherent suggestion that the notion of moral responsibility requires there to be a person within a person – an inner controller of character, the product of neither heredity nor environment. The fact is, however, that persons are simply the persons that they are, as defined by character, abilities, disposition, potentialities, and so on. What is more, it would be hard both to claim that intellectual and moral qualities are valuable and also to insist that society should be arranged so as to deny them their natural rewards.

A merit criterion, then, is compatible with the notion of justice in both its formal and its social aspects. It also has the advantage of offering a solution to the problem of the 'free rider', a problem besetting 'outcome' theories. The 'free rider' problem arises because there are many situations in which one person can get away with trading on the rest. For example, if you secretly ignore requests to turn down your central heating in a fuel shortage while everyone else complies, or if you continue – once again secretly – to water your garden in a drought, you might seek to justify this by pointing out that this makes for an overall social advantage – you gain, and no one else loses out perceptibly. Nevertheless, such conduct is widely held to be unjust or unfair. Unqualified 'consent' theories, however, provide no answer to the question why rational egoists should *not* act selfishly when they can get away with it. And as long as there are only a *few* selfish people, utilitarian theory, too would seem to justify – indeed demand – their selfish happiness being *added* to the total. In contrast, only a theory of justice which takes merit or desert as a criterion has no difficulty in (ethically) unseating the 'free rider'.

CONCLUSIONS

It should now be possible to return to the question of how the two kinds of justice, together with the wider notion of universal justice, apply to the three categories singled out as central to environmental considerations. And first, it will be clear from the above discussion that a localized notion of justice is not the one at issue in cases of international, intergenerational, or even interspecies justice. For these three cases, it is the universal conception that must be invoked as a guide to formulating appropriate local laws and just international agreements. Second, it is worth noticing that formal justice may conflict with social justice, since the latter can generally be achieved only by redistributive taxation – essentially, the compulsory removal from some people of wealth, rights or possessions, which are in principle protected by formal justice. This is just as true at the international level as it is at the community level. In both cases, only widespread approval of redistributive aims can, by turning a compulsory levy into a voluntary donation, avoid this conflict. It is not, however, impossible that such approval may be forthcoming once there is a general understanding of the issues involved, particularly in relation to the three groups singled out for discussion so far: the distant poor; future generations; and non-human animals.

Justice for the distant poor

There is a place for the requirements of formal justice amongst nations: not only does formal justice impose a framework of constraints of fair dealing in international relationships; it also dictates a common concern for respect for human rights, thus justifying interference in flagrant cases such as genocide, slavery or arbitrary tyranny. In contrast, the case for economic aid must be made on the basis of the notion of distributive justice. Could such a notion be used to justify international redistribution from rich countries to poor? Garrett Hardin (1979) presents a dramatic metaphor to describe the situation. The rich nations may be compared to a lifeboat surrounded by desperate swimmers – the world's poor – trying to get on board. Hardin uses this analogy to ask practical as well as theoretic questions: What would happen if the numerous poor did climb aboard? Would the lifeboat sink? Applying such questions to the North/South issue, some argue for cutting aid and for the adoption of strong population policies extending even to compulsory measures. From a purely environmental point of view, however, such recommendations come uncomfortably from the rich countries whose citizens are each individually massive consumers of world resources and energy compared to villagers in, for example, Peru or Bangladesh.

   In Hardin's analogy, the situation is painted in terms of stark alternatives: to help or not to help – to retain one's standard of living or to be completely overwhelmed. Singer (1993), in contrast, proposes a compromise based on the ancient notion of the tithe. He proposes, that is, that the inhabitants of the richer nations should individually give up a generous proportion of their income, whilst not rendering themselves or their families destitute, or even excessively uncomfortable. But in deciding the actual allocation of whatever aid is made available, it is still likely to be necessary to be selective. For this purpose, triage is sometimes proposed as an alternative principle of distribution. Triage involves identifying the cases where aid can be most useful and offering it there, rather than to cases which are so desperate that aid will be fully consumed, leaving the situation to return to what it was before. This, too, is a harsh programme to adopt in practice, since it involves ignoring the most needy and most tragic cases, helping some who are better off, whilst knowingly leaving the worst off to die. For this reason, it would hardly qualify as a principle of justice, even if there are situations in which it would be chosen on grounds of expediency or cost-effectiveness.

Implicit in Hardin's analogy is the idea that, whatever distribution strategies ae adopted, it would not be possible for everyone to achieve the standard of life of the western world, and Singer's compromise, too, implicitly recognizes this fact. It is a view shared by Ivan Illich (1971, 1976), whose own recommended solution involves a scaling down of the requirements and expectations of the developed as well as the developing world – in medicine, in education, in transport. There is also a potent argument that limits may be set not only by resources but by the logic of people's competitive desires: in other words, as Fred Hirsch (1976) has pointed out, some goods – *positional* goods – cannot of their nature be made equally available to all. Just as it is not possible for everyone to be the first person to climb Everest, for example, so it is not possible for everyone to enjoy preserved National Parks and wilderness areas, or raised standards of living, since in the latter case, the raising of standards may destroy the very conditions that are necessary for living the kind of life that people aspire to live.

What, then, does justice require here? Robert Nozick (1975) argues against all redistributive theories and in favour of a minimal state which acknowledges and defends the rights of people to what they have legitimately acquired, whether by work, gift, inheritance or otherwise. A Nozickian sense of justice confines us to asking the question: Are they *entitled* to share what we have? It has been suggested here that the notion of distributive justice may rightly take account of the equality of people's basic needs. It may also look critically at the question of whether the rich deserve what they have. But as critics have pointed out, inequality as such is not objectionable. What is objectionable is poverty at a level which makes the ordinary conditions of human life impossible. Satisfying basic needs, then, can be taken as in principle a just goal. Nevertheless, many will argue that in practice this goal may be turned into an unattainable moving target by uncontrolled population growth. The population objection, however, must be balanced by what might be described as Malthusian considerations in a modern context. There are countries which face a real danger of depopulation by AIDS, whilst long-abolished ills are returning to parts of Eastern Europe in the wake of social upheaval. These include diphtheria, cholera, tuberculosis, and even the Black Death. Ordinary health threats, too, apparently overcome in recent decades by the development of antibiotics, are returning in resistant strains to Western Europe and the USA. At the same time, a proliferation of weapons – nuclear, biological, chemical – is in the hands of unpredictable rulers and irregular groups all over the world. In these circumstances, Hardin's lifeboat may be less secure than it looks, and its occupants may perhaps permit themselves the luxury of extending well-considered aid, recognizing that, after all, the hypothesis of permanently increasing human numbers is the more optimistic of the alternatives confronting humankind at the present time.

Justice for future generations

What does justice require of us in relation to future generations? Here the principle of formal justice plays an important role through its requirement of impartiality. For the idea that it is wrong for an individual to make an exception of themselves can easily be extended to the principle that it would be wrong for one generation to privilege itself, leaving nothing for future generations. The understanding of injustice as taking too much, more than one's fair share, has been part of the analysis of justice from the outset. There may also be a require-ment of gratitude asymmetrically or transitively applied – gratitude to the past repaid to the future. Dworkin argues that there is an elementary obligation of justice to posterity, following Rawls, who says that each generation is obliged to replace the stock of capital goods it has inherited on a 'just savings' principle. The idea behind these claims is that we owe our progress to previous generations; this debt cannot be discharged backwards to our ancestors, so we must repay it forwards to future generations. In other words, we express our gratitude to our parents and grandparents in care for our children and grandchildren. For Rawls, as noted above, the goal of justice between generations is related to the needs of the least advantaged individual of each generation.

The principles which may be applied in this area, then, seem to be (1) not closing down options for future generations (for example, by making irreversible changes, including the elimination of species, or the using up of resources) and (2) maximizing future choices by making a considered judgement as to what are the most central, significant or important things to preserve and protect, for example, clean air, energy. Recent commentators have summed up the principles involved here as (1) conservation of options, (2) conservation of quality and (3) conservation of access (see, for example, Weiss 1989). This last principle aims at balancing justice requirements *between* and *within* generations. Alex Mauron (1993) writes: 'An environmental conservation programme that would benefit future generations generally but whose burden weighed mostly on the poorest countries of the present world, would violate the principle.' Here the complexity of causal relationships has to be borne in mind in the case of both present and future people. Chernobyl provides probably the best example of the extensive and unpredicted effects of contemporary technologies, affecting, as it did, world-wide interests from vegetables in Sicily to reindeer in Lapland. But future conse-quences of this and other incidents and policies are likely to be even more extensive, long-term, and essentially unpredictable.

Justice for non-human animals and nature

At first sight, the idea of applying the notion of justice to animals is doubtful. In previous centuries animals were tried by courts – often religious courts – some-times found guilty of 'crimes' and executed. Dogs were hanged from lamp-posts in Revolutionary France. It would be bizarre and absurd to return to the idea behind such practices – that animals are moral and legal persons in the same way as humans. The argument that nothing ethically significant distinguishes us from other animals is too strong for another reason too: that it would seem to mean that they were of equal concern. But few would hesitate to sacrifice a snake or a rat which was attacking a child. Equally, however, as previously noted, it would be wrong to count non-human animals as negligible. Attfield's argument, previously mentioned, which distinguishes moral standing from moral significance could offer a way round this dilemma. An alternative solution is encompassed in the notion of stewardship. The idea that human responsibilities for animals and for the natural world are responsibilities of stewardship has support from a religious as well as a moral perspective. But where some religious views would suggest that we care about them because they are for our use, others, as well as some non-religious viewpoints, allow that this may be simply *because they matter*. This leaves open, however, the contested questions of whether practices such as vivisection and the raising of animals for consumption are permissible. Some conservationists would allow for human use and consumption of animals as part of the general pattern of nature, in which species feeds upon species; Aldo Leopold's (1949) influential 'harmony with nature' form of conservationism, for example, took for granted the hunting, fishing and eating of animals. But others believe that only a complete change of human dietary and consumption patterns can preserve a viable world environment.

These are questions to be dealt with in detail in further chapters. Here the intention has been merely to sketch in questions concerning the range and application of justice. There is a sense, I have suggested here, in which something is indeed owed to the contemporary poor, to posterity, to other living creatures. In so far as justice is the idea of moral reciprocity, it coincides with the Golden Rule – what is owed to others is nothing less than what you would wish for yourself in their position. The question remains, Is a liberal approach based on justice and rights sufficient to cover this? Or is a new biocentred ethic needed? The liberal approach is the ideal of civil justice – *justitia communis*. Such a notion may indeed be adequate, but only if the conception of 'community' it embodies is sufficiently widely interpreted. It will need to extend first to mankind as a whole, and then, in Leopold's words, to 'soils, waters, plants and animals, or, collectively: the land'.

The environmental debate forces us, then, to focus on the interconnectedness of things. As far as other living creatures are concerned, this means awareness of the 'Great Chain of Being' that ties our interests firmly in with theirs – an earth which contained only humans and their artifacts would rapidly become a dead world. As far as the poor nations of the world are concerned, it means recognizing that the world has become an economic global village in which the rich live increasingly precariously, balancing appeals for aid against pressures for immigration and at the same time attempting to quell civil unrest beyond their frontiers, aware of its potentiality to destabilize not only those distant regions but their own, to affect their own lives through terrorism, or to lead to the use of horrific weapons of mass destruction. In relation to posterity, it means being conscious of the connectedness of past and future and the pointless ephemerality of a one-generation view. It also means endorsing the notion of a partnership of generations – in Edmund Burke's words – 'a partnership between those who are living, those who are dead, and those who are to be born' (1955: 140).

In practical terms, it means adopting policies of global conservation, of eco-management to preserve forests and savannahs, and seeking to develop alternative technologies and new sources of energy. The emphasis for the future is likely to be on a dynamic, changing ecology as opposed to any attempt to impose a stable equilibrium; hence the term 'conservation' is likely to take on an entirely new meaning as the judicious management of change.

The importance of making a judgement as to what it is that matters – the true meaning of 'value-judgement' – has been emphasized here. Such a judgement can be made only by a combination of intuitive sensitivity on our own part and persuasive argument in relation to others. Earlier the question was raised as to whether the appropriate moral response here is justice or compassion. Kant held that actions done from compassion or affection lacked moral worth, and gave pre-eminence to the motive of duty. However, feeling is essential to the type of judgements that environmental considerations raise. Hume's famous dictum takes on a more literal meaning here: 'It is not contrary to reason to prefer the destruction of the whole world to the itching of my little finger.' Since compassion for those we do not know or who are not yet born is a potentially elusive sentiment, there is a strong case in the environment debate for appealing to justice. As Anthony Skillen (1991: 206) puts it, 'Justice . . . counter- vails our tendency to tread on and exploit those to whom we are indifferent or opposed.' However, the sense of justice itself may require the motivation of sentiment to be added to it. The same author continues: 'The sense of justice requires not only the imagination and the intellect but the capacity to care about, to respect, the more or less conflicting needs, interests and claims that are at stake' (1991: 211).

2 Just ecological principles?

Joy A. Palmer

The concept of the environment embraces three natural units: individuals, populations and communities. No organism or group of life-forms can exist without an environment. It is the complexity of the interactions among individuals, other organisms and their physical and chemical backcloth for life which is the subject matter of ecology. Whilst it is certainly not the purpose of this chapter to provide a comprehensive text on the science of ecology, it is hoped that an introduction to some of the basic principles that govern the complexities of interactions in the environment will illuminate a number of the issues raised later in the book. In other words, ideas relating to individuals and the systems to which they belong will be set within an ecological framework.

The term 'ecology', deriving from the Greek *oikos*, meaning a house or home, presumably in an environment with which one is familiar, has become a household term in recent years. To some it conveys images of a precise mathematical science, which focuses on meticulous quantitative study of such matters as population sizes of living organisms, birth and death rates, and utilization of energy supplies and nutrients within natural systems. To others, it signifies rather more the practical application of an understanding of natural processes to the resolution of familiar environmental problems. Such application inevitably encompasses a wide variety of contexts, ranging from the biological to the social, economic, political and ethical. This chapter incorporates elements of both perspectives; it draws attention to fundamental concepts and principles of the discipline which can be researched by readers at far greater depth in specialist texts (see, for example, Ricklefs 1990; Ehrlich and Roughgarden 1987), and raises some key issues relating to their context and application for consideration and debate. Perhaps a useful approach to mapping out the theoretical terrain is by way of a glimpse into the complexities of the natural environment of our planet.

Scene one takes us to the 'bay shallows' of the San Francisco Bay area of California. Governed by tidal rhythms, the baylands are characterized by swimming crustaceans, fish and diving birds in tide; and worms, molluscs and mud-probing birds out of tide. Large amounts of mud sediment have been deposited through time on the floor of the drowned river mouth which is the San Francisco estuary. Mud is extensively exposed at low tides in various locations around the Bay, revealing two major types of water-logged environment: mud flats and salt marshes. Whilst some ecologists may use the terms interchangeably, there are differences between the two habitats: marshes are higher, usually above the average high-tide level. Their vegetation is adapted to the 'in between land and water' situation, with plant species limited by the length of time they can endure being inundated by water. Mud flats generally occur between high and mean low-tide levels. Many channels within them are permanently flooded, and vegetation is composed in the main of unicellular and other forms of algae. The major exception is zostera, or eel grass, whose habitat is almost always under water. Whilst eel grass, a seed plant, is able to tolerate an existence of almost total submergence, other plants such as cordgrass and pickleweed are indicators of marginally drier conditions. Cordgrass is able to endure up to twenty-one hours of submergence in water and may be seen as an indicator of the zone of transition between mud flat and salt marsh. Above it, pickleweed thrives around the level of the average high-tide line, in an environment that would best be described as marshland. Let us consider the adaptive devices and characteristics of these plants in a little more detail. Water itself provides the supporting medium for eel grass; air spaces in its stems and leaf blades respond to the buoyancy of the surrounding water as well as store oxygen for metabolism. The grass provides a stable habitat for many other forms of life: species of algae cover its blades, bubble snails cling to its stems, and species of shrimp and tube-building worms are sheltered by the vegetation. Cordgrass survives prolonged periods of submergence as a result of various physical adaptations: for example, hollow passages in its leaves and roots enable air to move readily throughout the plant even when it is surrounded by water. As a halophyte, it is able to tolerate soils of a high salt content as found in the bay shallows; excess salt is excreted by means of special glands, and the observer can often see white patches of salt crystals on the surface of the plant's leaves. Cordgrass has a crucial role to play in helping to stabilize new mud deposits in the upper tidal zone. Pickleweed, also a halophyte, demonstrates even more successful adaptation to the salt-marsh environment. Whilst lacking tissues for air storage, it resembles cacti and succulent plants in that it stores water in fleshy, leafless stems. In the process of osmosis, water generally moves from a less concentrated solution to a more concentrated one. The sap of plant cells is usually more concentrated than soil water, and so the flow of water is into the plant. In a salt marsh, however, when the surrounding water is of high salt concentration, osmosis is reversed. Whereas most plants would die under such circumstances, halophytes such as pickleweed have the ability to concentrate and store certain salts in cell fluids, so maintaining the imbalance required for successful osmosis. In higher locations of the shallows where the salt content of the soil drops below a certain percentage, pickleweed gives way to other halophytes, notably jaumea, a succulent, and salt grass, which prefer less saline and better-drained conditions.

Research on the Bay's tidal shallows has revealed their surprisingly high levels of fertility in terms of nutrient flows and abundance of life-forms. In part this is attributable to the regular tides, which both deliver oxygen and nutrients to the shallows and also remove wastes. The community also produces its own vegetative food supplies in the forms of plankton, algae, grasses and other plants. Anaerobic bacteria of the muds contribute to decomposition of decaying vegetation and subsequent organic enrichment of the habitat. Other forms of life also contribute to fertility: mussels in particular excrete phosphate, a fertilizer which greatly enhances the quality of the mud deposits for plants.

Animal life is rich and varied in the shallows. Permanent residents are dominated by invertebrate forms. Extensive beds of mussels, clams and cockles are either sustained by plankton carried in on tidal currents, or ingest nutrients from the mud. Mud-flat crabs and hermit crabs scavenge alongside burrowing anemones, clams and bristle worms; crawling horn and purple snails; bedded oysters and waiting whelks. Higher up the natural food chains are the flocks of waterbirds, which await the outgoing tide's exposure of mud-dwelling invertebrates. Coots, gulls and pintails forage with avocets at low tide; whilst herons, egrets and diving ducks hunt in the shallows throughout the day in search of fish and swimming crustaceans. Simple and complex food-chain and web relationships harmonize with the rhythms of day and night, high and low tides, winter and summer seasons.

The Bay shallows of San Francisco illuminate key ecological principles and interactions associated with biotic communities. Competition and predation, for example, characterize the relationships between many species. Invertebrates must avoid being eaten, as well as death from drowning or dehydration. Commensalism is displayed by inhabitants such as the burrowing flat innkeeper tube worm, which can shelter other organisms in such a way that they can feed or gain benefit without harm to the host. Food chains and food webs exist in both simple and complex forms. The fundamental principle of adaptation, that is the successful meeting of and living with environmental conditions, governs the range and diversity of life. The salt-marsh, mud-flat environment imposes limiting conditions on members of its community. Adaptation is thus one of the key principles associated with this immediate present-day community; a central tenet of evolutionary history. No individual or species adapts to local conditions readily; those best fitted to meet specific physical and biological conditions will survive through gradual acclimatization and evolutionary changes which accommodate characteristics of the given surroundings. Inevitably environments too will modify and change through time, leading to changes in species of plants present, and corresponding changes in the species of animals. The sequential changes which take place constitute a community's 'succession', with the rate of succession being dependent upon a variety of factors including climate and the availability of suitable plants that can 'move in', adapt and colonize the area. If the persistent infilling of the San Francisco Bay by natural as well as deliberate human deposition continues, this will inevitably lead to long-term changes in both flora and fauna of the region. Succession will be marked by a gradual shift from aquatic to water's-edge forms of life in many Bay perimeter locations. As a whole, the Bay shallows comprise a series of thriving biological communities. They display a complex range of interdependent relationships and self-stabilizing mechanisms, and are characterized by short-term internal balance alongside natural longer-term evolutionary changes.

Scene two focuses on the region of Africa known as the Sahel, which includes the countries of Mauritania, Senegal, Mali, Chad, Niger and Upper Volta (now Burkina-Faso). Throughout the years 1968–73 this region suffered catastrophic drought, killing thousands of people and millions of animals, and drawing world attention to the issue of desertification. Prior to this diaster, years of exceptionally good rains in the Sahel region had resulted in the spreading of arable cropping practices on to otherwise marginal lands, and the expansion of cattle herds on to poor arid lands on the desert's edge. Both of these practices – cropping and grazing – were of such intensity as to be in excess of sustainable levels. Nomadic pastoralists had traditionally adopted a regular pattern of movement in order to make the best possible use of the poor grazing options available in the Sahel region. Their pattern was to move cattle herds south in the dry season in order to graze on the farms of the settled cultivation in the South. Animals would feed on the fields of stubble left over from the preceding harvest whilst usefully manuring the land. At the onset of the rains, the cattle would be moved north to seek available pasture. This proved to be a mutually beneficial relationship between the nomadic pastoralists and the southern cultivators.

A combination of factors led to the Sahel drought disaster. In the first instance there was severe (though not unprecedented) drought. Early and heavy rains fell in 1968, then ceased in early May. Crop seedlings died before the return of the rains in June. As a result, cattle were already dying of hunger by the end of the dry season early in 1969. In 1970 the rains failed again, and the nomadic herdsmen who had moved furthest north during the rainy season were most affected. The rains of 1971, 1972 and 1973 were also below average. As the rains began to fail, herds of cattle were left with ever-shrinking pastures, and animals began to die at great rates as a result of lack of food rather than the direct shortage of water.

By the end of 1970, some three million people in the six nations of the Sahel were in need of emergency food aid. It is estimated (UNCOD 1977) that the drought as a whole claimed the lives of between 100,000 and 250,000 people. Millions of cattle and sheep were lost: the United Nations Food and Agricultural Organization estimated that 3.5 million cattle died in the year 1972/3 alone, with a total loss in excess of ten million. The drought concentrated scientific and public interest on the problems of the Sahel, and in particular on its climate. Resultant analysis suggests that in fact climatic change was not to blame for the disaster. Climatologists agreed that there was no evidence for a trend in falling rainfall in the Sahel area. Indeed, historical evidence shows that rains have failed through time in the region: a drought in the years 1910–14 was more severe than that of the 1968–73 period.

Whilst low levels of rainfall were clearly a major contributing factor in the disaster, they combined with various other causes which may firmly be attributed to human activity. For example, national governments in the newly independent nations in the Sahel region interfered with or even terminated the seasonal migrations of nomadic pastoralists, putting far greater pressure from grazing on key areas of land, whilst eliminating the mutual benefits of the long-established system. Parallel to this trend came pressures to reduce fallow periods and to grow more cash crops rather than staples; all at a time when greatly improved medicines and access to human and veterinary health care resulted in vast increases in the numbers of people and animals in the region. A situation had arisen where the natural environment had reached the absolute limits of its 'carrying capacity', the ability of an environment to support a population. Cattle numbers had reached such a level that available pastures could no longer sustain them. Furthermore, so-called aid programmes were controversial; some funded the provision of cattle water holes, which actually had the effect of concentrating vast numbers of cattle in selected areas, leading to complete destruction of the pasture in these places by the animals' trampling and grazing. The causes and impact of the Sahel disaster are thus complex. The attention of readers wishing to pursue this case study in detail is drawn to the 'Plan of Action' of the UNCOD (1977) Conference; also to commentaries on the Sahel drought and desertification issues (for example, Grainger 1986; Caldwell 1975; Club du Sahel/CILSS 1981; Jaiswal 1977; Tolba 1982). In short, it may be concluded that land degradation and the disastrous results of drought are largely attributable to human action in four particular forms: over-grazing, over-cultivation, bad irrigation and deforestation. Once again, basic principles of ecology are illuminated in this example, and it could be argued that the Sahel tragedy could have been avoided if closer attention had been paid to ecological balance and related governing principles. In particular, the concept of carrying capacity has already been mentioned. The resources of any environment include energy and nutrients; with limits to their availability. Individual members of a community compete with each other for energy and nutrient supplies as well as for physical space. An individual's chances of survival must therefore depend upon how many other individuals are present and competing for resources at any one time. Other factors will also influence an organism's chances of survival – the ability to escape predators, to find shelter, to maintain appropriate body temperatures, and so on. The carrying capacity of an environment includes everything that influences or regulates the size of a particular population within it. If the carrying capacity is reached, then the population will be regulated at a fixed level. In the case of the Sahel drought, the carrying capacity was reduced as a result of greatly increasing numbers of both animals and people; many did not survive, and long-term or permanent environmental degradation resulted. Two of the 'limiting factors' affecting the size of the cattle and human populations were, of course, availability of food and availability of water. The Sahel disaster is also a vivid example of the adverse impact of human life in an ecological framework, a theme to which this chapter will return. The nomadic pastoralists had traditionally practised successful grazing patterns which reflected an understanding of the complex and extremely delicate ecological balance of the region; a balance destroyed by a series of actions which took little or no account of ecological considerations.

Scene three tells of the introduction of the European rabbit, *Oryctolagus cuniculus*, into Australia. This animal, which originated in the western Mediterranean area, was recognized as early as Roman times as being a serious pest because of its grazing and burrowing habits. Yet traders continued to transport rabbits around the world on board ships as a source of fresh meat. Accounts differ in their reporting of how and when the rabbit first arrived in Australia. Some tell of the pastoralist Thomas Austin, who allegedly arrived in Australia with rabbits in 1854, desiring to recreate scenes of traditional English hunting sports. Some report the arrival of HMS *Lightning* with around a dozen rabbits in Melbourne, on 25 December 1859; whilst others claim that European settlers brought rabbits into the country as early as 1788. It seems that by the mid-nineteenth century, they were in every major settlement in the land, and had been liberated into the bush; yet for some years populations remained localized. Within three years of the HMS *Lightning* shipment arriving in Victoria, however, the rabbit population began to spread at a pace, following the destruction by a bush fire of fences enclosing one colony. During the period 1870–1900, *Oryctolagus cuniculus* spread 1,000 miles to the north and west, having considerable impact on the ecology of south-eastern Australia (Myers 1971). By 1910, an area of some one and a half million square miles had been colonized, covering a vast range of natural environments including stony deserts, wet coastal plains and subtropical grasslands. Two factors contributed to the very rapid colonization of the land by this species: natural dispersal and human interference. The thriving fur trade motivated trappers to move ahead of natural colonization, establishing rabbit colonies with animals carried across land in saddle-bags. Thus within a few decades, the small numbers of rabbits initially introduced had multiplied into millions. They burrowed and grazed their way through pasture land and natural habitat alike, becoming the most serious pest ever to be encountered in Australia. A devastating impact was made upon sheep- and cattle-grazing land. Hunters were paid to try and eradicate the problem: millions of rabbits were trapped, shot or poisoned, yet these efforts made little or no impact on numbers in the population. The widely held belief that killing large numbers of a population will control or eliminate its members was proved to be wrong. Trapping, shooting or poisoning rabbits selectively removes the dominant animals, as they tend to be more mobile and visible. As a result, territorial aggressiveness and dominant breeding stock are reduced; and subordinate females will then breed. As there are more subordinate females than dominant ones in the total rabbit population, the net result is that the overall reproduction rate goes up rather than down, even though many individuals are being killed. Attempts to control the rabbit population of Australia actually made the pest situation worse rather than better; a scenario often repeated in pest-control efforts generally. A key message conveyed by this account is that attempts at species control will be successful only if ecological processes and principles are understood and addressed. As with the Sahel case study, the Australian rabbit story is a classic example of human interference underpinned by ecological ignorance. No attention was paid to ecological processes (relating to the social structure of the rabbit population) that act as natural controls; indeed, rabbits were released from natural controls by human intervention. As for the broader question of the wisdom of introducing rabbits into the land mass of Australia at all, again the message parallels that illustrated by the Sahel disaster: it is essential to understand and apply basic principles and processes; to weigh up the advantages and disadvantages and the positive and the negative impacts from an ecological perspective *before* action is taken, rather than when the consequences are evident.

The case study from Australia illustrates a number of basic concepts and principles that have already been referred to, including the natural selection and adaptation of organisms within particular elements, the regulation of populations, the importance of carrying capacity, food chains, competition for basic needs, and the potential for adverse human impact in an ecological framework. The case study also illuminates a further fundamental principle, which is that if populations are unconstrained, they will grow very rapidly. When a species of plant or animal is placed in a supportive, even if unfamiliar environment, it may proliferate unchecked until ecological constraints (for example, limits to food supply) halt further growth of the population. This capacity for plants and animals to increase very rapidly in numbers is often referred to as exponential growth. Examples of exponential population growth may be based on evidence of geographical spread (for example, spread of disease organisms during an epidemic), or on the actual numbers of organisms involved. A key principle linked to exponential increase is the attendant tendency for the resources upon which the population depends to become depleted exponentially. If the resource is renewable, then the tendency will be resisted to an extent, for instance, grass pasture will generally be replaced by more grass until carrying capacity is exceeded. If the resource is not renewable, then it will be depleted at a great rate as the demands of the population increase.

A study of the structure and dynamics of populations is a major concern of ecologists, involving investigating births, deaths, immigration and emigration, and attempting to find out what controls these processes. No population increases without limit, and four components of the environment serve to influence population changes: food, weather, other organisms and having a niche or place to live. Such a simple statement inevitably conceals considerable ecological complexity, the teasing out and understanding of which is a major challenge of the science.

Each of the three key units studied by ecologists, individuals, populations and communities is exemplified by one or more of the case-study examples. The individual organism is the fundamental unit of interest, perhaps a dominant female rabbit; a population is all of the members of a single species in any particular location, for example, *Oryctolagus cuniculus* in Australia. Many different populations make up a biological community, such as a salt marsh, which is an assemblage of all the plants and animals found in a particular environment. Communities cannot be isolated from the chemical and physical aspects of our world: all organisms are composed of chemicals, and they obey the laws of physics. The combination of a community and its non-living environment is termed an ecosystem. Two fundamental areas of interaction between the biological and physical components of an ecosystem are climate, and the cycling and recycling of energy and nutrients. Ecosystems are independent of external sources of energy, other than the sun; and have the capacity to circulate all materials necessary for the continuation of life-forms, including water and other inorganic matter. Ecologists may well apply the term 'ecosystem' on a variety of scales with no limit to size or complexity. It may, for example, describe self-sustaining life centred around one particular plant (the ecosystem of an oak tree, of pickle-weed); it may explain interactions centred around an assemblage of populations in a specific environment (the ecosystem of a tidal mud flat, of a tropical rain forest, of a range of coastal dunes); or it may be used to refer to the entire living world, the biosphere of planet Earth. Whatever its scale or complexity, an ecosystem provides a framework within which solar energy is captured and channelled through a variety of forms of life. Within a stable ecosystem, a dynamic internal balance is maintained, i.e. there is no tendency for one species to decimate another, despite predation, competition and adaptive change. Key concepts integral to balance within ecosystems are interdependence, carrying capacity and sustainability.

Figure 1 provides a diagrammatic representation of components of the biosphere. Solar energy is the only energy form to enter and leave the closed system. This is captured and utilized through the process of photosynthesis in natural ecosystems, where it is channelled through a complex series of interdependent life-forms. Populations and communities within natural ecosystems interact with their geophysical surroundings in the take-up and recycling of nutrients and materials. Most significantly, Figure 1 draws attention to the distinctive role of human life in the ecological framework. It illustrates a central theme of this chapter which is the peculiar place of human life in planetary ecosystems; the inequality of *Homo sapiens* as producer and consumer, and the injustice which typifies many of the relationships and activities in which humans are involved. It is interesting to note how few texts which contain a wealth of theory on ecology provide adequate (or even scant) coverage of humans' unique role in the biosphere. All of the basic principles and processes relating to ecological balance and stability can potentially be altered and disrupted by human activities. Such activities are peculiar in that they encompass biological, technological, industrial, economic and social interactions. Whilst, like all other species, people are dependent on natural ecosystems and the geophysical environment, we alone modify natural ecosystems, deplete non-renewable resources, generate pollution, and produce non-recyclable, hazardous waste substances. The impact of human life is edging natural systems close to the limit of the planet's carrying capacity, with international, interspecies and intergenerational implications.

The three chapters in Part III of this book focus on matters of international justice, leaving little doubt that internationally, the world faces major ethical dilemmas. Many environmental-problem impacts have no respect for territory or boundaries. Air pollution is but one example. The accident at the Chernobyl nuclear power-station in the Ukraine, USSR, which occurred in April 1986, started a great fire, and released radioactive debris into the air. Uncontrollable clouds

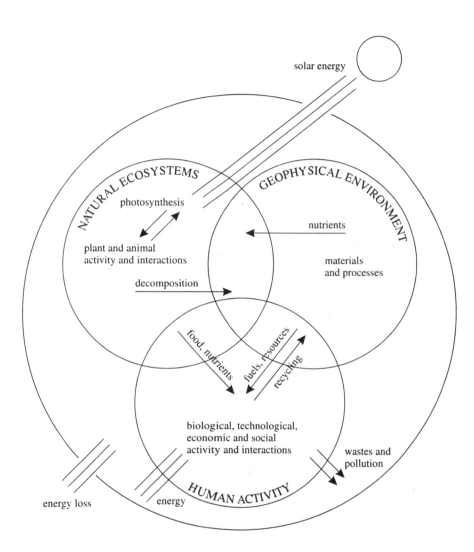

Figure 1 An ecological framework: the biosphere

trailed and dispersed their lethal deposits over the land of some twenty countries, up to 2,000 km from the reactor site. It is impossible to provide an accurate estimate of the impact of the disaster in terms of casualties. Thirty-five people died in their immediate attempt to control the inferno; hundreds were taken to hospital in the first day after the event. Some thirty-six hours after the explosion, 4,000 vehicles commenced the task of evacuating people within an 18-mile zone around the station. Some 130,000 people were eventually evacuated, many of whom had received their death sentence. It has been estimated that 24,000 citizens of the then USSR will die from Chernobyl-caused cancer-related deaths; that during the next fifty years there will be up to 60,000 Chernobyl-caused deaths around the world, 1,000 birth defects and 5,000 cases of radioactive-related genetic abnormality (Elsworth 1990). Radioactive emissions continued to be released from the power-station for a period of ten days. The extent of their impact depended upon wind strength and direction and rainfall; any rain had the effect of washing down radioactive materials to the ground, wherever that might be, with devastating effects on natural ecosystems. The impact across Europe certainly spread over an area from southern Italy to northern Scotland, and included Scandinavia. In the UK, the main areas affected were North Wales, Cumbria and Scotland, as a result of moderate localized rainfall. Official reactions varied from country to country, and were no doubt influenced by local attitudes to nuclear power. The Secretary of State for the Environment in the UK at the time denied health risks associated with the clouds. Yet in May 1986, levels of radioactivity in lambs in Cumbria were found to exceed the agreed safe limit; in June 1986, movement of lambs was restricted in England and North Wales because of contamination; in April 1987, 300,000 sheep were still under restriction; these restrictions were extended in England, North Wales, Scotland and Northern Ireland during 1987; and in March 1988, 322,000 animals were still covered by controls, with no indication of when restrictions would be lifted (Elsworth 1990). As far as human health risks are concerned, a gloomy scenario was outlined by the National Radiological Protection Board in the UK. Their figures suggest that a quarter of a million babies and young children in northern Britain could have received more than the recommended annual dose limit of radiation during the Chernobyl event (largely as a result of drinking fresh milk); and many of those children run a high risk of developing thyroid cancer. Independent researchers predicted that the Chernobyl disaster would cause 450–500 cancer deaths in the UK over a forty-year period, as well as thousands of non-fatal cancers (Elsworth 1990).

Regrettably, the Chernobyl incident was attributed in the main to human error; a tragic example of the ability of human life to interfere with natural ecosystems with disastrous results, and to generate hazardous substances which have far-reaching international impacts. Whilst Chernobyl may be something of an extreme example, the ethical dilemma of international injustice applies across the spectrum of global environmental issues. Environmental degradation, modification of ecosystems and their adverse impacts upon life-forms and societies are not equally shared among nations. The polluter, the exploiter, the degrader does not necessarily pay the cost of damage or carry the burden of responsibility. Wealthy countries do not necessarily bear the consequences of their actions; often it is economically developing countries which have to. A substantial proportion of the world's waste and pollution, including the so-called greenhouse gases and ozone-destroying gases, emerge from developed nations. The impacts of pollution, via the oceans and atmosphere, are global. Similarly, whilst developed nations continue to exploit the soils and forests of the tropics, the consequences are borne by indigenous populations and at a global level.

Whilst a sense of justice appears to be lacking on the international environmental scene, the inequality of human life compared to other life-forms dominates an analysis of interspecies considerations, aspects of which are discussed in the chapters in Part IV. The skills, power and technology available to people has allowed exploitation and squandering of both renewable and non-renewable resources, causing damage to or even extinction of life-forms. Damage to the critical ecological balance between humans, other forms of life, climate and the physical world was illustrated by the case studies of the Sahel drought and Australian rabbits; both demonstrated the ability of people to edge carrying capacities to their limits, with attendant disaster for other species.

Extinction is accepted as a natural feature of the evolution of life-forms. Yet it is hardly a just and accepted part of the natural evolutionary process that human activities have been responsible for the loss of most of the plant and animal species that have disappeared from our world during the past four hundred years. Thousands of insects, plants and small mammals have become extinct in this period, alongside seventeen species or subspecies of bears, five of wolves and foxes, four of cats, ten of cattle, sheep, goats and antelopes, five of horses, zebras and asses, and three of deer (Elsworth 1990). Wilson (1988) hypothesizes that some 17,500 species disappear from our planet each year. The process of extinction occurs in both the developed and developing worlds as a result of human activity. Some species are literally hunted to death: the panda, the rhinoceros and the African elephant amongst them. In most instances, animals and plants are endangered as a result of the degradation or destruction of the habitats on which they depend. Elsworth (1990) identifies three of the most significant environmental impacts: (1) the destruction of tropical rain forests, where an estimated half of all the world's species live; (2) the loss of wetlands; it is estimated that half of all the world's wetlands have disappeared this century, together with a rich range of life-forms; (3) countryside changes, as semi-natural and natural land has been taken over by agriculture, pesticides have destroyed habitats, the building of towns and roads has obliterated natural habitats, and over-intensive agricultural practices have led to land degradation. Such impacts have resulted from the ever-rapid and excessive growth of the human population and its ever-expanding needs for space and resources.

Interestingly, the ecological imbalance between humans and their environment and the scale of disruption caused by interspecies inequality has only become evident in the fairly recent past. In her seminal work *Silent Spring* (1962), Carson drew attention to human decimation of other life-forms in the biosphere, and raised awareness of the continuing disruption of ecosystems and the delicate interspecies relationships within them. One of the first major reports on environment and development, *World Conservation Strategy* (IUCN 1980), emphasized the global scale of ecological imbalance, the impact of human endeavours on the carrying capacity of the planet as a whole, and the need for a global agenda for change.

The United Nations World Commission on Environment and Development (WCED 1987) extended the message of *World Conservation Strategy* by examining the notion of limits within an ecological framework. It argued that the exploitation of natural resources must be constrained if it is to be sustainable for future generations. Thus it focused not only on the present-day carrying capacity of the planet, but also on intergenerational obligations and issues; the subject of the chapters in Part II of this collection.

Ecosystems cannot support sustained increases in resources to human life without causing deprivation for other species in the short term, and long-term threat to the viability of the system to support life at all. From its earliest days on earth, the human species has overdrawn against the 'capital' of the natural world, by the squandering to a greater or lesser extent of fuels, forests and soils. The greatly expanded population of recent times now faces an exhausted capital, an inability to respect the planet's carrying capacity, and the major ethical dilemma of responsibility and concern for generations yet to come. Presumably any sense of fairness and justice will come about when *Homo sapiens* accepts and adopts lifestyles and practices which are maintained *within* rather than beyond the carrying capacity of the biosphere.

We suggest that before such lifestyles and practices ever come about, the seeds of justice must be rooted in an understanding of an ecological framework for survival. So many issues are viewed and debated from a human-centred perspective. Take the threat to species and biodiversity as an example. We so frequently read of the implications of the loss of plant species for the human race, of loss to medical research, of loss of a genetic pool that is required for scientific advances. A sense of justice that extends to all species, in all locations, and which is not tied to the short-term needs of present generations must surely encompass a planetary, ecological dimension.

This chapter has drawn attention to the operation of basic principles of ecology, and has placed some of the environmental problems affecting our planet in an ecological framework. It is suggested that an understanding of this framework is essential if any movement towards a fairer and more sustainable use of the resources of our planet is to be achieved. It is somewhat paradoxical that it is those same principles which illuminate the critical truth that ecosystems and their delicate relationships can be altered, disrupted and even destroyed by human activities. A study of ecology reveals the peculiar role of the human species in world ecosystems: the inequality of people when compared to other forms of life and even to other members of the same species.

To what extent can principles of justice operate in a world in which many may sit comfortably and view colour images of children starving or being beaten to death; in which one year's pastures are the next year's barren desert; in which we take pleasure in a sun-drenched summer sky without thought for the impact of its increasingly harmful rays on generations of the future?

If ideas are to be transformed into action, then ecological thinking will form an essential part of the transformation – thinking, it is to be hoped, which takes account not only of the incredibly intricate and multiple patterns of survival, of communities and systems, but also of the individuals in all their forms which comprise those systems – their place in the world's biological heritage, their true needs and their quality of life.

3 The interrelationship of population and environment

John I. Clarke

CHANGING INTERRELATIONSHIP

The interrelationship between population and environment, which is of concern to so many people today, is not a new issue. Most societies since ancient times have worried about it, anxious about the availability of food, resources, space and standards of living. Many people have developed ways of adapting their numbers, customs and economic activities to the exigencies of their environments, endeavouring to achieve harmony or homeostasis (Abernethy 1979). Cultural adjustments have been made over time to balance population numbers with resources, a task which was easier among traditional societies before the rapidity of modern change.

The interrelationship was also conceptualized long before statistical data were available, regular censuses were taken, and scientific analyses were possible. Philosophers and thinkers as adverse as Confucius, Aristotle, Ibn Khaldun, Machiavelli, Rousseau and Malthus all considered the problems of numbers of human beings living within the limitations of their physical environments, relating them to principles of a moral, ethical and philosophical nature (Parsons 1994; Teitelbaum and Winter 1988). Increasingly, they sought laws linking population and resources (Davis and Bernstam 1990), and positivist explanations of complex diversity.

The nineteenth and twentieth centuries – the period since Thomas Robert Malthus wrote his *An Essay on the Principle of Population* (1798) – have witnessed changes in the history of humanity so dramatic that they have transformed the interrelationships between populations and their environments. As people have become less bound to the land, the impacts of environments upon populations have diminished, while the impacts of populations upon environments have increased, both processes being much more evident in the more developed countries (MDCs) than in the less developed countries (LDCs).

Among the many social and economic changes which have triggered transformations in population–environment interrelationships are (Clarke 1989):

- accelerating technological advances;
- changes in sources of energy;
- industrialization and its dispersal;
- mechanization, intensification, extensification and commercialization of agriculture and the decline of more traditional forms of agriculture;

- improvements in transportation and greater human mobility;
- territorial division of the world into states, and the nationalization of their populations;
- growing economic differentiation of countries and populations;
- spread of education and the universalization of information flows resulting from improved communications;
- huge growth of the service sector, particularly concentrated in cities; and
- growing globalization of markets.

Each of these changes has had manifold effects upon the distribution, composition and growth of populations and the ways that they have interacted with their environments. Among the major population changes that have taken place during the last two centuries are (Clarke 1989):

- the peopling by Europeans of many of the previously lesser populated areas of the world (Americas, Oceania, Central Asia), effecting a rather more even continental population distribution;
- widespread and large-scale urbanization, rising from about 2 per cent of the world population in 1800 to over 43 per cent today, including the recent rapid growth of mega-cities, particularly in the LDCs;
- growing concentration of population in economic core areas of countries, and relative and absolute depopulation of harsher and peripheral environments, such as deserts, mountains and tundra;
- differential demographic transition from high to low birth and death rates, initially transforming population growth rates within MDCs, and latterly affecting most LDCs to a greater or lesser extent, so that the world's population multiplied 5 1/2 times from under 1 billion in 1800 (Biraben 1979) to over 5.5 billion in 1993;
- accompanying socio-demographic changes, notably the spread of the nuclear family system, the rising status and changing roles of women, and the ageing of populations, all affecting the MDCs in particular; and
- greater direct and indirect influence of governments upon population dynamics, and much greater availability of population data through the spread of censuses, vital and other registration and surveys.

These various processes have led to widely varying populations – socially, economically, politically and demographically – perceiving, utilizing, altering and degrading their own and other environments, whose rich diversity but fragile vulnerability are now gaining widespread awareness.

Demographic diversity has increased particularly since about 1970. In the period 1950–70 world population grew from about 2.5 billion to 3.6 billion, and the average annual rate of increase rose from about 1.7 per cent in the 1950s to 2.0 per cent in the 1960s, but by 1970 the rate of growth in the LDCs was as high as 2.5 per cent in contrast to only about 1.0 per cent in the MDCs. At that stage the demographic contrast was at its greatest, owing to previous demographic transition in the MDCs and declining mortality and sustained high fertility levels in the LDCs.

GLOBAL ISSUES

By 1970, rapid population growth in the LDCs and its effect upon world population growth had become a matter of global concern. That concern stimulated large-scale international action by United Nations organizations and numerous NGOs as well as government action by LDCs assisted often by MDCs, all with considerable success. While MDCs have generally experienced continued lowering and convergence of vital rates, there has been a marked divergence among the demographic rates of LDCs. Some, like China, Taiwan, South Korea, Hong Kong, Singapore, Thailand, Indonesia, Sri Lanka, Cuba, Puerto Rico, Chile and Uruguay, have achieved remarkable progress in demographic transition; while at the other end of the scale many of the poorest sub-Saharan countries and some in Asia (for example, Afghanistan, Nepal, Yemen) have achieved little reduction in fertility and mortality. In between lie many LDCs which have succeeded in reducing mortality more than fertility, for example some of the Middle Eastern Muslim countries. The result is that diversity of demographic growth has never been greater.

Apart from population growth, we have also seen a major increase in global awareness, arising from dramatic changes in transportation, telecommunications, transnational production and trade, tourism and travel (Alger 1988). The emergence of the space age, with its remotely sensed images, has also been a contributory factor.

More than ever before, people have become aware of world-wide phenomena and issues, often related to the existence of a modern world system that is based upon the development of a capitalist world economy emanating initially from Europe and functioning without any single political control (Wallerstein 1974). People have become conscious, for example, of the growth of cities, rural out-migration, the disadvantages endured by women, the growing distinctions between rich and poor countries and people (however defined), the problems of ethnicity, and the impacts of human populations upon the physical and biotic environment. Global awareness has inspired a broad spectrum of international social movements concerned with issues like family planning, the environment, solidarity, peace, human rights, women's rights, children, youth and consumers (Friberg and Hettne 1988).

All this is in spite of the fact that we live within a state system which fragments the earth and its peoples most unevenly, a few macro-states contrasting with a growing multitude of micro-states. The state system has impeded to a greater or lesser extent the movements of peoples, goods and ideas, as well as the successful evolution of international and transnational structures and actions. Through national self-interest, manifested at the 1992 UN Earth Summit Conference at Rio, it is now impeding concerted intergovernmental action to cope with the global environmental change that scientists are measuring and about which the literate public are gaining knowledge.

Most of us live and operate in localities within states, but by being urged to 'think globally but act locally' we are becoming gradually more aware that our individual actions affect the world system, which involves a series of interconnected processes and phenomena: social, economic, political and environmental. Our planet is a fragile system composed of natural and human systems where elements do not function in isolation.

Traditionally scholars tended to consider global phenomena separately, viewing them from their own particular academic disciplines. Where the latter were cognate, like demography, economics and sociology, the chances of overlap were high; where they were not, the chances were low. Hence, population changes were often studied in relation to social and economic processes but much less in relation to environmental phenomena. The gap between the social sciences and environmental sciences is bridged with difficulty; even within the subject of geography there is a strong tendency to dichotomize the human and physical aspects.

Awareness of global environmental change and the recent occurrence of large-scale disasters such as those in the Sahel and Horn of Africa and the deltaic zones of Bangladesh have emphasized the interrelatedness of global processes and phenomena, their causes never being entirely natural or human, but generally a complex combination of factors difficult to unravel. Consequently, the study of population–environment interrelationships has attracted a recent resurgence of research interest (Zaba and Clarke 1994; Stern, Young and Druckman 1992; Jacobson and Price 1990).

Past studies of population–environment interrelationships had focused either on how the geographical distribution and movement of population are related to the spatial variations in the nature of places, the stuff of population geography (for example, George 1959; Clarke 1965; Beaujeu-Garnier 1966), or on the more contentious and controversial topic of the relationship between population and resources, and the linked concepts of minimum, maximum and optimum population, underpopulations, overpopulation and carrying capacity. As Teitelbaum and Winter (1988) have stated, the latter topic has deeply polarized roots in western intellectual traditions, where for centuries scientists, philosophers, theologians and politicians have all made contrasting contributions, and where 'social thought and scientific analysis have cohabited, albeit uneasily for as long as these enquiries have gone on' (Teitelbaum and Winter 1988: 1). Dominated by a human-centred view of the world with materialist and rationalist themes, western philosophy has accorded relatively little attention until recently to ecological perspectives; to the nature and needs of ecosystems and the urgency to reorder social values in order to reduce the prospects of ecological disruption, not least because of its drastic consequences for human health and well-being.

As Davis and Bernstam (1990) emphasize, the field is interdisciplinary and the spectrum of approaches wide to what has been frequently but inadequately termed 'the population problem'. Demographers have generally given much less attention to population-resource problems than to more centrally demographic matters concerning fertility and mortality. Consequently, they have tended to eschew involvement in the popular Malthusian–Boserupian debate – in simple terms, between those who see population growth as a negative factor in economic and social development, and those who see it as a stimulus – and have left it to others, particularly to economists and biologists.

LOCAL REALITIES

One reason for the limited incursions by demographers into the debate between the optimists and pessimists has been the great and growing diversity of populations, whose interrelationships with immense environmental diversity have never been so varied. Traditional societies were greatly dependent upon and influenced by their immediate environments, to which they were more territorially tethered. Modern societies have progressively liberated themselves from environmental constraints and are much less directly dependent upon them; although they tend to use ever larger amounts of the earth's resources from ever more remote locations and cause ever greater environmental degradation.

Local populations have distinctive interrelationships with their environments, influenced greatly by a wide range of intervening social, economic and political factors. Cultural heritage and customs, level of technological development, income levels, welfare, economic activities, trade, exploitation of natural resources and the nature of government policies (local and national) all play important roles. That population–environment interrelationships are more diverse than ever before is perhaps symbolized by the huge contrasts in population density, ranging from largely uninhabited areas like Antarctica to more than a quarter of a million persons per square mile in cities like Hong Kong, and by the contrasting use of resources epitomized by Wall Street and a nomadic pastoral tribe. Moreover, population–environment interrelationships are always changing, especially under the influence of rapid technological progress, more numerous catastrophes and disasters, and abrupt shifts in social, economic and political processes.

Consequently, there are still some populations which are almost totally dependent upon their local resources and environments, and others which rely almost exclusively upon external resources. Some cause local environmental degradation; some cause degradation elsewhere. Thus national comparisons of population–environment interrelationships, say between Singapore, Sri Lanka and Sierra Leone, or between Iran, Israel and Ireland, are not very meaningful. At household and community level, the diversity is even greater.

Hence there is a major problem of linking findings at one scale with another (Gallopin 1991). Local causes of population dynamics, composition and distribution may not be the same as those for larger populations. For example, at local level climate plays less part in influencing population distribution than at continental level; while migration tends to play a much greater part in overall population change at local level than at continental level. Local-level population rates and ratios diverge markedly from the demographic means of states and world regions (Clarke 1976).

A similar scale-linkage problem occurs with environmental phenomena, the causes of local processes differing from those at more general levels. Thus earthquakes may have severe local effects but be insignificant nationally, whereas a volcanic explosion and climatic changes may have widespread transnational effects.

Population–environment interrelationships may therefore be studied at different spatial and time scales, the level being influenced by the nature of the environmental phenomena under consideration (Clarke and Rhind 1992). Generally, however, it is felt more rewarding to undertake micro-level studies in order to understand how population is linked to environmental degradation (Little *et al.* 1987). The problem is to find global-level generalizations from local-level studies.

VARIETY OF POPULATION IMPACTS ON ENVIRONMENTS

A number of global environmental changes have manifested themselves strikingly during the second half of the twentieth century, and they appear to have severe long-term implications:

- *the greenhouse effect*, caused by burning of fossil fuels and biomass, methane production from domesticated animals and rice cultivation, emission of CFCs and use of synthetic fertilizers, leading to global warming, other climatic changes and sea-level rise;
- *stratospheric ozone depletion*, caused by emission of CFCs and other forms of air pollution, producing increased UV-B flux at the earth's surface;
- *acid aerosols*, caused by fossil-fuel combustion and burning of biomass, leading to acid rain;
- *loss of biodiversity*, through destruction of terrestrial and marine habitats, leading to less genetic diversity and weakening of ecosystems;
- *land degradation*, associated with intensive agriculture, deforestation and over-grazing, leading to soil erosion, sterility and salinity;
- *decline in water quality and quantity*, caused by pesticide and herbicide use, toxic and human waste disposal, deforestation, irrigation, siltation, etc.; and
- *growth of urban concentration*, especially mega-cities, producing concentrated energy, pollution, resource extraction and toxic wastes.

All of these changes are related to human population growth, and this has been stressed particularly in the popular literature, but the relationship is usually indirect rather than direct, and operates through a variety of intermediate factors of social, economic and political significance.

It is important to emphasize that there are many other environmental impacts of human populations, not all of them negative. They include the dispersal, domestication and conservation of plants and animals; deforestation and extension of bushlands, grasslands, scrub and deserts; changes in water-tables, flows and flooding; mining and quarrying; subsidence and slope movement; and coastal erosion and deposition.

Such changes do not result exclusively from human interference, and environments vary greatly in their sensitivity to human impact. They are always changing through natural causes, but at different rates. Indeed, different processes, human and natural, can lead to the same environmental result – the principle of equifinality

(Goudie 1984). It is one reason why it is difficult to define land degradation, as distinct from land change.

Along with others, Goudie (1993) has also emphasized the high level of uncertainty that surrounds future environmental changes, owing to a variety of factors including the great complexity of natural systems; ignorance about previous environmental experience; the role of catastrophic events and unsuspected mechanisms (for example, CFCs); the imperfection of models, especially of general circulation; and the problem in predicting crucial events like rainfall.

Resource depletion is an environmental impact associated with population growth, but as in so many cases, technological progress plays a very important intervening role. Increased technology with the Industrial Revolution enabled a massive expansion in the availability and use of resources to serve a growing world population. This is illustrated by changes in energy use and its geographically uneven spread, the MDCs using vastly more per capita than the LDCs, where use is highly localized. Unfortunately, many of the resources used are non-renewable, like fossil fuels; but particularly regrettable is the loss of biodiversity of living species and complex systems, as not only do we benefit in innumerable ways from the diversity, but genetic variation is the basis of nature's adaptive capacity (Morowitz 1991; Wilson 1989).

The globalization of markets has meant that resources have global as well as local significance, especially in relation to world population growth and the desired aim of raising the living standards of the people of the LDCs. The latter comprise over 77 per cent of the world's population and account for nearly 94 per cent of its growth, so any rise in their living standards will be at the cost of increased use of resources.

Fortunately, technological progress is now facilitating some reductions in resource use, in a number of overlapping ways:

- greater technical efficiency, as in engines and electronics;
- dematerialization, in which heavy, bulky and costly raw materials like iron and steel are replaced by lighter and cheaper materials like plastics; and
- creation of new materials such as fibre-reinforced composites and advanced ceramics.

The MDCs used vast quantities of resources in the development of their basic infrastructures, which far exceed those of LDCs. They are now benefiting also from the substitution of materials through technology. It is hoped that they will facilitate technology transfer to LDCs so that they may benefit as well, especially in the field of improved energy efficiency, which would not only reduce resource depletion and environmental degradation but also facilitate the development of LDCs. The decarbonization of energy sources is seen by many (Kanoh 1992) as an essential task for the future.

DISCONTINUITIES AND DISASTERS

One of the difficulties in analysing population–environment interrelationships is that changes do not take place in a linear fashion, but more by shifts, discontinuities or 'jump effects'. These occur when there is an abrupt decline in the capacity of an environment to sustain populations at current levels of well-being, and when the ecosystem is severely disrupted; acid rain, laterization of tropical soils and desertification are obvious examples.

Ecological disruptions are often associated with disasters, which are generally defined as sudden catastrophes affecting populations (Clarke *et al.* 1989). They result from many different causes – environmental, technological, social, economic and political – and frequently from a combination of physical and human factors, as in the Sahel drought and deforestation in Nepal, where ecosystems are fragile. Human costs of disasters vary enormously, but generally those which are essentially non-natural (for example, warfare and bad political decisions like China's Great Leap Forward) are more devastating than so-called natural disasters.

Certainly population pressure can trigger disasters, particularly in marginal environments which are unable to cope with extra people and where over-cultivation and over-grazing have led to greater poverty or out-migration. The volume of out-migration is such that the term 'environmental refugees' has gained currency in recent years for those forced to leave their traditional habitat because of marked environmental disruption (Richmond 1993), though the term has no legal standing and it is very difficult to distinguish from other forms of migration.

It is apparent that there are limits or thresholds of population density above which economic and/or ecological deterioration takes place. As long ago as the mid-1960s Allan (1965) devised a critical density of population for tropical African subsistence societies based upon a conservationist approach to population pressure, defining it as:

the human carrying capacity of an area in relation to a given land use system, expressed in terms of population per square mile; it is the maximum population density which a system is capable of supporting in that environment without danger to the land.

This was a precursor of the concept of ecological carrying capacity or population-sustaining capacity, which means the ability of an area to sustain a population over a long period without major environmental discontinuities or irremediable damage to the environment. Although it is apparent that in many parts of the world populations are exceeding carrying capacities by over-utilizing resources and living off their capital rather than their interest, the concept of carrying capacity is more useful theoretically than practically (Zaba and Scoones 1994). While it is possible to calculate carrying capacities for relatively 'closed' populations living from traditional land-based activities, populations have a unique ability to modify environments and to develop external links which negate the search for fixed carrying capacities for local populations. This is especially true for more developed populations with global links, such as Japan and the United Kingdom, whose natural resources alone would not sustain large populations. Even when carrying capacity is calculated for the world as a whole, the diversity of results (7.5–50 billion) inspires little confidence. So for human populations the term is more notional than formal (McMichael 1993). Nevertheless, it is important to retain the concept, for there are limits to population pressures upon environments, however changing and difficult they are to determine.

THE CONCEPT OF SUSTAINABILITY

Analysis of population–environment interrelationships inevitably raises the issue of sustainability or sustainable development, a valuable concept popularized by the Brundtland Commission (WCED 1987: 43), whose definition has proved the most acceptable:

> Sustainable development is development that meets the needs of the present without compromising the ability of future generations to meet their own needs. It contains within it two key concepts:
>
> > – the concept of 'needs', in particular the essential needs of the world's poor, to which overriding priority should be given; and
> > – the idea of limitations imposed by the state of technology and social organization on the environment's ability to meet present and future needs.
>
> In essence, sustainable development is a process of change in which the exploitation of resources, the direction of investments, the orientation of technological development, and institutional change are all in harmony and enhance both current and future potential to meet human needs and aspirations.
>
> (WCED 1987: 46)

Sustainable development is, of course, a grandiose ideal and is sometimes scorned or discarded as too vague and ambiguous. Moreover, different specialists have different views about what is to be sustained. While biologists stress the preservation of the environment and biosphere, economists stress economic growth and consumption levels, and sociologists stress demands on the environment that are culturally determined (Brooks 1992). Consequently, there have been varied interpretations, some less environmental than others.

The Brundtland Commission called upon all countries to adopt the following principles to guide their national policies:

– revive growth, because poverty is a major source of environmental degradation;
– change the quality of growth to achieve sustainability, equity, social justice and security;
– conserve and enhance the resource base by reducing per capita consumption of resources and developing non-polluting processes and technologies;
– ensure a sustainable level of population through population policies which are integrated with programs for education, health care and raising standards of living, especially for the poor;
– reorientate technology to pay greater regard to environmental factors and costs;

- integrate environment and economics by requiring decision-makers to be responsible for the impact of their decisions upon the environmental resource capital;
- reform international economic relations to help developing countries to diversify their economic and trade bases and build self-reliance; and
- strengthen international co-operation for sustainable human progress.

Despite widespread support, the Brundtland Report did not receive universal acclaim. In particular, it did not accuse the MDCs of being responsible for many of the most severe environmental problems, nor did it emphasize the need to redistribute the world's wealth. Nevertheless, it did stress that a change of approach was required, reflecting that:

- the true costs of resource depletion and pollution should be calculated rather than just short-term costs and profits;
- future needs must not be neglected; and
- long-term economic development and environmental protection are inextricably linked.

Putting sustainability into practice is difficult, globally, nationally, locally and for specific purposes. Unfortunately, individual, community, national and global interests tend to conflict, and NIMBY (not in my backyard) attitudes tend to prevail. Society at large too often pays for the pollution and personal interest of the few.

A merit of sustainability is that it emphasizes an integrative approach in which there is no simple solution, but a whole basket of necessary measures which include the reduction of fertility, achievable not only by family planning, but also by improving the social status, health and education of women. Tetrault (1992: 31–5) has stressed the integrative approach in his report for the Canadian International Development Agency (CIDA), stating that

establishing a sustainable development hinges upon several commitments such as:

- tackling poverty and the debt issue
- planning the human family
- investing in people
- achieving food security and preserving soils and forests
- caring for biodiversity, water and oceans
- making sound energy choices.

In this way we shall gain the long-term food and environmental security that many would like to see on the international agenda, replacing past obsessions about military security.

WEALTH, POVERTY AND THE ENVIRONMENT

Widening inequalities in income levels in the world lead to vast differences in consumption levels, use of resources and ability to invest in environmental protection. The slowly growing wealthy populations of the MDCs consume more and more in their persistent search for ever more affluence, but their polluting technologies which cause so much global environmental degradation have been quite resistant to change (Commoner 1988, 1990). They have turned attention particularly to the important role of population growth as a proximate cause of environmental change (Shaw 1989). Manifesting itself mainly in the LDCs, it reduces their prospects of sustainable development, but also increases their potential for environmental degradation.

Much environmental degradation in the developing world today arises from poor people seeking the basic essentials for human life: food, water, fodder and fuel. The rural poor living from subsistence agriculture are very affected by environmental vicissitudes, especially in marginal areas. They suffer from inadequate housing, sanitation, water-supply and waste disposal, as well as ill health caused by environmental diseases (for example, tuberculosis, dysentery, malaria, trypanosomiasis, onchocerciasis, filariasis and schistosomiasis), a phenomenon which has been greatly reduced within MDCs. The plight of women and children is particularly problematic, women managing not only reproduction but many aspects of production as well: collection of fuelwood and water, farming and many craft industries.

Among the least developed countries, especially in sub-Saharan Africa, there are many unsustainable enclaves or crisis areas, identified by FAO studies (Higgens and Kassam 1985). For the poor, out-migration has become a major outlet to environmental pressures, but often the poorest in rural areas have been the least able to avail themselves of the opportunities offered by migration.

The outpouring from the countryside into LDC cities has led to huge increases in the numbers of urban poor; during 1975–90 they grew by 81 per cent in Africa and more than doubled in Latin America. Their urban environments, usually slums and shanty towns, are often worse than those in rural areas through the proximity of industrial plants and waste-disposal sites producing air and water pollution and engendering environmental diseases. While urban growth in the developing world averages 3.6 per cent per annum and mega-city growth continues largely unabated, the problems will not be reduced.

In these circumstances, it is vital to use the synergism which exists between population growth, the persistence of widespread poverty and environmental degradation, by investing in the poor. They should be targeted with investments in their environments (for example, reafforestation, water-supply, land improvements, waste disposal), education (especially of females) and health (for example, tackling environmental diseases). In this context, there is much to be said in favour of population education and environmental education, both sponsored extensively by international organizations (for example, UNESCO, UNFPA), as well as population–environment education involving analysis of the multifaceted interrelationships between population and environment at local and global scales, and which might be incorporated most readily within geography curricula (Clarke 1993).

CONCLUSION

In some ways, the experience of the UNCED Conference at Rio in 1992 was a set-back to a more holistic approach to population–environment problems in the world. The manifest reluctance of the MDCs to assist the LDCs in their environmental and developmental challenges, except in the area of population control, widened the gaps. Although undoubtedly important, population control is not the answer to all environmental and developmental challenges – Eastern Europe alone exemplifies this. Debt relief, technology transfer and more open trade, for example, are all essential. Scientists are beginning to stress the need for much broader strategies aimed at economic growth, environmental protection and sustainable development through the reduction of rapid population growth, widespread poverty, water wastage and dangerous resource use along with greater management of population redistribution, increased promotion of renewable energy sources and more responsible attitudes to the world's ecosystems.

Global environmental change has highlighted not only the dangers of rapid population growth but numerous other unfortunate features of our time, some of which threaten the future survival and the well-being of our planet. A major shift in values is required to rectify this situation.

Part II

Intergenerational issues

4 The environment and justice for future generations

Barry S. Gower

In recent years many countries in the developed world have, to a greater or lesser extent, introduced programmes intended to limit, prevent, and where possible reverse the damage that people inflict on the environment. Some have imposed strict controls on emissions of harmful gases from power-stations and from vehicle exhausts. Some have introduced controls on the disposal of toxic wastes from factories, and of radioactive wastes from nuclear installations. Some monitor the quality of the air people breathe and the water they drink. Some educate and encourage citizens to recycle as much as possible of what they discard. Some support and provide incentives for ventures which conserve non-renewable resources or which enable those resources to be used more efficiently. Some ban the manufacture and use of destructive chemicals. Some use planning regulations to control the kind of 'architectural pollution' which can occur in, for example, popular tourist resorts (see Prosser 1992: 42). Some, indeed, say they do all these things and more. And there are numerous local, national and international pressure groups which exhort governments and the people they represent to implement programmes of this nature. When governments respond to this exhortation they do so, no doubt, because there are powerful and practical political motives for promoting policies which conserve scarce resources and reduce pollution; political parties which seek power need to adopt at least some so-called 'green' policies.

But many would see 'green' policies as worth pursuing independently of any party political advantage their adoption might bring. To aim for an unpolluted environment is to aim for a better environment, and in so far as a government achieves this aim it promotes the well-being of its citizens. Pollution is an evil, and by reducing or eliminating it, governments make people's lives 'go better'. No doubt the benefits of reduced levels of pollution can be achieved only if the members of a society constrain activities which they would otherwise wish to pursue; there are, that is to say, social costs which will have to be paid. Nevertheless, the knowledge we now have of the extent of the damage pollution creates has persuaded many people that some way of meeting these costs should be found.

How, though, will the benefits of programmes intended to prevent pollution and protect the environment be distributed among those affected? And how will the costs of introducing and developing these programmes be distributed among those who pay? These are questions about whether, and if so why, a particular way of distributing benefits and costs is a fair distinction, and the way they are answered in a society tells us whether the virtue of justice is to be found in that society.[1] Success in implementing 'green' policies is not, by itself, a reliable indication of the presence of this virtue, for even if the benefits of such policies far exceed their burdens, some ways of sharing them out would not be fair. For example, it would be unjust to promote socio-economic arrangements which lead to a prosperous minority enjoying the benefits of a pollution-free environment whilst the impoverished majority bear the costs of providing it. Yet sometimes this can be the effect of environmental protection policies. Hazardous wastes, together with the factories and power-stations which produce them, are more likely to be found in the neighbourhoods of the poor than in those of the rich; the prevalence of diseases caused by air pollution will be greater for the poor than for the rich; the costs of living in an environment with inadequate recreational facilities will be proportionately greater for the poor than for the rich (see Krieger 1970: 311–24 and Sagoff 1988: 56). In these and other ways, social arrangements intended to benefit members of society by improving their environment can be unjust because they make life worse for some of the already disadvantaged members of that society.

Questions of distributive justice arise not only within a society, but also between societies. For instance, in some parts of Western Europe, where pollution from heavy industry was considerable, the costs of providing a healthier environment are being paid, at least in part, in other parts of the world now suffering from the pollution caused by the introduction and development of those industries. With the growth of multinational corporations, the injustices arising from exporting the costs of benefits enjoyed in the affluent West seem likely to become more pronounced. Again, until recently, chloro-fluorocarbon (CFC) gases were freely used in some countries and played a significant part in economic development, but because of the environmental damage these gases are now known to cause, countries in the Third World cannot use them so freely and their economic development is, to an extent, hampered. The benefit of the effects of past use of CFC gases are enjoyed by relatively few; the direct and indirect costs of the damage they have created and of the disadvantages that their ban brings are distributed among a great many people and in a way that bears no relation to the distribution of the benefits. Financial intervention by rich economies may help to alleviate some of the effects of these injustices, but it cannot compensate for the loss, damage and destruction which is their immediate cause.

We recognize, too, that the burdens and benefits of the steps taken to exploit the environment, as well as to protect it from exploitation, should be distributed fairly between people who live at different times as well as people who live in different places. We therefore need to ask what one generation can reasonably and fairly be asked to sacrifice for the sake of a clean and safe environment for subsequent generations. We need to ask how far the costs of environmental policies promoted for the benefit of our generation should be paid by future generations, as well as how far the costs of policies introduced for the benefit of future generations should be paid by our generation. In practice, of course, responses to these questions become entangled with international justice; in so far as effective policies for the protection of future generations are introduced, it is more than likely that their costs will be disproportionately greater for poor economies than for rich ones.

To answer these questions we require general principles, or at least guidelines. A society which adopts an environmental policy does so because the benefits it brings are thought to outweigh the burdens it imposes; but scarce benefits and heavy burdens have to be shared, and it is principles of justice which determine whether a particular way of sharing them is said to be just or unjust. Who, though, are we to count among those who share? It may be possible for many people to receive the benefits and incur the burdens of the policy, but should our principles of distributive justice be concerned only with those who contract, in some sense, to live in the society in question? If so, 'reciprocity' will be a necessary condition for judgements about the justice of distributions; where there can be interaction, interdependence and reciprocal advantage between societies, questions of social justice can arise; where there cannot be interaction, as between non-overlapping generations, they cannot. According to this view, justice is a virtue which has application to the social arrangements for the sharing of advantages people gain as a result of co-operating with each other, and of any disadvantages which that co-operation may entail. Since members of non-overlapping generations are unable to co-operate with each other in order to secure advantages which can be shared, the effects of one generation's actions on another cannot be described as either just or unjust. So, although it may be wrong to require future generations to enjoy less than their fair share of the advantages of our environmental policies and to bear more than their fair share of their disadvantages, it is not a requirement of justice that we avoid arrangements which bring about these effects. We can be said to have obligations of humanity or of beneficence to future generations, but we cannot be said to be acting unjustly if we fail to discharge them. By adopting environmental policies which enable us to prosper at the expense of future generations we act selfishly and wrongly; but we do not act unjustly.[2]

The difficulty with this approach is not so much that it restricts the scope for considerations of justice in a way that many would consider mistaken (for example, Mill 1954) as that it conflicts with the ways in which we use the concept of justice. In particular, we think that a decision affecting other people can be appraised as just or unjust irrespective of when, as well as of where, the people affected live. Thus if an environmental policy results in very few enjoying its benefits whilst very many endure its burdens we would count it as unjust, and its injustice would not depend on when it is implemented any more than it would depend on where it is implemented. We naturally and intuitively suppose that we have a duty of justice towards future generations to conserve scarce resources, to preserve rain forests, to ban chemicals which damage the protective ozone layer in the atmosphere, etc. Our concept of justice is such that one society can, and often does, behave unjustly towards another even though there may be no means of rectifying the injustice; an understanding of justice which fails to reflect this cannot be satisfactory. Principles of justice should, we think, be impartial, and part of what this means is that they should be as 'blind' to differences in generation as they are, or should be, to national differences. We need to recognize, of course, that judgements about justice and injustice are made in particular contexts, and that it is only by attending to the diversity of contexts that we can ensure that principles of justice are applied sensibly. At a practical level, differences of place and occasion are relevant; people have different interests and objectives partly because the places where, and the times at which, they live are different, and our judgements about people cannot entirely overlook these differences. However, to overemphasize the particularity of judgements about what is just and to understate the universality of principles is to endorse the traditions, assumptions and prejudices which define the differences of time or place, and so to compromise impartiality. With regard to intergenerational justice it matters how we place the emphases. For we need, in the interests of impartiality, to overlook the diverse contexts of peoples' lives in different generations; and we also need, in the interests of fairness, to be sensitive to these same differences (see O'Neill 1993: 303–4 and Thompson 1992: introduction).

It might be objected that by basing these intuitions on 'our' conception of justice we beg the relevant questions. We are, in effect, appealing to the supposed authority of our conception, and unless this supposition can be defended little or no confidence should be placed in these intuitions. But where the intuitions are considered convictions they cannot be easily abandoned, and we shall want to explore a less peremptory response to the conflict. For most people it is a considered conviction and not just an uncritical intuition that our environmental policies can be described as just or unjust in respect of their effects upon people who will live in the future. We need, therefore, to develop a conception of justice which allows that the benefits and burdens of an environmental policy can be distributed in ways that are just and ways that are unjust, irrespective of whether those benefited or burdened can be said to have consented to the policy. *Mutual* advantage is no longer crucial. What remains central is the issue of whether the way benefits and burdens are distributed is fair.

For the sake of simplicity consider two societies, the Greens and the Blues, which have settled at widely separated places but both on the banks of a particular river. The Greens, we suppose, live upstream from the Blues, and the two settlements are sufficiently far apart for them to be, at first, ignorant of each other's existence. We suppose, also, that the two societies have quite different social structures, different traditions of moral and political thought, and that they enjoy different levels – perhaps very different levels – of prosperity. So long as the two societies remain unaware of each other's existence neither can accuse the other of behaving unjustly even though the actions – or inaction – of one may in fact have harmful effects on the other. For example, it may be that the Greens dispose of pollutants, produced by industries essential to their economic development, by discharging them into the river, and that as a consequence of this some of the Blues suffer from ill health, or the economic welfare of the Blues is undermined. All of the benefits of the Greens' policy are enjoyed by at least some of the Greens; all of the burdens of that policy are shouldered, albeit unknowingly, by at least some of the Blues. We may wish to censure the Greens' actions as thoughtless or uncaring, especially if they have been made aware that their policy *could* affect those who live downstream, but we cannot condemn their actions as unjust. Suppose, though, that the Greens become aware of the Blues' existence and of the effect that their environmental policy has upon them. Then, it seems, an obligation of justice does arise; not only *should* the Greens desist from discharging pollutants into the river, but they have an obligation of justice to do so. Whether or not there is any authority which can oblige the Greens to cease polluting the river, it is clear that this is what justice requires. This conclusion appears to stand whatever else may be true of the two societies. It would not be overturned by the fact, or by knowledge of the fact, that the Blues' level of prosperity and general well-being is higher than that of the Greens. It would not be overturned by the fact, or by knowledge of the fact, that if the Greens were to desist from polluting the river, their well-being would improve whilst that of the Blues would decline. Such facts may well have a bearing on what we think should be done. It may be that the weight of other considerations would lead to the conclusion that the Greens should not abandon their practice, but we would reach that conclusion knowing that it requires us to condone an injustice.

This example shows that considerations of justice not only arise when the effects of *mutually* advantageous policies are in question. The Blues play no part in the formulation or implementation of the Greens' environmental policy, and yet it seems that the Greens are behaving unjustly if they continue discharging pollutants into the river once they become aware of its effects on the Blues. The example also draws attention to an important practical problem. In sharing fairly the benefits and, especially, the burdens of an environmental policy it is crucial that we appreciate their nature and extent. So long as the Greens and Blues remain ignorant of each other's existence there will be no understanding of the damaging effects of the Greens' policy as costs of that policy which have to be paid by someone. But even when the two societies do become aware of each other's existence, the extent of their knowledge of these effects and of their understanding of them as costs will remain limited. The injustice of the Greens' policy will be recognized, but its moral significance will depend upon how much knowledge and understanding there is of the extent of the policy's burdens and of the particular way they are distributed.

The analogy with intergenerational justice is plain. The generation to which we belong has some understanding, albeit conjectural, partial and uncertain in many respects, of the effects that our environmental policies will have upon future generations. On the assumption that those policies remain unchanged and that other relevant factors will vary in certain ways, we can make predictions about the circumstances in which the lives of future generations will be lived. We can anticipate the levels of ultra-violet radiation reaching the earth's surface which will result from our use of chemicals which harm the earth's protective ozone layer; we can anticipate rises in the sea-level as a result of the production of 'greenhouse gases' and the consequent 'global warming'; we can anticipate a greater incidence of respiratory and coronary diseases caused by air pollution in urban environments; we can anticipate that imperfections in our current methods of storing radioactive waste will result in an increased risk of radiation-induced diseases. No doubt some of these predictions are less reliable than others, and in every case our confidence depends upon how far into the future our anticipations extend. But though our understanding of the effects of our policies is incomplete, the analogy suggests that we are not thereby absolved from considering the justice of our policies in so far as they affect future generations.

Before we can draw any conclusions we need to see what account of justice might support our belief that the Greens can behave unjustly towards the Blues. In the writings of Plato, Aristotle, Aquinas, Hume and many other philosophers we can find such accounts. But it will be claimed that the views these philosophers express about justice, whether or not they take a contractarian form, have a 'local' or 'limited' character in that they reflect and encapsulate historically specific views about human life and about social relationships. Thus, Aquinas' account of justice reflects the complex interactions between sacred and secular interests in thirteenth-century Paris and cannot be fully understood independently of a knowledge of those interests (see MacIntyre 1988: 389 and 1990: 142). And in John Rawls's recent influential theory of justice we recognize the ideals of modern democratic liberalism, even though the theory is presented as the conclusion of objective and disinterested enquiry (see Rawls 1972: 516; cf. Rawls 1985: 223–51). But if this is so, then it would appear that we search in vain for an objective standard of justice which could be used to determine whether, and how, the behaviour of the Greens in so far as it affects the Blues can be just or unjust.

The difficulty may be put in the form of a dilemma. When considering justice we must either find and use principles which abstract from differences, like the geographical difference between the Greens and the Blues, or we must suppose that such differences can make it impossible for there to be such principles. We must either suppose the availability of a moral point of view which transcends boundaries and the particular ways of thinking about justice which are tied to them, or concede that no such 'objective' point of view is possible because moral thinking is always historically and geographically specific. We must either accept that there is a difference between the Greens' geographically local belief that it would be unjust to, say, dispose of radioactive waste in such a way as to harm people in a neighbouring community and its actually being unjust; or alternatively we must accept that there can be no such difference because there is no 'standard' by which judgements of justice can themselves be judged. We can say what we, with our liberal-democratic tradition, would consider to be just and unjust in the behaviour of the Greens in so far as it affects the Blues, but unless the Greens share our tradition and take a similar view about the nature and aims of human life, they will take a different and perhaps incompatible view about the requirements of justice.

The same dilemma faces us in our understanding of intergenerational justice. We seek an account of justice which will enable us to determine the nature and extent of what that virtue requires of one generation in respect of its responsibilities to later generations. But any such account is bound to reflect features of our generation's historical context and of our generation's tradition of thought about the explanation and evaluation of human behaviour and social interaction. Other generations, in their different contexts, will have cultivated different traditions, and aspects of social and practical life which are unimportant for us will be important for them, and vice versa. We can expect this to happen in the case of intergenerational justice if only because we can see that it happens in the case of international justice; witness the very different emphasis given to the protection of so-called human rights in different states. Future generations will not share our conception of justice, or if they do, they will not value it as we do. What is more, the steps we take to evaluate rival conceptions of justice are themselves determined by allegiance to a tradition and will therefore be different for a different generation. The verdict on our conception of justice from a future generation may be quite at variance with our own verdict.

These considerations might seem to make it impossible to provide an objective basis for, and therefore make progress in understanding, our convictions that the Greens have obligations of justice to the Blues and that our generation has obligations of justice to future generations. The differences in tradition and ideology which invite this conclusion cannot be ignored. But similarities and connections should not be overlooked either. It will be part of the reason why the Greens have obligations of justice to the Blues that the Blues, like the Greens, are a community of people with ambitions, emotions, intellects, imaginations and needs, which can be recognized as human even if they are not all shared. There may be many differences between the Greens and the Blues in what they believe about themselves, about their fellow citizens, and about the political, social and cultural structures they have created, but however extensive these differences may be, there will still be similarities. People in both communities will share a biological need for food, for clean air and water, for an uncontaminated environment, etc. Similarly in the case of non-overlapping generations. However great the differences in tradition and belief between us and future generations, some value will be placed on human life and upon the means necessary to sustain it. An account of justice cannot, perhaps, yield principles which are altogether blind to differences of time, of place, and of society; but nor should it take any and every such difference as relevant.

Moreover, even though no objective basis for our considered convictions may be available, there can still be point and purpose in exploring the reasons we have for them. For by seeking general principles which will help explain these convictions we shall be able to achieve a better understanding of our conception of justice, even though it be local and limited. Explaining why and how the Greens are required by justice not to pollute the river on which they live will help us to understand our conception of justice, and help us to understand why and how we are required by justice to adopt environmental policies which are fair in their impact on future generations. We now have the power to affect the lives of people living in the future, and we have some knowledge of what the consequences of our decisions will be; it is not surprising that we should want to know whether and why our decisions are just or unjust. The question is not idle but practical, for whether we recognize it or not, we have some part in the decisions that are taken and we seek assurances that they are just.

Consider again the case of the Greens and the Blues. The Greens, we are supposing, recognize that they have obligations of justice towards each other. They have adopted principles which determine how the benefits and burdens of co-operation are to be distributed justly. But the benefits they share and the burdens they bear are relevant not just to their well-being but to that of other people – such as the Blues – as well. And it may be that the well-being of other people is affected by the consequences of co-operation between the Greens. This does not in itself imply that the principles of just distribution should determine how the consequences of the Greens' co-operation should be shared among all who are affected. But on the other hand it draws attention to a general principle, or rather a 'proviso', which seems especially relevant to this case. The river is, so to speak, an unowned 'resource' which is of value to both the Greens and the Blues, but because the Greens have discharged pollutants into it before it can be used by the Blues, they have decreased its value to the Blues. The Greens have, to use John Locke's terminology, appropriated and used an unowned resource without there being 'enough, and as good left . . . for others' (Locke 1963: second treatise, ch. 5, para. 27).[3] If, as in this case, the distribution of the benefits and burdens of the Greens' environmental policy requires the acquisition and use of an unowned resource – the river – then a necessary condition for the justice of that distribution is that the acquisition leaves 'enough, and as good' for the Blues, i.e. that the Greens' use of the river conforms to the Lockian proviso. It is because the Greens' policy does not satisfy this condition that it is unjust in its effects on the Blues.

Perhaps any adequate account of distributive justice would have to include something like the Lockian proviso. But at any rate, it would seem to have an important part to play in our conception of justice. Its relevance to future generations is clear. Clean air, clean water, fertile land, a protective atmosphere, an environment free of toxic and radioactive wastes, etc. are resources which we can damage and destroy so that it will not be true that 'enough, and as good' will remain available for future generations. Given the importance of these resources for human life as we know it, damage to any or all of them caused by the environmental policies we adopt will worsen the position of people living in the future, and our use of them will not be just because we fail to leave 'enough, and as good' for those people.

At the heart of this way of explaining our convictions is the idea that clean air, clean water, a protective atmosphere and a safe environment are essentially unowned and should be equally available to all people. Our concept of a human life is such that whenever it may be lived resources of this nature must be accessible if it is to be lived well. Aristotle put this in terms of what he called good fortune being a necessary condition for a good and worthwhile life (Aristotle 1976: 1100a10–1101a20); others may express it in terms of entitlements or rights. It would be unjust if people living in the future were deprived of the good fortune made possible by these resources, or of their entitlement or right to these resources, by our environmental policies. By not leaving 'enough, and as good' for future generations we ensure that the distribution of the benefits and burdens of our policies is unjust.

This conclusion, which attempts to do no more than specify a necessary condition for our policies to have the virtue of justice in so far as their effect upon future generations is concerned, is subject to some important qualifications. In the first place, the demands of intergenerational justice need to be reconciled with the requirements of inter- and intra-national justice, for it is clear that there could be disadvantages – in the form of sacrifices or lost opportunities – for our generation in applying the Lockian proviso for the benefit of future generations. These disadvantages will have to be shared in a just manner, and it may be that political and institutional arrangements make it hard to do this. In practice we may be faced with a choice between implementing just environmental policies for the sake of future generations and implementing just economic and social policies for the sake of those who, whether members of our society or not, are of our generation. No doubt a properly unified account of justice would allow us to make a reasoned choice, but given the strength of the political forces at work in national and international contexts it seems likely that the nice balance of potentially conflicting factors that this would require would be difficult to sustain. The institutions we currently use to distribute benefits and burdens cannot ensure that, so far as we have it in our power, all members of our generation have the 'good fortune' they need to live well; when we require of those same institutions that members of future generations also have the 'good fortune' they need to live well, we can hardly expect greater success.

In the second place, as has already been indicated, there are important limitations on what we can know, or reasonably believe, about the consequences – especially the long-term consequences – of what we do. It is true that our knowledge of the effects of environmental policies is growing, and our confidence in the predictions we make is improving. But the sheer complexity of the ecological systems affected directly or indirectly by those policies must curtail the extent and the reliability of what we can believe about their effects. The implications of our limited knowledge is that the predictions we make about the effects of an environmental policy must be 'discounted' to a greater or lesser extent. We believe that discharging 'greenhouse' gases into the atmosphere can lead to global warming in the more or less distant future, but whether global warming will occur depends upon how a number of relevant factors, some of which are beyond our control, interact with each other. We are rightly concerned with the long-term effects of deforestation, of disposing of radioactive waste in the oceans, of reduced genetic diversity, and of other practices and negligences which seem to violate the Lockian proviso. But the confidence we can place in any reasonably detailed predictions about their long-term effects is limited. Moreover, the expected benefits of our current environmental policies tend to be short term and therefore higher than their longer-term expected burdens.[4]

Accurate prediction is, in many ways, the key to securing justice for future generations, for without it the extent to which we are able to take into account the effects of our policies on future non-overlapping generations will remain restricted. It is, no doubt, for this reason that those who have wanted the interests of future generations to play an important part in our decision-making have tended to underrate the difficulties of accurate prediction.

But there is a different and perhaps better way to achieve this end. For justice is a virtue to which we are drawn not only by our intellect but also by our emotions. We feel affronted, dismayed, and sometimes angered by injustice. We know that sometimes acting justly involves acting courageously or selflessly and in these ways engaging our emotions. Using our intellectual powers we can undertake the kind of abstract reasoning which results in general principles which have application to intergenerational justice, but an important part of our response to practical decisions about what is just and what is unjust for future generations is emotional. We need to use our increasing knowledge of the consequences of what we are doing with our environment to educate that emotional response. If we succeed, future generations will at least be able to recognize our concern for their interests, limited though it may be, as a human concern.[5]

NOTES

1 Throughout this chapter I shall be concerned only with justice in distribution and not at all with justice in retribution, or criminal justice. For the distinction, see Ryan 1993: 9.
2 This, it has been argued, is the conclusion that John Rawls is driven to by the assumption in his 1972: 140 that all persons in the 'original position' belong to the same generation even though they do not know what generation that is; see Barry 1991: 252–3, and Bayles 1980: 113–14.
3 The term 'Lockian proviso' comes from Nozick 1975. A proviso of this nature features prominently in Gauthier 1986: ch. 7, but it is there used as a constraint only on agents co-operating for mutual benefit.
4 I explained and used the idea of expected benefit (and by implication the idea of expected burden) in Gower 1992: 9–11.
5 These hints of a different, less rule-bound, way of approaching practical ethical issues are explored in Nussbaum 1990: 54–105.

5 Nature, culture and history
'All just supply, and all relation'

I. G. Simmons

In 1611, the poet John Donne published his lamentation[1] that the world was, following the death of Elizabeth Drury,

> ... all in pieces, all coherence gone;
> All just supply, and all relation:

for the new philosophies of Brahe, Copernicus, Galileo and Kepler had thrown into question all the familiar models of the universe and its relationships. Perhaps similarly, we find ourselves in a period of doubt, when the polarities of socialism and capitalism, the superiority of First-World technology, and the very epistemological foundations of the empirical sciences that have underlain these ideas since the Enlightenment are also under piercing scrutiny. Yet environmental debate has recognized and incorporated ever more frequently the need for 'just' supply in the sense of a fair distribution now and a decent future for our descendants.

The aim of this contribution is to discuss the relations of the human population, its use of natural resources and the subsequent impact on the natural environment, together with some parts of the web of ideas that bind them together, especially in the West. They are all interconnected: the whole can be visualized as a double helix of ever-widening diameter (i.e. the material ecologies of resources and environment, driven by population growth), with a third strand of intangible thoughts and cognitions somewhat irregularly threaded through the others; here, *inter alia*, we find the idea of justice. What appears to emerge is that most ideas and institutions have changed through time and that our beliefs about what is, for example, just may not themselves be immutable. To take one imaginary example, what might the 'just' distribution of food resources be in a world with twice the present population?

'AS THE AGE WAS LONG': A PERIODIZATION

A number of divisions of the last 10,000 years are possible (Goudsblom 1989). For the present purpose, we shall use a simple segmentation based upon access to energy sources. The relevance of this is clear: as human societies gained control over sources of energy such as fire, the growth of plants and animals, the fossil fuels and nuclear power, their capacity to garner resources and in turn to change the natural world increased enormously. If this uncomplicated idea is used, the following periods can be delineated:

Hunter-gatherers	Recent solar energy from plants and animals: fire	Per capita availability: *c.* 3,000 kcal/day
Agriculturalists	As above, plus concentrated solar energy of domesticated plants and animals	Per capita availability: 12,000–26,000 kcal/day
Industrialists	As above, plus energy from coal, oil and natural gas, hydro-power	Per capita availability: 77,000 kcal/day
Post-industrialists	As above, plus nuclear power and 'alternative' sources	Per capita availability: 230,000 kcal/day

The dating of these periods cannot be exact. Early agriculture started to overwhelm hunting and gathering as early as 8000 BC, but there were still non-agricultural people with little industrial technology as late as the 1920s, for example, in the high Arctic. But by *c.* 500 BC agriculture was a world-wide and expanding phenomenon. Likewise, industrialization based on fossil fuel had earlier roots than those of eighteenth- and nineteenth-century England, but were ineradicably established in what are now the developed countries by 1900. The civilian use of nuclear power dates from the 1950s, with the somewhat more recent, and currently more marginal, addition of passive solar collectors, photo-voltaic cells and wind farms, to give a few examples of 'alternative' energy sources (Odum and Odum 1976). So in any one period there are always the early shoots of the next, just as there are places which, so to speak, 'lag' behind the rest of the world. The current designation of the less developed or technology-poor countries is an example of that type of labelling.

'TO CIVILITY AND MAN'S USE': THE PROGRESS OF HUMANIZATION

For each of these energy-related periods, it is possible to describe the essential characteristics of the material ecology in terms of resources gained and environments altered (Simmons 1993).

Hunter-gatherers

In 10000 BC, all the members of the human species were hunter-gatherers; now, perhaps 0.001 per cent or fewer live that way. Most hunter-gatherers ate as much plant material as they needed and as much meat as they could get, with the possible exception of those in regions like the High Arctic. Their success is attested to by the very wide range of environments in which they survived: literally from tundra to tropical forest. This was made possible by a low population density and, often, by a propensity for seasonal movement so that plant and animal resources were not overused. The low density was brought about by having to live off relatively dilute solar energy, and so the average hunter-gatherer needed access to *c.* 26 km^2 of terrain for food. Having to move encouraged a family size in which there was never more than one child who had to be carried.

The energy relations are usually marked by the control of fire in the landscape: few of the ecosystems in which they lived will not burn at some season or other, and it was often advantageous to burn the vegetation. At the very least it would flush out animals to be killed; at best it would encourage higher densities of food-bearing plants or a vegetation that would attract game.

Examples are well attested of the power of hunter-gatherer groups to change their environments permanently. Permanent reduction or extinction of plant and animal species may have followed heavy use, especially where climatic change put populations of species under stress. Permanent landscape changes were produced by repeated management practices to the point where fauna, flora and soils may all be said to be adapted to the management technique, for example, the repeated use of fire. Hunter-gatherers probably also developed early husbandry in such forms as the yearly gathering of seeds from certain stands of wild grasses, the taming of young animals, the diversion of water on to stands of plants and cutting of ditches to encourage eels, for instance.

Although they enjoyed an apparently robust and sustainable way of life, most such societies quickly adopted cultivation when it became available; most of our knowledge of these people comes from times when they had had prolonged contact with agricultural or indeed industrial economies.

Agriculturalists

The ecology of agriculture depends upon the concentration of food energy by bringing the plants and animals in, rather than going out for them. The field and the herd are high concentrations of energy compared with the wild systems that preceded them. To maximize energy surpluses, particular strains and character-istics of plants and animals were selected by humans to thrive under the new conditions, and this is called domestication. The earliest Old World domesticates, like wheat, barley, rice, cattle, sheep and the pig, are still key species in today's agriculture, supplemented by New World domesticates such as maize and the potato.

Agriculturalists produced the first totally humanized landscapes outside actual dwelling places, as land clearing, irrigation and the use of domesticated plants occupied intensely cultivated fields and gardens. The movement between culti-vated and wild was not all one-way in the sense that irrigation systems failed and silted up, as their soils became salinified and unusable. The wild lost some of its ecologically pristine character where the river valley economies were surrounded by nomadic pastoralists. These groups grazed enough beasts to exert gradual changes on the vegetation in the directions of more xeric communities, for example, or produced areas dominated by plants resistant to grazing and browsing.

With the development of political empires, transmission of land-use patterns and of technology was facilitated, so that there were larger geopolitical units which transferred materials within them: grain, from North Africa to Rome, silver from Mexico to Spain, for example. The empires used both irrigation and rain-fed agriculture and understood the role of domestic animals in providing manure for crops. Most land uses ever known were implanted during this phase, including metal-based industry. So much of the world outside the truly marginal cold, high and dry zones was made over by communities practising agriculture, some of it terraced, and having parks, gardens, canals, reservoirs, managed forests for ship timber as well as implement handles, fish ponds, whaling and cod-fishing fleets in deep waters, mines and smelting works, and prosecuting wars. Quite large cities with complex social stratifications were made possible by agricultural surpluses.

It seems impossible to judge the sustainability of this way of life. In some places at some times, famines point to an apparent reaching of Malthusian limits, even in the absence of stochastic features such as climatic extremes or the breakdown of civil order. There was, however, always a likelihood that population growth would exceed agricultural production, especially when a degree of immunity to major trans-continental infectious diseases had been acquired; Gellner (1988) suggests that agrarian societies are always in conflict since they are in continual danger of experiencing the Malthusian limits to population but are ideologically pro-natalist since their societies need young men for the farms and the forces.

Industrialists

In the industrial era, the access to energy sources which had been dominated by solar sources is now subsidized by immense amounts of stored solar energy as fossil fuels. Of these, coal was the first to be developed on a large scale, especially in Europe after the discovery in the early 1700s of how to smelt iron with coke. Oil was added to the repertoire in the late nineteenth century (initially, it was sought as a replacement for whale oil used in lighting), and then natural gas (Table 1).

Mobility is greatly increased via many technologies: conceivably the only really novel experience of humanity between classical antiquity and today is that of rapid travel. On a global scale, there are core areas and peripheries where the impact has been much less. The North Atlantic is the type locality, but there are others, notably Japan, South Africa and other high-income economies. The environmental changes wrought derive in many instances from concentrations of the use of energy and materials, either as goods or as wastes. Technology has made possible the synthesis of substances not present in nature. When these are led off into the environment there may be no natural breakdown pathways, and so they are prone to accumulation with results that are toxic to life or detrimental to biogeochemical processes.

The application of energy through technology has made environmental alteration much more thorough and widespread. The getting of energy itself necessitates

Table 1 Growth in population and energy use, 1870–1986

Year	Industrial energy use (TW)	Per capita (watts)	Cumulative use since 1850	World population (millions)
1870	0.2	153	3	1,300
1910	1.1	647	25	1,700
1950	2.9	1,160	100	2,500
1970	7.1	1,972	200	3,600
1986	8.6	1,720	328	5,000

Notes: 1 TW (terawatt) = 1×10^{12} watts. The table refers only to *industrial* energy use: not therefore to biofuels like wood and dung.

local environmental change, as around a deep coal-mine or even more so at the site of open-cast mining. Steam power meant the transport of materials and ideas over larger distances much more quickly, and indeed consolidated empires whose purpose was to supply home countries with materials. Thus a periphery of less developed countries experienced the transformation of subsistence agriculture or pastoralism into commercial plantations.

For the first time, some of the consequences of human activity became truly global rather than simply world-wide at discrete points. The outstanding examples are those of toxic chemicals with very slow breakdown rates now found in the atmosphere (as aerosols), on land and in the seas, together with gases which have a long residence time in the atmosphere and enhance radiative forcing. These comprise the 'greenhouse gases', and of them carbon dioxide is the most important, with atmospheric concentration rising from 275 ppm in 1850 to 356 ppm in 1992. Methane is also important, and quantities are rising from rice paddy extension, the greater number of cattle in the world and positive feedback from peaty environments.

Many a writer has questioned the sustainability of any *genre de vie* which is so clearly based upon non-renewable resources. Given the economists' view of sustainability, the best that can be expected is that the knowledge gained by the use of the fossil fuels can be turned into the wisdom of how to do without them. The technological solutions seem to be nuclear power and/or 'alternative' energy sources, but the alternative of using a great deal less in the rich countries is also available, if there is the cultural and political will to pursue it.

Post-industrialists

Even more concentrated than the hydrocarbons is the energy in the atomic nucleus of elements like uranium, first released in controlled chain reactions in 1942, used militarily in 1945 and in civil power since the 1950s. In the latter application, it produces only electricity (and a great deal of waste heat not usually used since the installations are normally sited well away from dense settlements), and so there are no discernibly new patterns or processes; it tends to reinforce existing configurations. In contrast, the environmental effects of fossil fuels and fears over their future supply have led to the development and small-scale introduction of 'alternative' or equilibrium energies based on direct but dilute solar energy (for example, passive collectors, photovoltaic cells), wind energy and the movement of the sea in tides and waves. Few of the latter have yet produced an energy surplus above their development and manufacturing energy inputs.

This phase is quite new, so differentiating its effects must necessarily be speculative. Steam has been replaced conceptually by electricity, and this force has made instant electronic communication available virtually everywhere via satellites. One consequence is the rise of the world city: a place where key decisions of the capitalist economy are made which then have the capacity to affect the ecology of any part of the earth. A major change may well come soon as result of changes of consciousness in low-income economies brought about by the ubiquity of electronic communications. In parallel there is a stronger awareness in the world of the web of effects of any given process and of the virtues of protection of some of the richness of species and ecosystems resulting from organic evolution. This awareness is made keener by the new-found ability to accomplish genetic manipulation of organisms with predictable biological if not ecological results.

It is nevertheless, a world of considerable unevenness of access to resources, as shown, for example, by the differences in per capita energy use during recent years or measures such as GNP per head. Whether these indices have anything to do with the real quality of life, or whether they are simply measures of the breakdown of complex molecules into simpler ones, has been the focus of investigations into alternative economic measures which use data not only on income but on, for example, literacy and health. But low income does not necessarily mean low environmental impact, as poor people are forced into marginal environments by the pressures of population growth or landlords' use of land for cash-crop production.

An overview

The outcome of 10,000 years of resource use has been a humanizing of the earth. Very little is now in the kind of pristine condition which maps of 'biomes' or 'world vegetation' in atlases might suggest. There is still a large area of dry land which shows only minimal human effects, most of which is desert, tundra or ice; the rest has been transformed by the human hand and its mechanical extensions. Table 2 shows the extent to which human-led appropriation of natural biological production has taken place: some 45 per cent of the land surface has undergone such change. The role of population growth is summarized in Table 3, where the millennia of agrarian economies are given their due; in environmental terms, these are put in the shade by the data of Table 4, where the access to energy of the industrial world provides for a giant leap upwards in the simple index of impact calculated there.

Table 2 Human appropriation of net primary productivity in the 1980s

World NPP	
Terrestrial	132.1
Freshwater	0.8
Marine	91.6
Total	224.5
NPP directly used by humans	
Plants eaten directly	0.8
Plants fed to domestic animals	2.2
Fish eaten by both	1.2
Wood use for paper and timber	1.2
Fuelwood	1.0
Total	7.2
NPP used or diverted by humans	
Cropland	15.0
Converted pastures	9.8
Others (cities, deforestation)	17.8
Total	42.6
NPP used, diverted or reduced	
NPP used or diverted	42.6
Reduced by conversion	17.5
Total	60.1

Source: J. M. Diamond, 'Human use of world resources', *Nature, Lond* 328 (1987): 479–80

Even some of the wilder parts have occasional concentrated reminders of human presence, as in the recent (1993) attempts to remove some of the debris of climbing expeditions from Mount Everest in the Himalayas. There are, in fact, subtler traces detectable by the right instruments: aerosol lead stratified into the Greenland ice sheet, for instance, and radioactive nuclides from pre-1963 atmospheric nuclear weapons testing in the slow-growing lichens of Arctic tundras. The seas are often omitted from such discussions. The continental shelves are without doubt altered considerably, since they receive the contents of the continental rivers as well as being the scene of hydrocarbon extraction and the most intensive fishing. The open oceans are more like a true wilderness, though spilled oil and pesticides are found in the water and some whale species have been brought to the brink of extinction. So Donne's 'western treasury, eastern spicery, / Europe, and Afric, and the unknown rest / were easily found' turns out to be true, and indeed these areas have been seen to be lands whose 'plenty and riches is / enough to make twenty such worlds as this'. Current concerns revolve around the future of the plenty and riches and the identity of those who will enjoy them. Is it a just world, for instance, in which the world's richest 20 per cent of nations absorbed 70 per cent of global income in 1960 but increased that share to 83 per cent by 1989, and in the same period diminished the share of the poorest 20 per

Table 3 Population and longevity: proportion of years lived

Date	Population × longevity	Period covered
10000 BC	8.6	From evolution of species
AD 1	34.2	10000 BC–AD 1
AD 1750	28.2	AD 1–AD 1750
AD 1950	16.8	AD 1750–AD 1950
AD 1990	12.2	AD 1950–AD 1990

Source: Livi-Bacci 1992

Notes: The second column shows a percentage of all the people who have ever lived, not an absolute number.

Table 4 Environmental impact as a function of longevity and energy use

Date	Population × longevity	Per capita E use (W)	Index of impact
10000 BC	8.6	50	430
AD 1	34.2	100	3,420
AD 1750	28.2	300	8,460
AD 1950	16.8	1,972	33,130
AD 1990	12.2	1,720	20,984

Notes: The index is obtained by multiplying the two previous columns and is obviously crude; it nevertheless puts into perspective the data in Table 1.

cent from 2.3 per cent to 1.4 per cent? Are systems which favour economic growth and consumption rather than equity and the alleviation of poverty just?

'NEW PHILOSOPHY': THE DEVELOPMENT OF IDEAS

Down the ages, each new philosophy has always had the potential to put 'all in doubt', and there is no denying that humans' ideation of their surroundings has been very varied from place to place and time to time (Simmons 1992). That these interpretations intertwine with some of the material changes is undeniable, yet it must always be remembered that what people say and write is not always what they do: Taoist philosophy of a quietist kind pervaded China just as the people were engaged in large-scale transformations of land use and terrain cover.

The metamorphoses of thought

For pre- and non-literate groups there is only a hazy notion of their conceptualization of their surroundings in the distant past. For more recent times and for the present, the work of anthropologists and ethnographers has shed much light, though what chronological depth can be attributed to the notions expressed is usually unknown. When it comes to written sources of evidence, apart from the West since the classical period, there are materials from the Indian subcontinent, China and Japan, but nothing from aboriginal American foundations.

For instance, has the hunter-gatherer phase of human history (which must account for about 95 per cent of the species' evolutionary time) had any permanent psychological effects, comparable to the ecological ones? Traits of aggression amongst males useful when there were large mammals (and their predators) to be hunted will be of negative value in a more crowded and sedentary world if they have persisted. The cosmic world-view of such groups suggests eternal and recurring patterns and that there are many worlds of being and meaning (for example, religion is polytheistic) in which life can participate. This may lead to an acceptance of the diversity of human personality and ways.

In early irrigated agriculture, the contrast between the river valleys and the semi-arid surroundings must have been very great, and some locate the home of western thought in the desert/cultivated margins, with it becoming first codified in the Hebrews of Palestine. They occupied a niche between the pastoralists and the farmers: they accepted transience but not fatalism from the nomads. They also rejected much of the agriculturalists' ways since they appeared to lead to con-scription, enslavement, famine and disease. The farmers of the valleys contrast, too, with hunters. Whereas the hunter moves through the land, the farmer is centred in it and can overview it as a whole. Nature can withhold: no matter how great the drudgery, failure at some point is inevitable (Shepard 1982). All im-portant things are human-created and all else is *other*. History became linear and so might lead somewhere. An infusion of Zoroastrian duality transformed ambi-guity into polar opposites.

The desert landscape of the previous phase sustained a vision of a split world in which images of opposition flourished: Christian Gnosticism plus Zoro-astrianism provided a Manichaean expression of an unresolved tension and division of the world (Peters 1987). Mainstream Christianity kept up the idea of the Fall to explain undesirable places and events and then was implicated in the rise of Renaissance humanism and then of science, which promised the reclam-ation of a pre-lapsarian state and, eventually, the perfection of mankind. The second world created by humans would therefore also be perfect since man was the measure of all things. Monotheism and Utopianism led to authoritarian, imperialistic thinking informed by philosophies which were unambiguous, di-chotomous and unmetaphorical. Historical events became unique and interpretable through envoys with control of the written word which could be used politically to control the 'true' version of events and of history. Gellner (1988) stresses the need for manpower of agrarian societies (for labour and defence) and thus their propensity to conflict as well as a Malthusian relationship with their productive environment.

The great change of the industrial phase is that humans exist within a tech-nologized world rather than being in control of technology. In science and technology is sought the answer to problems, whether of resource shortages or environmental pathologies. They were also the crucial factor in the success of European colonization during the nineteenth century. The city favours knowledge of mankind, of physics and perhaps chemistry, but not biology, and certainly sanctions a machine paradigm of the universe since nature to the city child is much less coherent than the constructions of humanity. Then to the adult, the city looks more organized than a wilderness. It seems as if those who are perplexed by the imperfections of society have a strong will to destroy what already exists as a first phase of reconstruction. As with pastoralists, transience is a feature, as is a detached sense of the value of things like work or soil. Indeed, single-shot activities and specialization are rational acts in a way which would not have been legitimized in hunter-gatherer societies and perhaps less so in agrarian times. Interestingly, the late nineteenth to mid-twentieth century seems to have been a period when less attention has been paid by major philosophers to the consideration of what their predecessors would have called the relationships of man and nature.

In the post-industrial world, the tendency to globalization, seen especially in the financial transactions of the world economy, is subject to countervailing forces which emphasize the virtue of the local and regional (witness the upsurge of nationalism in Europe in the early 1990s), so that small ethno-cultural groups assert their independence of the nation-states to which earlier mores bound them. There are some signs of a growth of a world consciousness that encompasses the non-human world at a level of intrinsic value rather than simply as an instrument for human use. This could equally bring the realization that humanity is not destined for a very long evolutionary tenure on earth: a short life but a merry one could be preferred. Sub-currents include the re-evaluation of holistic thinking (with some shifts within western religions) and the rise of feminist thought in environmental matters. There is also the opposite case of increased demand for production of all kinds, which results in the occurrence of unpredictable instabilities in major biogeochemical cycles and increased reliance on science and technology to produce solutions to any consequential problems at the same time as the realization that the findings of science are neither empirically nor epistemologically always reliable.

Meta-theories

In the last twenty years the notion of sustainability has come forward as the shibboleth to be included in all discussions of human–environment relations. In many discussions, it takes precedence over justice, since, it is argued, without a sustainable economy and environment, there is simply no chance of justice to either humanity or nature. Clearly, sustainability is a concept to be examined with a critical eye (Redclift 1993). In particular, it has to be analysed to see whether it is another avatar of the western world-view which currently holds sway over most of the globe's societies and their environmental relations. The foundations of the world-view are in a linear view of history, and in the beliefs that more is better and that science and technology hold the keys to more and better as well as the solution of perceived problems (Kates 1988). To these ends, any philosophy of the non-human world is strictly instrumental. Within this framework, any notions of justice have been dominated until recently by those with a utilitarian base, though others (see Chapter 1 in this volume) are now entering the picture. Unlike many of the more restricted philosophies of environment, however, the western world-view is widely, if implicitly, held by millions of people.

'THE FIRMAMENT IN EIGHT AND FORTY SHARES': RESONANCES

In most commentators' views, nature does not communicate directly with the human species. The features of nature 'out there' do not report to *The Times* what they think of being made resources or receptacles for wastes or vehicles for human pleasures. But the social cognitions of the strands of environment and resources are the cause of much discussion within society about environmental concerns. This is not all directly pragmatic in its focus, since matters like the ontology of nature and the concept of justice (to take two rather different examples) are both part of the intellectual explorations. This discussion could be compared to a resonance within society being set up by humans talking to each other about their surroundings and their meanings.

A major consequence of the last 400-odd years which is relevant is that of specialization. Not only is the getting of resources and the study of environmental processes specialized, but the way in which they are discussed is split among specialists as well. Furthermore, the languages used are often different (Luhmann 1988). The predilection of the natural sciences for mathematics is very different, for instance, from that of a deconstructive post-modernist talking about Rousseau. It might be useful to compare the situation with that of a pipe-organ, with sounds of different frequencies and volumes in pipes of varying length and width. One result of all the resonance which seems always to have occurred and always to have created a set of harmonics which do not apparently make sense is the desire to simplify them. In place of a unitary knowledge of humanity as ecological agent interacting with nature and ideas flowing into and out of such minglings (Kates 1988), we have a series of separate channels for the resonances, in the manner of the pipe-organ. These have separate labels and are the province of specialists, with their own languages: ecology, climatology, the economy, religion, law and education form part of the list. Again, in attempts to simplify the complexities of the relationships, western culture at least has found comfort in binary opposites, one of which ought to be overcome (often 'conquered') in the cause of the greater good. The origins of this cultural trait seem to be located in Persian Zoroastrianism, and the most notable pair is that of good and evil. There are other pairs which are of direct relevance here, such as humanity ↔ nature; determinate ↔ creators; technocentric ↔ Green.

So it seems as if any discussion of a concept such as justice relating to the environment will have originated as a resonance arising as part of a strand of ideation weaving in and out of the discussion by humans of the interaction of humans and nature. That resonance is likely to occur in a number of channels; it may well not be confined to the one marked 'law', for example. If it is, then it may well stay there, with all the drawbacks of intellectual isolation. A high probability (to be understood rather than eliminated, perhaps) is that attempts will be made to simplify the sounds into those heard as 'just' and those as 'unjust', which will make into black and white what presumably ought to display all shades of green as well.

'A NEW COMPASS': THE FUTURE

What meanings for today and tomorrow can be drawn out of a long-term historical-cum-sociological view of these complexities? A number seem evident. There is first the conviction that each human institution expresses at least an implicit philosophy of nature. This may arrogate to itself its own channel of resonance or may have to share with others: the evolving discipline of ecological economics would be a good example. As industrialization and urbanization have proceeded, most show an increasing detachment from natural processes, but this appears to be countered by a great deal of communication *about* the environment through various channels (Luhmann 1988). The electronic media, especially television, represent a new channel, with unforeseeable results.

Second, each new phase of human–environment relations appears holistically as possessing emergent qualities which are not easily, if at all, predictable from the features of the previous levels. What is there, for example, to predict that it would be Europe and not India or China that developed into industrialism? *Post hoc* explanations abound, but it would have been remarkable to find such a prediction (a) of the nature of the emerging economy and (b) of its location in, say, 1611. The same was doubtless true of the emergence of agriculture, and in fact it was in some places a reversible development.

Taking this further, the triple helix seems analogous to a *self-organizing system* in the sense of Jantsch (1980) and of Prigogine and Stengers (1984). These systems start with a set of interactions which are far from thermodynamic equilibrium and which dissipate concentrated energy in building up complexity. So while they cannot but create entropy, there are swirls and vortices, as it were, which allow the development of phenomena like life and human cultures. But such systems are essentially very complex, and their behaviour cannot be totally predicted from any set of initial states. The dynamics may well now include human purposes, but that is only one of the cybernetic loops which bind the system together and whose synergisms allow the creation of emergent properties which could not be predicted from hitherto existing states. This may serve as a reminder of the importance of contingency in any scheme of evolution, as brought out vividly by S. J. Gould (1989). He uses the word 'teleonomy' for changes which, while moving in a general direction, make use of contingency and chance and adapt in small increments.

These considerations may give us pause from blindly endorsing concepts with the label 'sustainable', desirable though they may sound. If at no stage in history could the future be accurately forecast, and the present is not a great deal better, what possible meaning can sustainability have? It seems founded on either outdated concepts of biological equilibria no longer held by ecologists, or on the role of capital in neo-classical economics, and neither may survive either the realism of the next doubling of population or the new ideas about humanity and nature which are bound to evolve. In history, every time something could be identified as 'sustainable', it was replaced (hunter-gatherers, solar-based agriculture) by an innovation which spread rapidly. Humanity could decide now to immobilize nature, resources and ideas at the present stage, but the probability of so doing seems vastly remote.

There is need for caution here: if we define justice to include future generations, but cannot forecast the nature of that future at all accurately, then how do we know what to avoid now? A simple *laissez-faire* fatalism seems inadequate, but exploration of some guidance for the adoption of a teleonomy seems desirable even if teleological behaviour is abandoned.

Overall, this reading of history suggests firmly that there is no going back to some Golden Age, when all was an Arcadian and pastoral idyll with humans and nature coexisting under a sunny sky. But the lack of predictability also suggests that future Utopias are also mirages: the systems are too chaotic for any one *telos* ever to be possible. For relatively stable systems, Treumann (1991) posits,

> the percentage of the time up to which the behaviour of the system can be predicted with say better than about 66% amounts to somewhere between 5 and 10% of the length of time the system has been continuously observed in the near past up to the present time when the prediction is made.

If we add to this the trampling that occurs in the pursuit of Utopias, such New Jerusalems may not be very desirable either. A teleonomy in which the capacity to utilize unexpected novelty and to innovate replaces a far-off teleology seems preferable in human terms (Berlin 1990). The notions of contingency and radical openness to the future have their parallels in recent thought of a post-modern character: the environment and our relations to it surely come into Bauman's (1993) category of 'moral agonies which no reason-dictated recipes can soothe, let alone cure'. In the same mode of discourse, Schatzki (1993) quotes Lyotard's view that justice is in the realm of opinions and not of truth and therefore must take its character from diversity (what echoes of Rio!) and all parties must agree locally on the rules. In the case of the environment, this simply brings us back to many of the central arguments in environmental ethics about standing and about the extension of value beyond the instrumental to the intrinsic (Birch 1988). But it does point us to the notion that self-organizing systems may spin concepts of justice which are the result of continual renovation and adaptation.

> Nor are, (although the river keep the name)
> Yesterday's waters, and today's the same.

NOTE

1 *An Anatomy of the World.* Each heading in this chapter also quotes from the poem. All spellings have been modernized.

6 Population prospects with special reference to the environment[1]

Léon Tabah

During the next thirty-five years the world will be the object of an unprecedented demographic evolution with considerable economic and social consequences, as well as impacts on the environmental resource base upon which sustainable development ultimately depends.

According to the United Nations (1988: 579) and the World Bank (1989: 421) demographic projections, we have started to witness a genuine change in the world with the beginning of what is called the demographic transition of the Third-World countries, that is their progression into a phase of declining fertility accompanying the declining mortality.

The generations born since the early sixties will experience during their early and adult life an upheaval in the world demographic map owing to the inevitable staggering of entry into the phase of transition, which, obviously, will not happen at the same time and at the same pace in all countries. Some countries, notably those in Africa south of the Sahara, have scarcely begun the process, and it would indeed be superficial to view this as merely 'historical backwardness', while almost all other countries are rushing ahead so fast that they will reach the end of the process two or three times quicker than many developed countries in the nineteenth and up to the beginning of the twentieth century.

The passage through the demographic transition signifies that the quantitative changes of the population would occur with qualitative transformations that would entail necessarily extensive repercussions on the world economy and on the environment. One wonders whether for the first time population growth would be intimately associated in the Third World with more 'affluence', and whether the theory of transition – a major theory of demographers – should not be entirely revisited.

Or, to phrase this basic question in another way: to what extent will the demographic transition of the Third World bring about subsequent increased demand for energy, food and water, and be linked with more stratospheric ozone depletion, greenhouse effects, and global spread of air pollution?

One argument which arouses scepticism about the application of the theory of demographic transition in the Third World is that for the industrialized countries the process was a 'silent revolution', extremely slow, induced by the progress of education and general well-being, while in many Third-World countries the process is deploying very fast, impelled by policies at governmental level with considerable exhortation from the mass media and without significant advance on consumption. To take the example of China – one-quarter of the entire Third-World population – the abrupt decline of fertility has been accomplished essentially thanks to government measures and surveillance at individual level. In all Asian countries, as well as in many Latin American countries, strong incentives towards family planning are playing a decisive role in the fertility decline.

If this reasoning is correct, the merit of population policies and of family-planning programmes resides not only in the acceleration of the demographic transition, which will achieve lower volumes of population faster when the transition is complete, but also in accomplishing this result with less industrialization, and generally less detrimental effects on the environment, than the industrialized countries, whose lifestyles are the sources of the primary risks to our common future. These have been the main beneficiaries of the wealth accumulated through the processes of economic growth that have produced environmental degradation and resource depletion.

It is not necessary to justify this assertion to consider that population growth is not the only, or even the main, factor in the deterioration of the environment. Other factors are also at play, especially the technologies utilized since the last world war and inequitable development, which have seen the economic and social situation of the South worsening, particularly since the 1970s.

Let us consider this aspect. The second part of this chapter discusses the demographic outlook and its environmental consequences.

THE EFFECTS OF THE POPULATION ON THE ENVIRONMENT

The question of the extent to which population growth and distribution create a distinctive impact on the quality of the environment has become extremely controversial.

Surprisingly enough, the subject has not greatly attracted the scientific community of demographers. At the 1989 International Population Conference in New Delhi, there was no mention at all of the subject in the eighty-nine papers presented and discussed. Only recently has a committee of the International Union for the Scientific Study of Population been set up. This deficiency in the demographic community is all the more regrettable as the global risks for the environment have their roots at the local level, which should normally fall under the competence of local or national institutions.

More and more economists consider that environmental consequences are not adequately recognized in economic accounts, and they are interested in the environmental factor as they start envisaging environmental resources as economic goods. The evaluation of net national product should include environmental resource use as other goods and services.

It has been difficult hitherto to assess the scope and scale of the linkages between population and the environment, and how they operate. One reason is that the necessary environmental data are generally absent, especially for developing countries. We have not reached the situation in which we are actually able to trace the causalities between population, environment, resources and development. Therefore, it is not surprising that extreme views are rife on the subject.

Some authors have concluded that population growth is an essential, and even dominant, factor of the environmental deterioration, for example, P. R. Ehrlich and A. H. Ehrlich (1990), National Academy of Sciences (1992), N. Myers (1992) and R. E. Bilsborrow (1992).

According to these authors, population pressures constitute a determining factor among many others. The three factors population, consumption and technology interact in a multiplicative fashion on the environment with other factors such as socio-economic inequities, cultural constraints, government policies and the international political order. Each of the three factors reinforces the others' impacts, but the role of the population is bound to be significant, even when population growth is relatively restricted.

Myers (1992) gives some illustrative examples in support of his assertion. During the 1970s and the 1980s, the amount of per capita arable land declined by 1.9 per cent a year, because of population growth surpassing the expansion of arable land, and led necessarily to the application of fertilizers and pesticides to cope with the growing needs of a growing population, consequently deteriorating the resource base.

Myers estimates that grain gained from the effects of the 'green revolution' – irrigation, fertilizers and other inputs – were worth 29 million tonnes a year, equivalent to the world need to feed the population increase (28 million tonnes at current nutritional levels), while the total loss from all forms of environmental degradation adds up to 14 million tonnes of grain output a year.

The emission of carbon dioxide is estimated at 2.4 billion tonnes in 1950, and at least 6.8 billion tonnes in 1985, with an average increase of 3.1 per cent a year. As the rate of population growth was 1.9 per cent annually, Myers draws from these figures the conclusion that population was responsible for two-thirds of the increase in carbon dioxide emissions, while the 'affluence' and the technology factors were jointly responsible for only 1.2 per cent a year.

According to a recent study by the OECD (1991: 297), for the time being, 30 per cent of emissions of carbon dioxide is produced by developing countries and 70 per cent by industrialized countries. These proportions are likely to be reversed by the end of the first quarter of the next century, according to the US Office of Technology Assessment (1990), with the population growth of the Third World on the one hand and with environmental conservation measures taken by the industrialized countries on the other hand. If this proves to be accurate, it signifies that the environmental problems stemming mostly from today's industrialized countries will turn out to be essentially caused by today's Third World.

As for the emissions of methane, which cannot be as readily reduced as emissions of carbon dioxide, methane production is bound to increase with population growth since it comes from rice paddies, ruminant livestock, biomass burning and natural gas, which are all expected to expand with the increased food needs of the growing population and dietary upgrading. To cater for the increased food needs, land productivity should increase by 50 per cent in developing countries by 2025 according to L. A. Paulino (1986), cited by Myers. Yet, in many parts of developing countries, especially Africa as a whole, food productivity has been contracting because of land degradation and poor agricultural planning.

The Third World currently produces 17 per cent of global chloro-fluorocarbons (CFCs), one of the main ozone-depleting chemicals, but with the growing demand for refrigerators, one of the major producers of CFCs, the Third World would expand CFC production tenfold under the joint effect of population growth and the amelioration of well-being. None the less, we might anticipate that the expected increase in numbers of refrigerators in the Third World will be due more to reducing the backwardness of consumption than to population growth.

We have to acknowledge that the population factor is playing an important role in deforestation with the need for cheap energy and the practice of slash-and-burn by landless farmers. An increase of 1 per cent in population has been associated with an increase of 0.5 per cent in deforestation in the Third World (Allen and Barnes 1989). If Allen and Barnes's econometric analysis is correct, it means that in all developing countries the deforestation rate is about 1 per cent a year, which is extremely high. In fact this is only an average, and in Africa the rates are much higher in countries such as Nigeria (14 per cent) or Ivory Coast (15 per cent). The two main proximate causes of deforestation in the Third World are new agricultural settlements on to increasingly marginal lands and the high cost of energy, leading to the use of fuelwood (Bilsborrow 1992), while the ultimate causes are population growth and poverty. A study by FAO (1991), based on a statistical analysis for sixty developing countries, concluded that population growth is significantly associated with deforestation. And the future is not promising: according to the UN demographic projections, almost 80 per cent of the population of 2025, some 6 billion inhabitants, are expected to be living in tropical areas of the world, putting pressure on the remaining forests.

Population growth and redistribution, especially the absolute increase in human numbers each year and migration to cities, are also playing a direct substantial part in water shortage. It is already estimated that as many as 2 billion people live in areas with chronic shortages, with the water often contaminated by pollutants and pathogenic agents. Human consumption of water has doubled this century and it will at least double again with the population growth during the next three decades (Falkenmark 1990).

If the analysis of the authors convinced of the responsibility of the population factor in the deterioration of the environment were confirmed, the resolution of environmental degradation should rest, at least partly, in the control of population growth, and therefore essentially in the Third World.

Barry Commoner (1991), also in search of the respective influence on environmental quality of the three factors, population, consumption and technology, drew the opposite conclusion. Discussing through decomposition analysis the number of automobiles as an indicator of the pollutants emitted in sixty-five developing countries over the period 1970–80, he came to the conclusion that, in the annual rates of change of the environment, the population was responsible for 2.5 per cent, affluence for 0.2 per cent and technology for 5.4 per cent. In sharp contrast to the previous authors, Commoner concluded that the influence of technology on environmental impact is more than twice as high as the influence of the population factor. He arrived at similar conclusions concerning the production of electricity (effect of population: 2.7 per cent, average annual change in GDP per capita: 0.7 per cent, average annual change in electricity with respect to GDP: 8.1 per cent), and concerning the impact of nitrogen fertilizer (population: 2.5 per cent, agriculture production per capita: –0.6 per cent, nitrogen use per unit of agricultural production: 6.6 per cent). In all these calculations, the effect of population seems in harmony with the rate of population growth, while the effects of the two other factors – consumption and technology – are essentially dependent on the nature of the technology used. What is surprising in this analysis is the very low, or even negative, impact of the consumption factor. We shall see later that it might be very different in the future with the deployment of the population transition.

Whatever the quantitative impact of the population on the environment may be, two conclusions emerge from the literature. First, population growth is not the sole force that undermines the environmental resource base, but one among many, and especially the technology used. What is at variance is the respective shares of responsibilities, and we should recognize that the statistical tools to deal with this basic question are extremely rudimentary. Second, the three factors, population, consumption and technology, interact in a multiplicative fashion, and it is these interactions that will matter in the future as the last two factors will have increased influence. Environmental economics and population growth and distribution will be tied to each other in an intricate web.

Let us turn now to the time horizon, as we can assume that the next four decades will definitely witness a different demographic path from the past. As the populations of most of the Third World, except sub-Sahara, are entering into lower fertility rates with growth rates none the less·extremely high by past standards, the interactions of population and the other two factors will exercise their full strength, unless two conditions are met, jointly or independently.

These two conditions are:

1 The development of the Third World will be achieved in a different way from that of the industrialized countries, with alternative options resulting from 'clean technologies'; and
2 The decline of fertility will not be accompanied by much affluence, contrary to the theory of demographic transition, as was experienced in the past by the industrialized countries when the concerns of the environment were almost absent.

Concerning the first condition, we should recognize that some growth in the use of energy by developing countries is inevitable and, for the present, development scenarios for these countries follow the same material-intensive patterns as the industrialized countries. In fact, the economies of the Third-World countries that are experiencing strong economic growth are all adopting an energy-intensive heavy industrialization phase.

Bangkok, Beijing and Manila rival Taipei as far as pollution is concerned. Throughout Asia measures to safeguard the environment are absent or ignored. The decision-makers consider that the costs of environmental protection are too high and are having constraining effects on their development strategies. In all developing countries, development concerns eclipse environmental ones, at least for the time being. Preventing soil degradation at the village level has less priority than the increase of food production to feed a growing population.

The poor do not in general have the means of undertaking soil-conservation measures that would preserve their resources. Their first task is to meet immediate basic human needs. To do so, they are often compelled to overexploit the natural resources on which their long-term development depends.

Preventing carbon dioxide emissions by restricting automobile transport in cities like Mexico, Cairo, Bangkok, Rio de Janeiro or Sao Paulo, is attempting the impossible. Exerting pressure on developing countries to shift to environmentally sound technologies is putting a burden on the economies of these countries. At the present time, the technologies of industry, agriculture and transportation are basically the same in developing countries as they are in the rich countries, without the resources for the adoption of measures to protect the environment.

If it is true that industrialized countries contribute more to environmental damage than the developing countries, the latter also suffer more than the former. The Bhopal catastrophe is a case in point which, unfortunately, is bound to be repeated in developing countries if industrialization occurs without the necessary financial means. The Brundtland Commission stated that the common need for global environmental security requires a substantial and sustained increase in the flow of financial resources to support the broad development needs of developing countries.

The main question is: is the date of reaching the end of the population transition too close for permitting most current technological constraints to be overcome? At this stage, is it likely that the expansion of agricultural production will be feasible on the world scale without dire environmental effects if the present technologies, such as those of the 'green revolution', are modified? We should remember that, in Asia, the increase in agricultural production is possible only through increased productivity rather than through an increase of arable areas.

THE DEMOGRAPHIC OUTLOOK AND ITS ENVIRONMENTAL IMPLICATIONS: AN OPEN-ENDED DEMOGRAPHIC FUTURE

The world's future in demographic terms would seem to be very open-ended, judging by the United Nations' projections, since the high and the low variants put the population in 2025 at 9.42 and 7.59 billion respectively, i.e. a difference of 1.83 billion. The truth probably lies somewhere between the two. But it is obviously not a matter of indifference whether the actual figure will be closer to one or the other as far as resources and the environment are concerned, even if 91 per cent of this 1.83 billion difference is accounted for by today's developing countries and only 9 per cent by today's developed countries, which consume more raw materials and cause more environmental pollution. It is true, on the other hand, that a good number of developing countries are also responsible for damage to the environment as a result of poverty, and many of them will progressively experience a form of development, as will now be discussed.

The growing diversification of the Third World

Many of today's developing countries are and will be moving into the category of industrialized countries. We are witnessing a demographic diversification in the Third World. The simple two-speed pattern of population growth of twenty years ago has been superseded by one that is increasingly varied. All the signs are pointing to a world where demographic change is taking place at several speeds and giving rise to a vastly different geographical distribution of its population. The idea of a North–South demographic divide is no longer valid, as can be seen from both the United Nations and World Bank projections. It is equally obvious that, at the same time, we are beginning to see the end of a pattern of economic development of two or three speeds. The world scene is becoming even more varied and one where today's developing countries will move in different directions, with some rapid catching up on the industrialized countries from the demographic, social and economic standpoints. The 'old Third World' is split into successful developers of various degrees and the rest. And, looking at this more closely, it is obvious that those countries which are quickest in accomplishing the demographic transition are the ones best placed in terms of international competition. Take the example of the 'four dragons' so often referred to: they are now well into the post-demographic transition phase, and there is little or no difference between them and the countries of Western Europe in terms of both fertility and mortality. In the radical changes that are beginning to occur within the hierarchy of world powers it is clear that countries that were long considered underdeveloped will soon be up alongside the leaders.

It is equally clear that, while accomplishing the demographic transition will not in itself ensure development, without it development in the Third World is inconceivable.

A persisting poverty

Though the idea of an 'ever-widening divide', so widely accepted during the 1950s and 1960s, is by no means a thing of the past, the divide is no longer simply between the whole of the North and the whole of the South, but between the North plus a substantial part of the South, on the one side, and on the other side, large black spots that are likely to persist for a good many years to come. These areas include almost all of sub-Saharan Africa, where under-exploitation of natural resources, compounded by totally unrestrained population growth, political unrest and environmental damage, is isolating this sub-continent from the world economy.

In Asia, which comprises the most heterogeneous collection of countries from both the economic and demographic standpoints, the future of many populations looks scarcely more hopeful. Alongside the dramatic success stories there are, according to the World Bank, 600 million people living in 'absolute poverty'. This means not only low income and malnutrition but also lack of access to education, health care, housing, drinking water and main drainage. This poverty is rife not only in Bangladesh, Myanmar, Pakistan, Afghanistan and Cambodia, but also in countries where the overall situation is beginning to improve, as in the Philippines (where it is estimated that 35 per cent of the total population live in poverty) and Sri Lanka. In India it is reckoned that 40 per cent of the population, and more particularly the inhabitants of the north-eastern states, are below the poverty line. In China 130 million people, mainly in rural areas, are known to be living in penury.

In short, it can be said that a substantial proportion of the Third World's inhabitants, an estimated 1 billion at least, are untouched by the process of development, and, since this vast population has not yet gone through a process of genuine demographic transition, it is likely to double by the year 2025. In 1985 it accounted for 40 per cent of the lowest income group (below $480 per head, according to the World Bank), totalling an estimated 2.4 billion people. It is to be hoped, of course, that a proportion of this population will move out of 'absolute poverty' before it doubles. The way world demography evolves will, to a large extent, depend on what the future holds in store for this vast section of the world population, since it is destined to have the most prolonged and highest growth rate. Its magnitude, constantly renewed, has been singularly resistant to reduction in all parts of the world.

Demographers as well as environmentalists are keeping a constant eye on the poorest of the poor. Demographers do so for the reasons just mentioned, and environmentalists are also maintaining a strong interest in this fraction of the population because they consider that poverty and environmental degradation are closely linked, as are the opulence of the industrialized countries with the environment, with the difference that the poor bear the brunt of the environmental damage while the rich have the resources to try counteracting it. The poor living in absolute poverty are dependent for their survival upon the environmental resources of soil, water, forests, fisheries and biotics that make up their main stocks of economic capital. They have no alternative but to exploit their environmental reserve base at an unsustainable rate, causing irreversible injury, deforestation, desertification and soil erosion on a wide scale. It is well recognized that poor people are forced into ways of living which induce further destruction because of the complex cycles of poverty, inappropriate development and environmental deterioration.

A relatively new phenomenon: migration due to environmental degradation

There is likely to be a far higher level of migration from regions in the world with high population growth and low development into regions with the opposite characteristics, i.e. with a depressed demographic pattern but with very healthy economic development, particularly since, as recent years have shown, the former are in many cases politically unstable, thus prompting flows of workers and their families. The developed world will find itself with a diminishing and ageing labour force and faced with a young and abundant labour supply in the Third World prepared to cross the ocean in search of work. Migration, in fact, occurs from further and further afield, facilitated by increasingly less expensive means of transport. This is particularly true as regards Europe and the southern and eastern Mediterranean, where for the moment no real centre of development is emerging as is happening in Asia and to a certain extent in Latin America.

With the intensification of migration, internal or international, the human environment of most inhabitants will change drastically. And with the combination of differential fertility and international migration it will also change the ethnicity distribution of the population.

In certain years flows of migrants are also affecting regions of the Third World depressed by environmental degradation towards other parts of the Third World, or of the industrialized countries. Let us take one example even if it might be considered an extreme case: the Sahel region of Africa. In Mali a demographic survey conducted in 1985 provided information on the causes of migration (Thiam 1992): causes relating to drought accounted for 51.5 per cent, as compared with 45.7 per cent related to work or study and 2.8 per cent for family or other reasons. There are good reasons to believe that the Mali case is only one among many others, especially Brazil, and that with continuous environmental deterioration in the Third World the exodus could grow considerably. S. Ricca (1989: 10) estimated that, around 1983, 35 million Africans lived outside their countries of origin, i.e. 8 per cent of the sub-Saharan African population, one of the highest as compared with other large regions of the world. There are mass migrations into tropical countries due in part to both population growth and deforestation.

It is true that migration among African countries has been part of the African way of life for generations, pastoral nomadism being a distinguishing cultural feature of African populations, but here and elsewhere other, frequently environmental, reasons are gaining significance. One of the most extreme and striking cases is the migration caused in the areas of the Chernobyl catastrophe. R. Rybakovsky (1992) indicated that in the Kiev province, where the population got the information sooner than others, the positive balance of migration of 93,000 people in 1985 was replaced by a negative one of 49,000 in 1986. And many more inhabitants want to leave the areas, especially in the Gomel area of Belorussia. The economic factor is no longer the main cause of migration flows, and the environ- mental one could take on a sizeable dimension in the future.

The geographical distributions of populations within countries are far from optimal according to the resources and to the environment. Sixty per cent of the world population already live in coastal areas, and 65 per cent of cities with populations above 2.5 million inhabitants are located along the coasts. This growth in coastal populations is exerting strong pressures on the marine environment and its resources, and they become increasingly sources of pollution as sewage-discharge effluent goes directly into near-coastal waters. As more than half of humanity lives in coastal areas the potential changes in sea-level as a result of global warming should provide a very strong warning before these changes occur.

Also, with global warming, intra-regional shifts in agricultural productivity, and consequently in geographical distribution of population, will possibly take place which are beyond any forecasts at this time. Some adaptation of the population will necessarily have to take place.

Ecological risks due to a combination of climatic changes, rapid urbanization and high density of population – and we shall see that some densities in the Third World could reach high levels in the future because of population growth – could jeopardize life in many parts of developing countries should natural catastrophes occur.

The prospect of demographic transition in the Third World

What are the prospects for world demography during the next decades according to the United Nations and the World Bank projections? And when will the demographic transition be completed in these projections? It can be reasonably assumed that the demographic transition will be completed, or approaching completion, when the total fertility rate (TFR) is 2.1, since this generally goes with a life expectancy permitting population replacement. This does not, however, imply zero growth, because of the time-lag in the adjustment of the structure to fertility and mortality effects. For the world as a whole, the medium-variant projection of the United Nations, extrapolated to the year 2030 gives an aggregate TFR of 2.1, a growth rate of 1 per cent, a seventy-year life-expectancy at birth (for both sexes), and a 70 per cent rate of urbanization. This process of demographic transition would be almost completed in the Third World as a whole, the world containing 7.1 billion inhabitants in the countries of today's Third World and 1.4 billion in today's industrialized countries.

At the turn of the century, almost all Asian countries and much of Latin America should be well on the way to completing their demographic transition, while sub-Saharan Africa and part of the Near East will still be a long way off. According to the World Bank estimates, we cannot expect TFRs of around 2.5 for a large part of sub-Saharan Africa until the year 2050. Moreover, this is only an average, and a considerable number of African countries would still have TFRs exceeding 3: Niger, Malawi, Rwanda, Mali, Mauritania, Gambia and Sierra Leone.

What is striking is that, between now and the year 2025, the population of countries which will have completed, or almost completed, their demographic transition will amount to almost 6.8 billion, or five times that of today's industrialized countries. Thirty years is an excessively short period for a transformation of such amplitude, given that the countries concerned will also by then be industrialized to some extent and highly urbanized. A much longer time was necessary for today's industrialized countries to come to the end of the demographic transition process, and become both industrialized and urbanized. It seems an impossible challenge for the Third World, and the world as a whole, if the international community does not fundamentally change its ways of reacting and thinking, in particular from the environmental standpoint. Production, whether industrial or agricultural, should be conducted so as not to weaken or diminish our planet's capacity to sustain life and so as to protect our environment in both the present and the future.

Doubts about the demographic outlook

Should the United Nations and the World Bank projections be realized, there will be many more areas of development and environmental crises in the future. The crises could be such that they cast doubt on the longer-term materialization of the projections. Some distortions would necessarily occur, such as different trends in fertility, fewer improvements in health and mortality and intensification of migration.

First, these projections are presented as if they were vectors unaffected by any external factors, proceeding in a vacuum without any hindrance. It is this that makes them scarcely credible as soon as they go beyond one or two decades. One of the first certainties is that each of the following factors – population, environment, food and energy – has assumed global significance and interacts closely with the others.

The second reason for doubt is that it is not conceivable that some form of demographic equality will gradually emerge at the end of the demographic transition given that this situation will apply not only to the world population as a whole but also to that of each individual country. It is difficult to accept this idea since it would imply either that people will become equal in terms of economic and social conditions, or that differences in economic, social and even cultural conditions will no longer have any effect on either fertility or mortality.

So far, however, no hypothesis of any other kind has been put forward and perhaps, therefore, for want of anything better, we can accept the idea, provided the calculations are not extended too far into the future, following the example set by the United Nations.

A third serious doubt regarding these projections is the seeming implausibility of many of the results. For example, is it conceivable that Africa, with its many ecological and economic problems, where school enrolment rates and the number of doctors are the lowest in the world, where industry is limited and where there is a growing division between vast urban conglomerations and immense tracts of derelict land, is likely to see its population increase sevenfold between 1950 and 2025, and thirteenfold between 1950 and the end of the next century? The population of Africa, which represented less than 10 per cent of the world population in 1950, would see its share rise to over 25 per cent – unless, of course, it is assumed that there could be massive emigration, a hypothesis which demographers working in international organizations have not dared to put forward; or that mortality rates could cease to decline and would even rise as a result of the worsening of nutritional and economic conditions, the emergence of new diseases such as AIDS or the resurgence of illnesses such as malaria or cholera; or that there could be a combination of all these adverse circumstances – something that cannot be ruled out, at least in certain regions. It is predicted that the Sahel countries (Burkina Faso, Chad, Gambia, Mali, Mauritania, Niger and Senegal) will see their populations increase fourfold on average between 1985 and 2025, and by almost as much again between 2025 and the end of the next century.

The paradox with these projections is that the populations forecast to expand the most rapidly in the future are precisely those that are being subjected to the strongest demographic pressures, and which for a number of decades have been confronting problems that they are unable to solve and that are getting worse.

Admittedly, it has been true that, until now, the poorer a population was, the faster its growth. But tomorrow's world is unlikely to be a repetition of yesterday's, and it is very probable that populations facing difficulties, because of the deterioration of their environment, for example, will try to move into less hostile surroundings: in fact, we are already beginning to see migratory movements in Africa and Brazil caused by deterioration of the environment, as noted above.

A fourth source of doubt is just how quickly birth-control will become widely practised in the poorest part of the Third World, especially sub-Saharan countries, and it is this which leads us to believe that, for these countries, the high rather than the low variant of the United Nations projections is likely to be closer to the truth.

The United Nations and World Bank projections for a relatively steep decline in sub-Saharan Africa and the poorest regions of the Third World are likely to be proved correct only if recourse to contraception changes. So far, the use of contraceptive methods has been conditional on acceptance of them, determined to a great extent by the improvement in women's status and level of education, and the more general improvement in living conditions. It is not inconceivable that we may see the development of what might be termed the 'contraception for poor people'. It is not inconceivable that a fertility transition should take place in response to economic hardship, as was suggested for sub-Saharan Africa by E. Boserup (1985), helped by large-scale campaigns to promote birth-control using ever more powerful and wide-reaching mass media. It is virtually certain that the future will see the introduction of cheap modern methods of contraception within the reach of even the poorest members of society, and that the current inhibitions about their use will gradually disappear.

Concern about health and mortality, especially in sub-Saharan Africa

A fifth reason for doubt and concern about the projections of the UN and the World Bank concerns the mortality trends, about which five points may be made.

First, it is suspected that there has been an increase in mortality rates in tropical countries. It is virtually certain that malaria is staging a strong comeback, and there is a clear and steady rise in the incidence of this disease. The World Health Organization estimates that there are no fewer than 1.7 billion inhabitants of tropical regions facing the threat of malaria because the situation there is unstable and getting worse. The latest estimates put the current number of cases of malaria per year throughout the world at 100 million and the number of carriers of the parasite at 264 million, mostly on the African continent and in Central and South America, particularly Amazonia. In some countries where the disease is rife, such as Nigeria, Kenya and Gambia, between 20 and 30 per cent of the deaths of unweaned infants are due to malarial infection. The WHO also reports a recrudescence of venereal disease as a result of population movements or lack of health-care facilities.

Second, the extraordinary and dramatic appearance of AIDS on the world health scene is another growth source of concern. It is more of a pandemic than an epidemic disease and one which is liable to become a significant demographic factor. Unofficial figures for some sub-Saharan African countries put the number of infected adults as high as 20 per cent and even more in urban areas in West and Central Africa. It is estimated that 8–10 million children will be infected by the year 2000, most of them in sub-Saharan Africa.

The third cloud on the horizon in the Third World as far as health is concerned stems from these countries' economic difficulties. These are causing cut-backs in expenditure on health care, which already represents a far from adequate proportion of their total budget – rarely more than 5 per cent.

Fourth, environmental damage may make improved health an illusion, or partly cancel out its effects. The extension of deserts diminishes food supplies. Pollution and lack of water encourage the spread of water-borne diseases. Water also represents a danger in those regions of the Third World which are subject to flooding, particularly in tropical America and Asia (for instance, Bangladesh). Traditional barriers to infection often give way with migration to overpopulated and insalubrious cities, where health-care facilities cannot keep up with population growth, all the more so given the economic restrictions.

In the fifth place, many Third-World countries which are well down the path to development are rapidly joining the levels of health and mortality of the industrialized countries, so that what can be said now is that there is a widening gap in terms of health and mortality between, on the one hand, the industrialized countries and those countries of the Third World which are making economic progress and, on the other hand, those Third-World countries that are not managing to move into the stage of demographic transition and of development. This brings us to the idea that the differences between countries in terms of health and life expectancy are not tending to disappear.

Uncertainties about the rich countries

There are finally as many question marks about the demographic future of the industrialized countries as about that of the Third World. The industrialized countries have entered into what is termed the 'post-transition phase', for which there has been no precedent. Neither governments nor experts have any direct experience of this phenomenon, whose causes are rooted in society itself and could be eliminated only as the result of radical change.

As far as the demographic future of the developed countries is concerned, we are in the dark, as is evidenced by the vagueness of the term 'post-transition phase'. All of the alternatives outside the well-trodden paths are open. The industrialized countries no longer have the certainty of the transition theory that has been guiding them until now. The only certainty is that of an inevitable ageing of the population and of having become magnets for the poor and jobless of the South. The projections concerning these countries are more a matter of judgement than genuine science.

Overview and conclusions

Environmental concern, and the costs of dealing with it, is another factor widening the gap between industrialized countries and the Third World, as there is no doubt that population growth and its increasingly unbalanced distribution within countries are playing a definitive role in the deterioration of the environment. Admittedly, the true quantification of the relationship is subject to heated controversy and many intervening factors are operating with that of population in a complex web, such as poverty, modern technologies aimed at increasing production to keep up with population growth and the need to catch up on living conditions with the industrialized countries, uneven income distribution, and so on. It might even be that these factors are more responsible for environmental degradation than population.

It is likely that for the present time the Third World is more responsible for factors affecting the environment linked with population – deforestation and water shortages – whereas industrialized countries are more responsible for factors linked with industrialization. The relative impact could be around 1 to 3. Nonetheless, with the process of population transition of the Third World, and some forms of 'affluence' associated necessarily with it, the relation could change drastically, and even reverse in a not too distant future.

I observed above that many of today's developing countries are or will be moving into the category of industrialized countries and that there is a causal chain: demographic transition–development–industrialization–environmental problems. Never have we had so much evidence as we have today of the effect of demographic factors in development. If we take a close look at this, we see that it is those countries which are quickest in reaching the stage of demographic transition which are best placed on the international economic scene, and further ample evidence of this can be found in the contrary examples of sub-Saharan Africa and some Asian countries such as Pakistan, Bangladesh and Cambodia. It can also be said that it is those countries which are in the midst of this period of demographic transition that have the advantage as regards the development of their economy, benefiting as they do from a steady inflow of plentiful and cheap labour. The newly industrializing economies of Asia possess the three pre-requisites for success, i.e. emphasis on agriculture, a process of industrialization focused from the outset on exports and a demographic policy designed to curb population growth.

A major issue is whether the countries which have completed their transition, or are getting closer to that stage, will have the technological and financial resources to remedy environmental damage. An estimate based on the United Nations medium variant indicates that, by about the year 2025, the population that will have completed the phase of demographic transition, and thus have achieved some form of industrialization, will be 6.8 billion, with 1.4 billion in today's industrialized countries and 5.4 billion in today's developing countries. We can imagine what this means in terms of consumption of natural resources and efforts to prevent deterioration of the environment. What will the air we breathe and the water we drink be like if this population of about 6.8 billion human beings, which will have completed the phase by the year 2025, also manages to industrialize as the 1.2 billion inhabitants of today's 'rich' countries are doing? Going from 1.2 billion to almost 6.8 billion 'post-transition' inhabitants in the space of only thirty-five years will create enormous problems of adjustment. And the source of these problems will not be the size of this population, but its propensity to damage the environment.

Is the theory of demographic transition to be revised, since fertility may decline sharply without real development, and therefore without strong industrialization? This is what the case of China might suggest. But China is an exception, and its rapid fertility decline was the result of an unprecedented and vigorous policy. Further, China can be expected to reach by the year 2025, or shortly after, an advanced stage of development and industrialization. The country will be in a good position to recover during the next century the dominant position it occupied during ancient times, thanks to its massive population.

One of the basic questions is whether those countries which will be going through the phase of demographic transition will have the ability to develop in a manner different from that of today's industrialized countries, that is to say, consuming less energy than is required for development by today's industrialized countries. The question is well discussed by N. Keyfitz (1992):

> If a tight relation exists between energy use and income, and for unalterable physical reasons the correlation is as high as it is in the world today, then there is no way that the [less developed countries] can attain the incomes of the developed countries.

In this connection, the rich countries' pleas for good behaviour are likely to fall on deaf ears so long as they themselves are not setting the example of 'clean industrialization' or transmitting their 'environment-cleaning' technologies and, most important, the resources needed to apply them in the developing countries.

There are indications that the United Nations high-variant projections are more plausible than the medium-variant projections for the poorer countries of the Third World, at least as regards fertility. For sub-Saharan African or other very poor countries, the assumptions of both fertility and mortality decline on which the projections are based seem highly unrealistic. The health problems encountered by the poorer countries, with the AIDS pandemic and the resurgence of malaria and more recently cholera, translate the catastrophic health conditions prevailing in many of these countries, which could put a brake on population growth, as commented on by J. Caldwell (1991). Under the most pessimistic scenario, both fertility and mortality decline would slow down, delaying the end of the demographic transition. The medium-variant projection would be accurate only because of errors in both variables which would cancel one another out in the final rate of growth.

Whatever the case, these calculations show that there is something contradictory about a Third-World policy which consists in accelerating the demographic transition by encouraging family planning, while taking no, or very few, steps to preserve the environment. The nearer a country draws to the end of the demographic transition, the more urgently it needs action to protect its environment. The two policies, family planning and environmental protection, should be closely associated if the balance of the ecosystem is not to be severely disrupted, and the association must be a very long-term one. We may say that to support family planning in the Third World without providing the means necessary to protect the environment is to be guilty of disrupting this balance. In population and environmental policy alike, the rich countries are responsible to the developing ones, as they are to themselves, for transmitting the necessary technologies and resources for implementing them.

Clearly, it is first and foremost to the 1 billion inhabitants lagging behind as regards demographic transition and development that the information and education campaigns on contraception should be directed in order to slow population growth over the long term. During the second half of the next century, the growth in world population is likely to come almost entirely from sub-Saharan Africa.

Finally, the hypothesis of a move towards a certain degree of demographic homogeneity, with the scenario of stationary populations in almost every case by about the end of the next century, as forecast by some projections is unconvincing. As Paul Demeny (1989a: 54) writes, 'the idea of a trend towards a stationary population may be justifiable from a normative standpoint, but it lacks support from the theoretical, empirical and historical standpoints'. There is no objective necessity for a stationary population, and there is no historical basis for it. Future demographic trends are not programmed, and a stationary population is not their automatic outcome. And, in fact, differences in fertility and mortality have never been as marked as they are today: the ratio of the fertility rate of Germany or Italy and that of many sub-Saharan countries is 1 to 5. These differences have grown over time, instead of diminishing. Differential demography will continue affecting all sorts of relationships among countries.

ACKNOWLEDGEMENTS

This chapter has been reduced by the editors from the author's paper with the same title published in *Population and Environment* (Paris: CICRED, 1992). It has been reprinted by kind permission of the author and publisher.

Part III

International issues

7 International justice and the environment

Steven Luper-Foy

There are many strategies for defending claims of justice concerning the environment. Bits of the non-human world may themselves be the sources of moral obligations. A growing number of people argue that animals have the sort of moral standing that implies that individual animals must be protected from various sorts of abuse and whole species from extinction. People also argue that entire ecosystems or life itself have moral standing (see Chapter 10 in this volume). Some or all of these people may well be correct; if so, their arguments would provide powerful reasons to change the ways people treat the non-human world. But I shall not assume (or deny) that the non-human world has any sort of moral standing. Whereas I think that we ought to treat the non-human world quite differently than we do, I want to give other sorts of reasons for changing our behaviour. I want to exploit the evident fact that many of our obligations towards the non-human part of the world are determined by how human beings should treat each other. Even if human beings had obligations only to each other, and the non-human world were merely a resource (a collection of natural resources) for us to use as we wish, we would still have powerful reasons to change our behaviour, or so I shall argue.

I shall avoid making strong assumptions about the sorts of thing that have moral standing because these assumptions are highly controversial. It is critical to find as uncontroversial a basis for discussions about matters of global justice as possible, since agreement is a precondition for action, and the diverse peoples of the world find it extremely difficult to agree on anything. The conception of justice on which I shall rely is lean and, I believe, relatively uncontroversial, as far as it goes. It is libertarian, at least in spirit. To be sure, libertarianism *is* controversial, but the controversy is almost entirely generated by people who think that justice is *more* demanding than libertarianism says it is, not by those who think that libertarianism requires things that are not true obligations. Thus it is common for people to complain that libertarianism is flawed because it does not require people to help meet the needs of others. But few will disagree with the libertarian's claim that when I am doing something that has no impact on another my freedom to continue to do so should be protected. So people who disagree with the views I defend here are likely to do so because the views are not demanding enough. And even these people are likely to think that protecting the freedoms championed by libertarians is more important than meeting the other requirements that non-libertarians would link to justice. There is a long-standing tradition in liberal philosophy, going back at least as far as the publication of J. S. Mill's *On Liberty*, and including John Rawls's *A Theory of Justice* that assigns liberty a place of prominence over the other features of a just society.

Another reason I rely on a libertarian conception of justice is that I happen to think that it is quite plausible, especially on the global level. However, I do not have the space to defend my version of libertarianism. I can do no more than lay out the theory I recommend, and get right to the suggestions I shall use it to defend.

THE THEORETICAL FRAMEWORK

The libertarian view suggests that people (and organizations of people) have *negative* obligations in the sense that we must do everything we can to *avoid interfering* with each other's projects. The central task for the libertarian theorist is to work out a non-interference scheme, a scheme by which people may engage in their pursuits with minimal mutual interference. Of course, maximizing freedom will require restraints. For some to be free to arrange their private affairs, others must not (be free to) interfere. In particular, if some are free to acquire a particular set of natural resources others are not free to interfere, and hence not free to acquire them. Freedom in one area limits freedom elsewhere. But people should be as free as possible to believe, to value and to act as they wish, and a non-interference scheme is designed to tell us which combination of freedoms and restraints will allow individuals the greatest scope for their pursuits.

The claim that we ought to minimize the extent to which we interfere with each other's endeavours will be acceptable to a wide range of people. What people will find far more controversial is the libertarian's claim that we have *only* negative obligations. We have no *positive* obligations; we are not required to aid others except in so far as this is necessary to avoid interfering with their endeavours. We must abide by the terms of a non-interference scheme which tells us how to minimize interference, but otherwise we may freely refuse to join with others into schemes for mutual advantage. Fortunately, however, we may postpone deciding whether or not there are positive obligations. What I want to do in this chapter is to provide a framework for identifying our negative obligations and use it to clarify some of the requirements of global justice.

It is important to avoid a possible confusion concerning the libertarian claim that justice requires maximizing freedom. The sense of 'freedom' libertarians have in mind is a *negative* sense of freedom. The relevant sense of freedom is captured by Rawls (1972: sect. 32), who says that people are free to do something 'when they are free from certain constraints either to do it or not to do it and when their doing it or not doing it is protected from interference by other persons'. Accordingly, libertarians want to devise a scheme whereby we avoid getting in each other's way. Thus libertarians do *not* mean to devise a scheme whereby people are provided with as much help as possible to achieve their aims. The latter could be construed as a scheme for maximizing people's freedom to do what they want, a kind of freedom that can be thought of as 'positive'. People have this 'positive' kind of freedom when they have the means or ability to take advantage of their (negative) freedoms. But our having the kind of freedom the libertarian is interested in does not imply that we have the means to take advantage of our freedom. Libertarians think that just behaviour is a matter of not hindering people in their efforts to accomplish their ends, not a matter of *helping* them accomplish their ends.

One of the failings of many libertarian theorists is that after saying that everyone should be free to do what fails to interfere with the endeavours of others, they do not tell us how to work out how we may act when we *will* thwart the desires of others. For example, you and I cannot both gain exclusive ownership of a particular Pacific island; how do we settle this and other disputes? My suggestion is that we make our choice of non-interference scheme using some of John Rawls's apparatus. Rawls (1972) defends both a non-interference scheme and a scheme of mutual aid. He thinks that we have both positive and negative obligations, and uses his apparatus to identify both. My suggestion is that we use it to pick out negative obligations, not positive ones. My idea is that in designing a scheme of non-interference, we are looking to see what sorts of mutual accommodation should be insisted upon when people's plans clash. Presumably we want those mutual accommodations to be fair, since initially no one's plans have any greater claim to be realized than anyone else's. Rawls has given us a superb tool for fair adjudication; let's use it.

Briefly, I would apply Rawls's apparatus in much the way that he recommends. Aside from the fact that I would use the apparatus to evaluate only non-interference schemes, the one important change I would make is a change in who gets represented in the original position. In his own brief discussion of international justice (sect. 58), Rawls assigns entire nations representatives in the original position. For many reasons, including the fact that the desirability of the nation-state is itself an issue of global justice, I recommend that we instead give a representative to all those affected by the principles of non-interference we seek, namely, everyone in the world. The rest of Rawls's apparatus stays in place.

Let me sketch Rawls's apparatus for those who are unfamiliar with it. The idea is to evaluate principles of justice from the standpoint of hypothetical people who are in a hypothetical situation which Rawls calls the *original position*. Each party in the original position represents the interests of one person in the world, and, in my version of Rawls's apparatus, everyone in the world is represented by one party in the original position. The parties undertake the task of ranking alternative conceptions of justice on behalf of the persons whom they represent. By stipulation, the parties are rational, and hence strive to do what is maximally in the interest of their wards, and mutually disinterested, meaning that each is unconcerned about the interests of other parties and their wards. The parties have certain sorts of information. They have the general, scientific knowledge necessary to work out the consequences for normal human beings of the implementation of alternative conceptions of justice. But their knowledge of their wards is severely restricted. They know that their wards are normal human beings, and that they have a sense of justice, meaning that their wards have a normally effective motivation and capacity to act from principles of justice once these are made plain, even though acting justly will often call for subordinating their efforts to secure a good life. The parties also know that their wards have a conception of the good, which is roughly a plan for their lives that specifies how ideally their lives would unfold. But the parties do not know anything else about their wards. Thus, for example, the parties do not know their wards' idea of a good life or the specifics of their situations in society, and so are ignorant of their sex, race, income, occupation, generation and, since we want principles of non-interference which will apply across the globe, citizenship and place of habitation. Given these severe restrictions, the parties are unable to single out their wards and hence unable to contour their choice of conception of justice to the particular features of their wards. They must assume that their wards might occupy any of the social positions that would occur in a society that is ordered by the conception of justice they choose, including the worst social position. Hence they must select a conception that generates a society whose worst social position is fully acceptable to their wards. In effect, the parties are forced to treat everyone in society fairly, since for all they (the parties) know, the person they represent might be anyone. Rawls thinks that the fairness of his mode of selection of principles of justice transfers to the principles themselves; hence the aim of his slogan 'justice as fairness' is achieved.

REGIONAL AUTONOMY

So let us use Rawls's original position to sketch part of a global non-interference scheme, and see what we can learn about our obligations towards the environment. I shall be particularly concerned to question the idea that the present order of sovereign nation-states should be accepted, especially given the assumption that they own the resources within their boundaries.

Everyone in the world, past, present and future, is represented in the original position, so the representatives will consider everyone's interests to be equally important. But the representatives know the specific plans of no one. Obviously, then, they will want to choose a scheme that allows the greatest variety of plans to be realized, across the globe and across the generations. They will want to ensure that people are as free as possible to pursue their private goals, to be sure, but also that people are as free as possible to sort themselves into pairs, communities and other associations, and to author the rules that are to govern their interactions.

But what should be done to deal with the inevitable clashes of individual and collective plans? Clearly the most practical, freedom-expanding step to take is to preserve a high degree of regional autonomy, as suggested by the *principle of regional autonomy*: where clashes of individual and collective plans threaten to occur, let people sort themselves out into different geographical regions where like-minded people can govern themselves according to regional rules of association which they themselves construct, or emigrate in order to seek some other region with more attractive physical features or rules of association. There is no more effective way to arrange for a great variety of incompatible lifestyles to coexist peacefully.

Of course, we cannot expect all rules of association to be constructions at the level of individual autonomous regions. The principle of regional autonomy itself is a global, not a regional, rule, and other global rules will be needed as well. We need global rules because some sources of conflict are irreducibly interregional or irreducibly intergenerational. No amount of intraregional or intragenerational rule-making will solve certain conflicts. Conflicting claims to natural resources are the outstanding example. Region A cannot settle a conflict with region B over the world's resources by making laws that apply only within A. And pollution wanders across regional boundaries, damaging features of the planet (such as the ozone layer) on which everyone depends.

As things stand, nations have some policies for dealing with ownership of natural resources, and are on their way to developing policies for handling other environmental matters. At summits of the seven major industrial nations environmental issues have been given higher and higher priority. And the United Nations has sponsored discussions about environmental issues that culminated in the United Nations Conference on Environment and Development in 1992. These discussions have made it clear that many states recognize that environmental problems are urgent. However, it is not clear that they realize how urgent the problems are, or that they realize how serious some of the global injustices involving resources are. For example, the people of each nation regard the natural resources that happen to fall within its borders as theirs – as the property of present and future generations of that nation – to conserve or destroy as they wish. The presumption is that the land and other resources within the geographical boundaries of each nation belong to (the people of) that nation alone. This conventional presumption is endorsed by Principle 2 of the Rio Declaration made at the United Nations Conference on Environment and Development in 1992. According to that declaration,

> States have, in accordance with the Charter of the United Nations and the principles of international law, the sovereign right to exploit their own resources pursuant to their own environmental and developmental policies.

I do not know of a plausible justification for this conventional assumption. Michael Walzer defends a related thesis when he argues that communities such as states have a right to exist and hence a right to sufficient territory (1977: 53–8) and resources (1983: 42–52) to enjoy their way of life. But I have already argued that while the existence of communities (which are like states in some respects) is just, these communities should not have all of the features which states have, such as sovereignty. Sovereignty entails the authority to disallow emigration, a power no community should have. However, even if we agree with Walzer that states have a right to the use of the territory and resources that will make their way of life possible, it does not follow that they should be given *ownership* of that territory or its resources. For most communities could maintain their way of life even if charged rent for the use of territory and fees for resources. And let us not too quickly agree that states have a right to the territory and resources that will make their way of life possible. Doesn't it matter what sort of life they lead, and how much territory and resources they demand? Surely communities are not entitled to (buy? take?) *whatever* resources they need in order to carry on their way of life, regardless of how demanding it is. We cannot assume that ways of life are acceptable just because they are established. We need principles of justice to tell us which sorts of consumption patterns and hence which cultures are permissible.

In any case, the key point is that the parties in the original position would insist on equity in the sharing of the benefits of the world's resources, including the world's land. From their point of view, the conventional presumption that state boundaries establish ownership of resources is completely insupportable. As the parties in the original position will recognize, the presumption is doubly unjust. First, it wrongs people who happen to live in resource-poor regions, and second, it wrongs future generations. Representatives realize that their own wards might be citizens of resource-poor regions or members of generations whose predecessors have consumed and polluted so extensively that little remains. Yet as representatives also know, natural resources are critical means for anyone's life plan. Almost everyone wants as many natural resources as possible; why should the representatives accept an arrangement in which their wards might end up with comparatively few? Instead, the representatives would adopt the *resource-equity principle*: resources are to be handled in a way that is equitable both across the globe and across the generations.

Clearly enough, the resource-equity principle is incompatible with the idea that national boundaries establish the proper distribution of natural resources. None the less, the resource-equity principle could use some clarification. We need to know more precisely what an equitable resource policy will look like, both across the generations and across regions.

RESOURCES AND INTERGENERATIONAL JUSTICE

People want the benefits of far more resources than are available, and it is a safe bet that this will be true of future generations. But if resources are consumed too rapidly or if they are destroyed by pollution, then later generations must do without. Therefore the parties in the original position will want to demand that resources be consumed (and pollution allowed) at a rate that is indefinitely sustainable. Equity across the generations reduces to the demand for indefinite sustainability in the areas of both pollution and consumption.

Pollution is of great concern to the parties in the original position since it makes resources, such as land, air and water, unusable. As things stand, industries ignore many of these effects; the costs of pollution on present and future generations do not figure in the costs of their operations and are not passed on to those who purchase the products of the operations (the costs are 'externalized'). In view of the fact that any substantial level of pollution leads to high accumulations of harmful substances over time, the parties in the original position would want to prevent all but the small amounts of pollution that can be assimilated without harm by the environment.

The parties' concern about consumption patterns is the same as their concern about pollution: they will want policies that people can sustain indefinitely into the future. Thus the policy 'consume what you want' is unacceptable, since it allows any generation to consume everything, produce a future generation and leave it nothing. In securing sustainability, the parties' deliberations will have three main emphases: conserving, recycling and renewing resources.

In principle, most of the natural resources people absolutely require are indefinitely renewable. Energy from the sun is plentiful and for practical purposes inexhaustible. Food and many clothing and building materials derive ultimately from sources, such as plants and animals, that, suitably managed, are indefinitely renewable or replaceable. Justice calls for consuming renewable or replaceable resources only in connection with a policy of renewing or replacing them.

Often it will be legitimate to replace plants and animals living in a particular region with other, more manageable and productive life-forms, as when grasslands are converted into cattle or crop farms. Even future generations would be better off were such changes made. But changes in the flora and fauna of a region must be restricted since they eliminate a natural resource which otherwise would be available to future generations. The parties would allow major changes only when the changes would not result in the loss of species or in the loss of substantial areas of great biodiversity. The parties would protect species and areas of substantial biodiversity for the following reasons: first, the loss of species and biodiversity would have a powerful effect on the ecological order that sustains the world's life. Second, the plants and animals may have a wide variety of applications for people. And third, the particular plants and animals and the various species that are to be eliminated may have great aesthetic value.

Non-renewable resources are more problematic from the point of view of sustainability, but the main idea is to combine conservation with continual recycling. The way to handle water and air is clear enough: any water or air that is used must be reintroduced into the environment in its original purity. But it is harder to recycle resources like oil. Perhaps the best one can do is to insist that if such things are to be consumed, they must be converted into things which are themselves indefinitely recyclable, and also that they be gathered sparingly so that large quantities will be conserved and thus made available to many generations who will probably find them indispensable for many uses. It is impossible to justify the way fossil fuels are squandered today. Oil and natural gas are limited resources with an enormous variety of uses, yet present generations are consuming them in ways that future generations would certainly not endorse, especially when we consider the harmful effects of pollution which our children will have to endure.

Exactly what future generations there should be is an issue the parties must also settle. The vast majority of people consider reproducing to be of central importance to them. I think that it is reasonable for the parties to assume that future generations will also want to reproduce, so that one high priority for the parties is to insist on capping the global rate of reproduction so that it is sustainable indefinitely. No generation would be shown special consideration in this matter; the parties would want each generation to be able to reproduce at least at the rate of its predecessors.

A complication is that what constitutes a sustainable rate of consumption and pollution depends on the rate of reproduction, and vice versa. If people consume less and if they destroy less by pollution, they could sustain a higher rate of reproduction, and vice versa. So there is some flexibility in the policy the parties would impose. The general principle they would favour, the *sustainable consumption–reproduction principle*, could be put as follows: each generation may consume natural resources, pollute, and reproduce at given rates only if it could reasonably expect that each successive generation could do likewise. Arguably, my principle is expressed at least roughly by Principle 8 of the 'Rio Declaration':

> To achieve sustainable development and a higher quality of life for all people, States should reduce and eliminate unsustainable patterns of production and consumption and promote appropriate demographic policies.

When the population is too large to be sustained safely, the sustainable consumption–reproduction principle implies that it must be reduced. The pressing needs of a growing population are not acceptable grounds for lowering the planet's biodiversity or damaging its ecosystem. The parties would consider such steps to be a bad idea from the standpoint of even more distantly future populations, and would prefer to reduce drastically (and even reverse) the rate of population growth instead, as required by the sustainable consumption–reproduction principle.

The sustainable consumption–reproduction principle appears to have some dramatic consequences, given the growth of the world's population and the ways that population consumes resources. For it may be that the world's population level has exceeded the point at which it can be *indefinitely* and *safely* sustained, thus violating the principle. And if the population has reached that point, our situation is dire, for it is clear that the world's population will soon double. Most underdeveloped countries have tremendous growth, a doubling rate of thirty-three years. And even in countries where the birth rate is low, there are so many young people (who have not yet reproduced) that we can expect the populations in these countries to increase dramatically.

That the world's present population level of 5.6 billion cannot be indefinitely and safely sustained is not something I can establish. The relevant literature contains both optimistic and pessimistic assessments. However, a plausible case can be made against the sustainability of 5.6 billion people. The case I have in mind was made by William Ophuls and A. Stephen Boyan (1992), who argue for a considerably weaker claim, namely that 8 billion cannot be sustained. But I think that their data, if accurate, would support my stronger claim. Let us consider some of the relevant facts as they report them.

First, all land that is good for agriculture is already in use. In fact, already much land in use is marginal, and the marginal land is not very productive. Eighty per cent of the world's food comes from the better half of the land already in use. Second, land that is already in use is becoming less productive, not more productive. Third, not much new land can be made even as productive as the less productive land already in use. Clearing forests for cropland leads to a host of disasters, flooding, erosion and desertification among them, and new irrigation projects not only have the problems of the old ones (salinization, waterlogging, and fertilizer and pesticide contamination), but are also limited by the decreasing availability of good water. (Already, in one-fifth of the irrigated areas of the United States, water is being pumped faster than it is being replenished.) Fourth, the world's oceans, which are largely vast deserts except on the edges, are already yielding about as much as they can, and their present yield may be unsustainable, since overfishing threatens some species, pollution is accumulating at an incredible rate and tropical wetlands are being destroyed.

These facts suggest two conclusions. First, much of the present level of productivity of agriculture is due to unsustainable methods of farming. The use of fertilizers derived from petroleum products and heavy applications of insecticides are just two examples of agricultural practices that must eventually stop. Given that unsustainable methods of farming must stop, a second conclusion is hard to avoid: for the foreseeable future land is already about as productive as it is going to be. In view of the limitations on land productivity cited above, if a switch is made to sustainable methods of production, we should not expect that the world's capacity to produce food will increase much beyond its present level in the foreseeable future. To think otherwise is to assume an irresponsible attitude of faith that improved technology will rescue us.

The conclusion that land is about as productive as it is going to be for the foreseeable future is important given another claim made by Ophuls and Boyan: there is *already* a gap between available food and the number of people who need it, and certainly no safety margin to prevent many occurrences, such as insect plagues, drought, or other common natural catastrophes, from resulting in the starvation of millions.

So while Ophuls' and Boyan's conclusion that it would be completely irresponsible to expect to feed 8 billion, completely irresponsible to allow the population to grow that large, seems entirely justified given the empirical claims they make, I think it can be strengthened. Their data suggest that our present population level cannot be sustained safely. It is irresponsible to allow the population to remain at its *current* size. It is far easier to reduce the number of people who make demands on the world's finite resources than it is to find new ways to provide an ever-increasing population with access to the resources they need if they are to live a worthwhile life. If resources and land productivity truly are dwindling the way Ophuls and Boyan say, then justice requires extreme cuts in the population, which means immediately limiting the average family size to one child per couple, and preferably even less.

RESOURCES AND INTRAGENERATIONAL JUSTICE

Only after we are clear about what each generation owes the next can we work out what its members owe each other. By setting the ceiling on the resources that are available to each generation, and by delineating *how* resources may be consumed, the sustainable consumption–reproduction principle specifies what resources are available to us as a generation. However, we do not yet know how the benefits of our generation's share of resources are to be distributed among us. Who gets what? For guidance, we need principles of intragenerational justice or, to use a more common (though less desirable, since it takes for granted the framework of nation-states) expression, principles of international justice.

Of course, we are not completely in the dark about the matter of intragenerational justice since we have already seen that the parties in the original position would insist on a distribution of the benefits of natural resources that is equitable both across and within the generations. So what we need now is a practical scheme for realizing equity within a generation. My suggestion is that some international institution such as the World Bank should be assigned the responsibility of handling natural resources, and that its authority over the handling of resources should be a limitation on the power of communities to govern themselves. The World Bank would apply the sustainable consumption–reproduction principle to work out what resources were due to each generation, and then see to it that the members of each generation got their share of the benefits of those resources through the following policies.

First, the World Bank would sell on the open market the rights to recover resources that, unlike land and air, require recovery. Particular communities would have to allow free market forces to control the costs associated with natural resources and their recovery. In regions in which legitimate resource recovery was authorized by the Bank, the communities must allow access. By the same token, buyers of recovery rights would have to recover the items in ways that were virtually pollution-free, and use them in ways that were consistent with the conservation, renewal and recycling requirements of intergenerational justice, but otherwise would be free to keep whatever they recovered or to sell it to others (who in turn would be bound to meet the requirements of intergenerational justice). Forbidding pollution would, among other things, eliminate the possibility that the costs of dealing with pollution would be externalized by any industry, including the recovery industry. The recovery rights would be for limited periods of time, so that the Bank could maximize the revenues it gained from selling those rights.

Second, the World Bank (or whatever) would lease the world's land, itself a natural resource, on an open market in which competitive offers were made for leasing rights. No one would own land outright; everyone would be required to purchase the right to use land. The Bank would lease land in various packages and for various periods, always with an eye to maximizing its revenues.

Third, the Bank would subtract from its revenues its own operating costs, and then it would distribute the rest equally among the members of the generation at hand.

My suggestion about leasing arrangements is consistent with a range of plans by communities for raising the funds necessary to lease the territory they required. On one plan the community's governing body would lease an entire area using funds it collected through taxes or through subleasing parcels of land. On another the governing body would have nothing to do with leasing land, and would simply be elected by people who leased contiguous areas. On no arrangement is it likely that any community could control vast stretches of unused land that was needed by others, for market forces would tend to ensure that most useful land would find its way into hands that could put it to productive use.

My land-leasing arrangements would entail that communities that could pay the most for the most desirable areas of the globe would probably end up leasing them, but that result would not be unjust. When those who could pay the most to lease land did so, the proceeds available from leasing those areas would be as high as possible, which in turn would ensure that everyone's share of the benefits of the world's land was as high as possible. Note also that areas that were set aside for conservation purposes would not go completely unused, for people (such as indigenous populations) may occupy them and pay little or no leasing fee, so long as they maintained a lifestyle consistent with the goal of conservation.

Cultivated crops and livestock cannot be handled through the leasing arrangements I just sketched, for they are not natural resources and cannot be treated as such. The parties in the original position would favour equity in the distribution of natural resources since initially no one's claim to natural resources is any better than another's. But crops are a different matter. They are to some extent the fruits of someone's labour. However, the land on which crops and livestock are grown and the nutrients on which they feed are ultimately natural resources. These resources would fall under the same leasing arrangements as others. Farmers and ranchers would have to lease land and use it only in ways which did not deplete it, and the rest of us would benefit both from our share of the leasing fee that farmers pay and from the food available for purchase.

The sustainable consumption–reproduction principle provides a limit on the number of children each generation as a whole may produce, but does not tell us which individuals may reproduce or how many children they may produce. The number of people in a generation directly affects how many resources it may enjoy, so we also need to know whether and how our decision to have a family should affect our resource share.

Two points are crucial here. First, the parties would conclude that every competent adult's desire to reproduce is as important as that of any other competent adult. Each is entitled to no more offspring than the others, and the total is limited by the generation's ceiling figure. Second, people who forgo having children create an opportunity for others to reproduce. Here the parties have grounds for rewarding those who have few or no children.

A practical way to accommodate these concerns is to arrange for the sale of parental rights on an open world market. If I have the right to have one child, I may sell that right to someone else. Through this mechanism, childless parents are compensated, and parents who have especially high numbers of children are penalized in that they must purchase the right to have more children. At the same time, there is no absolute limit to the number of children parents may legitimately have, though they may have to pay dearly for the extra offspring. People who give their children up for adoption will not gain the right to have more children, since adopted children add to the population just as much as others. However, a family that chooses to adopt or abort retains the right to produce as many children as before, since adopting a child or aborting a foetus does not increase the world's population.

Implementing any limitation on procreation rights will require overcoming the widespread attitude that people should be free to have as many children as they like. It will require setting aside a growing mass of sometimes incoherent national and international law promulgated by officials who work hard to ignore the fact that the so-called 'right to reproductive freedom' which they are protecting guarantees the individual's right to help overpopulate the world. In the US, the legal basis given for the 'right to reproductive freedom' is the constitutional right to privacy (US Supreme Court 1972). So passing laws restricting procreation rights in the US would require a substantial change of Supreme Court policy, or even a constitutional amendment. Internationally, the situation is about as bleak. Even though the UN mandates guaranteeing the prosperity of posterity through such documents as the Child Convention of 1990 according to which children have a 'right' to a standard of living that allows for their physical, mental, spiritual, moral and social development (not to mention health care!), the UN has also declared reproductive freedom to be a 'basic human right' in Proclamation 16 of the 1968 UN Conference on Human Rights.

> The protection of the family and the child remains the concern of the international community. Parents have a basic human right to determine freely and responsibly the number and the spacing of their children.

But let us notice that the 'right to reproductive freedom' is questionable even from the point of view of its defenders. What is said in defence of the 'right' is chiefly that it plays an important role in protecting women's sexual autonomy, their health, and their opportunity to participate equally in the social and political arrangements of society (Hernandez 1991). However, the justifications are completely unconvincing. The so-called 'right to reproductive freedom' is the combination of a legitimate right, namely, the right to not have a child, with an illegitimate 'right', namely, to have as many children as desired. And while the justifications commonly given for recognizing the 'right to reproductive freedom' *do* support recognizing the right not to have a child, they do *not* support recognizing the right to have unlimited numbers of children. It is important for families and individual women to have the legal right not to (be forced to) have children. Truly, the right not to have children plays a central role in protecting women's sexual autonomy, health, and opportunity to participate equally in the social and political arrangements of society. But the 'right' to have as many children as desired does not play any such role.

REALISM AND 'LIFEBOAT ETHICS'

I have said that each generation may consume natural resources, pollute, and reproduce at given rates only if each successive generation could reasonably be expected to do likewise. The members of each generation must share the benefits of its portion of resources and its allotment of parental rights equitably. But these are radical demands. Can we imagine making the transition from our present global order to one that is just by these lights? Perhaps, but the considerations involved are complex, and people's foresight and commitment to justice are limited. There may even be powerful prudential grounds for resisting some of the suggestions I have made. Neo-Malthusians such as Garrett Hardin have argued that providing any sort of aid to people in nations whose population growth is substantial would be disastrous, so that any moral considerations that suggest such a policy should be rejected. Let me make some comments about Hardin's influential arguments, then move on to make some suggestions about how to move towards more just global policies.

In a series of essays (for example, 1968, 1972 and 1974) Hardin has argued that people in the United States and in other wealthy nations should think of their relationship to people in poor nations as analogous to that of people in a few well-equipped lifeboats surrounded by huge numbers of swimming people who have fallen out of hopelessly overcrowded and ill-equipped boats and are desperately looking to climb aboard the well-equipped ones. One might think that justice requires those of us who are in the boats to conclude that the boats are a common resource, so that we should let swimmers board. But the attitude that the boats should be shared – indeed, 'the fundamental error of the sharing ethics' – is that the attitude would put people in a Prisoners' Dilemma situation (for which Hardin's term is 'tragedy of the commons'): anyone swimming in the water would stand to gain by securing a place on the boat, even knowing that others are trying to do the same. But everyone is 'in the same boat', so to speak, and reaches the same conclusion. So everyone tries to board, and the result is that the boats are swamped and everyone is killed. Hardin's conclusion is that the people on board had best not share their boat, and that, by analogy, people in wealthy nations ought to deny those in poor nations the opportunity to immigrate. Hardin goes on to argue that people in wealthy nations should not send food and other movable resources to people in poor nations. Once again, the idea that these are resources people should hold in common leads to a Prisoners' Dilemma situation. Each poor nation's ruler would tend to conclude that the best (since most selfish) policy is to take from the common food supply, and that the matter of replenishment should be left to wealthy nations. The collective result would be that resources were exhausted. Meanwhile, resources given to the poor would result in a population surge that increased the need for resources in poor nations even more, and since the rulers of these nations knew they could simply take more food from the common supply, they would have no incentive to halt the growth. Since sharing is suicidally to create 'commons', people in wealthy states must avoid it. To a large extent this means ignoring other nations and what goes on in them, and turning their attention to eliminating commons that exist within their own nations, such as any commons that lead to any population problems there. There is no *global* population problem, Hardin says (1989), any more than there is a global street pothole problem; there are only separate population problems in separate nations.

Hardin thus makes two separate claims: first, the lifeboat analogy convincingly supports the claim that people in wealthy nations such as the US ought to ignore other nations and what goes on within them, and certainly that they ought not to aid people in poor ones, either by giving them food or by letting them in; and second, the 'ethics of sharing' in general and the idea that everyone is entitled to a share of 'our' resources in particular generates intolerable Prisoners' Dilemma situations. Both of these claims are false.

There are many respects in which the situation of the world's population is disanalogous to that of the people described in Hardin's lifeboat metaphor. In view of these, it would be a mistake to reason from the point of view of the lifeboat metaphor. Two disanalogies seem especially important.

First, many of the emergencies that prompt the lifeboat metaphor are ones that cannot be dealt with if people hunker down within each ship of state. Many of the 'commons' that need to be addressed cannot be eliminated simply by each nation refraining from interacting with others. Such a policy leaves critical 'commons' in place, such as the seas and the atmosphere, which will be destroyed quickly once each nation ignores the others. As Hardin himself realizes (1989), an acceptable policy for handling these resources must be truly global.

Another respect in which the lifeboat metaphor breaks down is that it suggests that almost all of the resources it is desirable to conserve are in the boats of the wealthy. Disasters such as population explosions occur when the wealthy share their resources. But at best the analogy works when we imagine the wealthy sharing their resources with people in nations like Ethiopia that have very few natural resources. But many of the disasters that are important from the point of view of global justice occur in resource-rich areas of the world, such as South and Central America. There is an overpopulation problem in Brazil, but it is not caused by tender-hearted outsiders feeding starving masses. There is a great deal of poverty and a very high population growth rate in Brazil, but the Brazilians want to deal with the problem themselves by developing the resources they have. What is worrisome from the point of view of global justice is that the vast rain forests of the world really ought to be conserved largely intact, and the populations there held as low as is consistent with that aim. Certainly some of the growth in South and Central America is the result of foreign aid, but in the long run the nations in these regions would be able to exploit their resources without any aid, simply buying the technology they need. If we apply the lifeboat metaphor to such countries, we seem to be faced with the conclusion that the people in such nations are doing exactly what they ought to be doing: exploiting their own resources so as to feed the populations they decide to produce, and conservationists elsewhere simply ought to butt out. That is the wrong conclusion to draw, so the metaphor must go.

However, if we put the lifeboat metaphor aside, aren't we saddled with a policy of indiscriminate sharing that creates disastrous Prisoners' Dilemma situations? Hardin seems to think so. He thinks that the creation of disastrous Prisoners' Dilemma situations is the 'fundamental error of the sharing ethics'. However, Prisoners' Dilemma situations are not created by the ethical view that sharing is appropriate. Rather, as Hobbes noted in *Leviathan* (using a different terminology), they arise among amoral agents who always attempt to maximize their own short-term self-interest. Such agents lack the moral capacity for co-operative activities such as taking turns harvesting each other's crops or using the same pasture for their cattle. If you and I were such agents, you would *agree* to help me harvest so that I will help you harvest, but if I were to help you harvest, you would not actually follow through, since securing my help *without* giving yours in return is better from the standpoint of your short-term self-interest than securing my help *and* giving yours. But if I realize that you are motivated in this way, I will not accept your agreement. Similarly for other co-operative activities. However, moral guidelines allow morally motivated people to escape Prisoners' Dilemma situations. They would follow through on their promises; hence co-operative activity such as sharing the burden of harvesting crops would be possible for them. Morality *solves* Prisoners' Dilemma situations. It does not create them.

Of course, many people *are* short-term self-interest maximizers, and many others, people who are capable of moral motivation, are short-sighted or just too busy to work out all of the consequences of what they are doing, and hence end up acting as short-term self-interest maximizers. Co-operation with such people can be difficult. But the way to handle the latter, the short-sighted, is to identify what justice requires and inform them, so that their normally effective moral motivation can lead them to act justly. And the way to handle the former (as Hobbes saw) is first to identify what justice requires, then implement coercive institutions to enforce those requirements, so that acting as justice requires *becomes* something that is in their short-term self-interest.

Earlier I suggested that the benefits of the world's natural resources must be shared in common, but it does not follow that these resources should be turned over to the short-term self-interest maximizers of the world. We require a policy that is *just*, and hence not disastrous for future generations. Its implementation must be coercive so that the self-interest maximizers of the world will comply along with the rest of us. In particular, as I have already argued, sharing the benefits of the world's resources must be accompanied by whatever restrictions are needed to avoid disasters such as population growth that is inconsistent with the indefinitely sustainable consumption of the world's resources.

INTERMEDIARY STEPS

Hardin's metaphor encourages us to persist in looking at global justice from the standpoint of the present order of nation-states. We should reject both the metaphor and the standpoint it encourages us to embrace. The assumption that the present structure of national prerogatives is legitimate is a substantial obstacle to realizing global justice, as I have attempted to argue. None the less, governments guard their authority jealously, and laying such a structure aside to make the changes I have been suggesting is not on the cards during the near future. Accordingly, we must begin the process of reaching global justice by making whatever changes are consistent with working within the structure of largely autonomous nations. The most obvious plan would be for each individual nation to undertake to perform within its borders the tasks I have assigned to the World Bank above. This plan, too, is unlikely to overcome the political pressures against it. But perhaps it is not too much to hope that some steps towards its implementation will be taken. The plan has three main components.

The first is the task of transferring the benefits of natural resources within nations. At a later stage, the transfers could go international, largely from the richer nations, which are doing most of the recovery, to poorer ones. But such transfers would occur only after the order of nation-states was de-emphasized.

The second is the burden of converting to methods of energy production and methods of consumption that are consistent with the sustainable consumption–reproduction principle. Pollution must be eliminated as rapidly as possible. All industries should be required to find virtually pollution-free methods of operating within the very near future. Operations that could not do so should simply be shut down unless substantial loss of life would result, and even if some lives would be lost it might still be necessary to shut down pollution-generating operations. Some loss of present life would be tolerable if there were strong reason to think that an enormous loss of future life would be caused by the pollution. Outlaw polluters should be fined more than the cost required to clean up the damage they caused so that there would be no incentive to pollute.

Moreover, the squandering of non-renewable resources must stop immediately, inasmuch as many of the known reserves are on the edge of exhaustion. Among other things, halting their consumption would involve the invention of (clean) methods of generating renewable energy (such as harnessing solar power), something that would happen only when inexpensive fossil fuels were relatively scarce, for only then would there be an economic incentive to find alternatives. One strategy is to institute a progressively increasing ban or tax on superfluous uses of non-renewable energy sources such as fossil fuels, so that their use for superfluous purposes would eventually be completely illegal or imprudent.

The third component is each nation's task of reducing its population level to one it could sustain indefinitely given its resources. The incentives provided by the family-planning policy suggested above would help towards this end, but the force of law would have to play a role as well. It is especially important that nations which have regions of great biodiversity such as rain forests reduce their population size. It is folly to expect these areas to survive the onslaught of ever-burgeoning populations.

Leaving it up to each nation to perform the task of the World Bank would, in effect, entail that each nation act as if it were the only nation in existence. This distortion would have obvious drawbacks, however. One especially salient drawback is that developed nations that have already squandered tremendous amounts of the resources within their territory would have to reduce their populations considerably and initiate enormously ambitious conservation programmes. There would be a different but equally imposing drawback for less developed nations, namely, that their development would have to be confined to forms that are pollution-free and consistent with the conservation, renewing and recycling requirements of the sustainable consumption–reproduction principle. Since the technology for such development is largely in its early stages and expensive where available, less developed nations could presumably improve their material situation only in severely limited ways.

These limitations can be overcome as soon as the importance placed by people on global justice is great enough to motivate them to restrict national sovereignty. At that time, it will be possible for everyone to view the benefits of the world's natural resources as something to be shared equitably, and to construct consumption and development strategies that make sense globally. Development will occur in areas of the world that have already been developed and that are not ecologically sensitive, and conservation will occur in areas of the world that are underdeveloped and ecologically sensitive. It will be possible to make a trade-off between people in highly developed but ecologically less important parts of the world and people in ecologically more important but less developed parts of the world. On the one hand, there should be transfers of funds generated by re-sources; largely these will be transfers from people in developed areas to people from less developed areas. Simultaneously, nations which are not environment-ally sensitive must greatly relax their immigration restrictions to accommodate people from nations that combine large ecologically sensitive areas with large populations. For the most part, this will mean that developed nations must take in far more people than they would like. However, they can better afford to deal with large numbers of people than less developed nations. Most importantly, the pressure of overpopulation will be removed from the ecologically most strategic parts of the world without simply requiring people who are now living in those areas to carry the world's conservation burden.

ACKNOWLEDGEMENTS

I thank Curtis Brown, Alex Neill and Robert Peterson for helpful comments on an earlier version of this chapter.

8 Power, control and intrusion, with particular reference to Antarctica

Robert Prosser

> No species has ever had such wholesale control over everything on earth, living or dead, as we now have. That lays upon us, whether we like it or not, an awesome responsibility. In our hands lies not only our own future, but that of all other living creatures with whom we share the earth.
>
> (Attenborough 1979: 308)

A crucial element in this 'awesome responsibility' is *ownership*. The concept of individual and communal ownership underpins all issues concerning the environment and human relationships to it at all scales. For instance, the Criminal Justice Bill which came before the UK Parliament in 1994 contains sections on trespass, whose objective is to strengthen the rights of and protection given to 'owners' of land and property. In this instance the State, through its institution of governance, was acting to reinforce the rights of individuals to exclude others from resources. Exclusivity lies at the heart of ownership. Conversely the State acts to contain the actions of individual, corporate and communal owners through the body of law, and specifically the planning system – legislation and an appropriate organizational and implementation structure.

This leads to the related concepts of *freedom* and *authority*: the extent to which owners of environmental resources do and should have the freedom and authority to use the resources they own and as they see fit. Freedom embraces autonomy of decision-making, and authority implies empowerment to act. In the United Kingdom the ownership of the 'freehold' of a parcel of land or property gives absolute rights for life, but ultimately ownership lies within the fief of the Crown and our 'absolute rights' can be exercised only within the frame of law. Ownership in these terms includes the three dimensions of owner rights (rights to transfer), user rights and occupier rights (rights to exclude others).

Freedom, authority and the notion of ownership are set, therefore, within a cultural framework enshrined in the body of law of the nation-state, nested within a more diffuse aureole of international law. This cultural setting based upon a shared value system, or the value system of an 'establishment élite', is crucial in determining the perceptions of and policies for the environment. Taking another example from the United Kingdom, the Countryside Commission estimate that on a typical summer weekend, there may be 18 million recreational visits to the countryside. This is indicative of cultural perceptions which value a rural heritage. This brings communal demand into direct confrontation with individual ownership, hence the high-profile, long-running debate on *access*, i.e. the right to enter and use land and water space, and on what terms. In the United Kingdom, ownership gives the right to exclude others unless they acquire a right of access – 'An Englishman's home is his castle.' But it need not necessarily be so: in Sweden, *allemansratten*, the right of common access,

> gives everyone the right to cross another person's land on foot provided no damage or disturbance is caused. The landowner or tenant does not have to give permission. Carefully defined exceptions ensure that walkers are not allowed to enter the private land surrounding a house, or cross newly-planted woodland, growing crops or other land likely to suffer damage.
>
> (Shoard 1987: 539)

From another perspective, there are intensifying conflicts surrounding the rights of resource owners to develop them for leisure use and so to increase the supply of opportunities for recreation and sport. For example, the addition of theme parks to country estates, the transformation of farmland to golf courses, etc. will increase supply and opportunity, but are generating concern over the desirability of such changes.

One response has come from the Countryside Commission, who have issued guidelines for developers and planning officers in relation to golf-course proposals:

> There should be a general presumption against laying out of golf courses in designated areas – National Parks, Areas of Outstanding Natural Beauty, and the Broads – and in the New Forest and on Heritage Coasts, unless it can be demonstrated that the proposed new course contributes to, and enhances, the special character of the area. Environmental assessments should accompany all proposals for golf course development in historic parklands, designated areas, the New Forest and Heritage Coasts'.
>
> (Countryside Commission 1993: 5)

Today the debate about environmental values is increasingly taking on an international dimension, often packaged within the philosophy of *stewardship*. This changes the concept of ownership from a kernel of rights to one of responsibilities, and from a focus on exploitation to one on *sustainability*. Under this philosophy, those with authority, i.e. the power of decision-making, over a geographically defined environment become stewards of its living and non-living components. Such responsibility carries with it the duty to ensure the lasting social, economic, aesthetic and ecological well-being of that environment. For all but a few societies, this requires a fundamental shift in value stance. This rings true especially for the developed world, or North, with its rapidly accelerating perceived power of ecological dominance:

> The urge to go on taking, to forgo restraint, has certainly afflicted our kind of civilisation for the past few hundred years. Indeed, the notion is now firmly

embedded in our culture that we have a right to exploit natural resources so as to further human progress and well-being.

(Bunyard 1991: 17)

This attitude is more pithily expressed in the credo of the American pioneers in the nineteenth century – 'Foul your nest and move on West!'

None the less, with the inexorable growth in the world population, this shift from an exploitation ethic to a conservation ethic still in reality means development, albeit sustainable development. As Bunyard has asked, 'What is development other than the transformation of the natural environment to suit human purposes?' Within a conservationist philosophy lie value systems and courses of action whose priorities and purposes are the sustained existence of something which is perceived as having 'value' in both qualitative and quantitative terms.

This belief system is exhibited in an extreme form in campaigns whose motives are centred upon conservation for its own sake. Existence value and the rights of *all* living species are paramount, and the aim is the rejection of ecological intrusion by human activities, although the issue can be muddied by the question of whether *any* human access is permissible once the conservation objective has been achieved. The 'Save the Spotted Owl' campaign in the US Pacific North-West is as much about saving the remnants of the primary temperate rain forests as it is about saving the owl and its habitat. The campaign strategy has been first to have the owl added to the 'endangered species' list. This status activates habitat-protection legislation which in effect bans logging in primary forests as the owl appears to nest and breed successfully only in old-growth forest. As commercial logging is the largest industry in Washington State and supports many communities, the 'exploitation' lobby is very powerful, but the 'conservation' lobby is well organized and vigorous. Ownership, authority and values clash head-on.

At times, campaigns to deny ecological intrusion achieve headline status, becoming genuinely global and adorned with celebrity campaigners such as David Bellamy or Sting. A classic case was the proposed Franklin River dam in Tasmania. In 1983 members of the Tasmanian Wilderness Society

> were prepared to risk injury, arrest and imprisonment to alert the world to the consequences of proposals to dam the upper tributaries of the Franklin River. At stake was a large area of temperate rainforest, containing a whole range of unique species.
>
> (Bellamy and Quayle 1986: 180)

The campaign became a world-wide symbol of the fight to turn back the tide of ecological intrusion and spawned a flood of scientific and emotional pronouncements:

> It [the river] is threatened by the same mindless beast that has eaten our past, is eating our present, and threatens to eat our future: the civil beast of mean ambitions and broken promises and hedged bets and tawdry profits.
>
> (McQueen 1983: 3)

The campaigners won, the dam has never been built, and the area is now protected within the Tasmania Wilderness World Heritage Area.

The clash is between two opposed philosophies of the human relationship with planet Earth. In the one corner there is what Pirages has called the 'Dominant Social Paradigm' (Pirages 1977). This paradigm he saw as 'a set of beliefs and values that included private property rights, faith in science and technology, individualism, economic growth and the subjection of nature and exploitation of natural resources' (McCormick 1989: 196). In the opposing corner is Riley and van Liere's 'New Environmental Paradigm' (Riley and van Liere 1978): 'an entirely new kind of society based on carefully considered production and consumption, resource conservation, environmental protection, and the basic values of compassion, justice, and quality of life' (McCormick 1989: 196).

Interpreted at the global scale, each delimits an unequivocally discrete stance and hence a seductively straightforward choice. When applied to specific environments, societies or resources, however, this clarity diffuses. The definitions do not address the issue of who can and should impose their authority – and hence values – upon an environment or set of resources. Should it be only those in geographical occupation of the defined space and its contents, i.e. the 'owners', or do 'outsiders' have the right or authority to impose their values, i.e. the 'stewards'? Once again, the ownership–stewardship issue moves centre-stage.

In Brazil authority over the future of the tropical rain forests of Amazonia has long aroused many-faceted debate at the heart of which lies the question 'Whose forests are they anyway?' One dimension of the debate is the perception of this huge ecological treasure house as an example of environmental resources so precious that they should be regarded as 'global commons'. This idea accepts the inevitability that most environments are and will continue to be under individual ownership and individual national sovereignty, but that certain regions are so special as to warrant supra-national control, i.e. to be acknowledged as part of 'the common heritage of mankind' (Davis 1992: 40). This is based on the public-heritage concept in Roman law, where a set of environmental resources is held in trust for current and future generations.

Not surprisingly, the Brazilian government has resisted the pressures from the international community to relinquish some sovereignty over part of Amazonia. One proposal not greeted with favour was the 'debt for nature swap', whereby some of Brazil's debts would be written off in return for international access to decision-making in Amazonia. The Brazilian response has been to introduce conservation-orientated policies and programmes in order to appease global environmental and humanitarian institutions, from the United Nations to WWFN and Greenpeace. Such assumption of authority and control by the federal government has not pleased several of the individual states. The opposition has been led by the outspoken governor of Amazonas, Gilberto Mestrinho, who has proposed the so-called Amazonian Code, which if approved would transfer environmental control over Amazonia to the nine states of the region. This alarms not only the Brazilian government but also global environmental organizations, especially in the light of views such as those expressed by Mestrinho in an interview for *Time* magazine in 1991:

Q. In order to improve the quality of life in the Amazon, you have to develop it?

A. Of course, but we plan to do so in a rational way. The problem is that anytime somebody talks about doing anything at all in the Amazon, there is this wild hysteria from the rest of the world and from certain sectors in Brazil telling us we can't cut down a tree. The fact is, the Amazon is the least destroyed place in the world. Since the arrival of the Europeans some 500 years ago, only 8.5% of the Amazon has been deforested. In my state of Amazonas, only 1.24% has been deforested. These are the facts. And the people here are living in misery, but nobody cares about them. All you hear is 'Save the Amazon, save the animals.' Environmentalists care more about trees and monkeys than people. It's absurd. I have my priorities straight. I value the lives of people more than those of animals and plants. Only after we have improved the lives of humans can we begin thinking of the fauna and flora. Those who disagree with me are against humanity.

Q. What of your accusation that ecology groups are controlled by outside interests?

A. Most environmental groups are defending economic interest, not nature. They are being used by multinationals and cartels to prevent us and other Third World nations from cutting into the developed world's profits. It was only in the 60s and 70s, when Brazil began to explore the natural resources of the Amazon and foreigners saw that we could extract the resources at a very low cost, that the whole campaign to preserve the Amazon began. We weren't destroying the forests, they know that. But we were threatening foreign businesses. They continue to fabricate stories and exaggerate the facts, say we are torching the Amazon, that there will be a greenhouse effect. The truth is, the amount of carbon dioxide released from forest fires is insignificant, while the more than 500 million motor vehicles of the world emit 56% of the carbon dioxide in the atmosphere.

(Maier 1991: 60–1)

The issues surrounding ownership, control, authority and intrusion are nowhere more vividly demonstrated than in Antarctica. This is the only continent with no history of human settlement. Even today the resident human population peaks at around 4,000 in the southern summer, falling to perhaps 1,000 during the long, dark winters. The first 'native' of Antarctica was born in 1978, after Argentina flew a pregnant woman to one of its bases so that she could give birth. This is the only land mass, too, which no one 'owns', although there are many 'claims'. As what is at stake is one-tenth of the world's land surface (5.5 million km^2), albeit with a 98 per cent ice cover, and surrounded by one of the most productive oceans, it is not surprising that Antarctica has been attracting growing interest since Captain Cook first sailed round its margins in 1772–5. In 1820 a US sealer and a

British explorer each claimed 'first sightings' of the continent. Another British explorer, James Ross, was the first human to set foot on the mainland in 1841, and Norway's Roald Amundsen was first to reach the South Pole in 1911. In 1990, *Time* magazine could write: 'The number of people who have gone to Antarctica is smaller than the attendance at this year's California Rose Bowl football game' (Lemonick 1990: 37). Human presence, then, may be embryonic, but human ambition is full-grown!

Thus, alone of all the continents, Antarctica is a genuine 'wilderness', nurturing no established indigenous peoples with communal or individual rights. Ironically, this absence of 'prior claimants' makes Antarctica uniquely vulnerable and 'up for grabs' by acquisitive societies without raising awkward ethical issues concerning conquest and colonialism. There will be no remnants of Native Peoples to fight for the last vestiges of their cultures and their lands, to become media stars and tokens of environmentalist campaigns. For these reasons, many perceive Antarctica as a crucial test case of the human will to overturn Pirages' 'Dominant Social Paradigm' and work towards McCormick's 'New Environmental Paradigm'.

> The despoliation of this last continental scale wilderness would signal the bankruptcy of our technological society in finding creative solutions to global scale problems.
>
> (Broady 1991: 9)

The uniqueness of this scenario is apparent if we compare it with the history of North America over the past three hundred years. The 'frontier' and hardy pioneers conquering 'the wilderness' are central elements in the cultural imagery of American and Canadian society. The settlement of North America by successive waves of predominantly European immigrants was undoubtedly a massive achievement, but it was a cultural and ecological intrusion on an unprecedented scale. What was 'conquered' was not a 'wilderness', but a sub-continent settled by a rich diversity of societies totalling perhaps 10 million people. To these indigenous peoples, the North American environment was not a wilderness, but their homeland. They, along with the ecosystems of which they were part, were swept aside, as literature from James Fenimore Cooper's *Last of the Mohicans* to Dee Brown's *Bury my Heart at Wounded Knee* records. Today the survivors of this intrusion, or invasion, struggle to retain or restore their identity and to regain control of land and resources which they claim as theirs by traditional right. Notice, however, that most stress communal rights, not individual ownership. Meanwhile, the dominant American society engages in revisionism and guilt assuagement by welfare programmes, enactment of entitlement laws and flocking to films such as *Dances with Wolves*.

Antarctica does not come with this cultural impedimenta. It is, however, enshrouded in the powerful logic of the new environmental ethic and enmeshed by equally powerful political and economic tensions. Antarctica 'has come to symbolise the conflict between exploitation and conservation, between claims to territory and recognition that no one single country should have rights to declare any part of that uninhabited continent its own' (Bunyard 1991: 17). No single nation does indeed 'own' any part of Antarctica if 'ownership' is defined as jurisdictional sovereignty accepted by the international community. None the less, ambition for ownership or at least the intention to establish territorial authority and control is expressed bluntly by the political map of Antarctica (see the map in *Time* 1990: 35). Seven nations have established 'territorial claims' – Argentina, Chile, France, New Zealand, Britain, Norway and Australia – while a number more, most notably the USA and the former USSR, operate scientific bases. The claims were made formally in the 1940s on the bases of proximity and prior history of exploration. The involvement of the USA and the USSR acceler-ated during the 1950s as the cold war built up and competition between the two superpowers intensified. Thus, the claimants responded readily to a US initiative that the twelve nations which had operated scientific bases in Antarctica during the IGY should construct an agreement which would govern all activities on and around the continent. The outcome was the 1959 Antarctic Treaty, fully ratified in 1961, and based upon four fundamental notions:

1 a moratorium on all territorial claims (a 'freezing', not a renouncement);
2 demilitarization of the whole region;
3 international scientific co-operation;
4 conservation of flora and fauna.

The Treaty remains the foundation of global policy towards Antarctica, although cynics see in it a pre-emptive strike by the United States to exert control and authority. It was certainly intended to prevent Antarctica from becoming an area for US–USSR rivalry and to reduce tensions between nations which claimed the same territories: for example, Chile, Argentina and Britain have overlapping claims across the Antarctic Peninsula. Yet 'it has become commonly regarded as one of the most successful international regimes of recent times' (Davis 1992: 39). By 1990, a further thirteen nations had joined the original twelve Treaty countries, gaining voting status by demonstration of 'substantial scientific research'. (For the purposes of the Treaty, 60°S. latitude is regarded as the boundary of Antarctica; hence it includes extensive areas of productive ocean.)

Like all such international agreements, the Treaty was a creature of its times. From the late 1950s through the 1960s, governments and corporations saw little immediate economic potential in the frozen continent, and it lacked the strategic geographical location of the North Polar region. Conversely, scientists had made a convincing case for Antarctica as a collaborative 'global laboratory'. So, individual countries saw that they had much to gain and little to lose by adopting the Treaty. It ushered in what has become known as the 'scientific phase' of Antarctica's modern history. This phase of the ascendency of science was in fact the fourth phase of human–environment interaction. First there was the age of *discovery*; second came the phase of *commercial whaling and fishing*, which overlapped with the third phase, that of *exploration*. In each, the value systems involved and the impacts/intrusions imposed were quite distinct and products of their cultures and times, for example, the confused altruism and jingoism of Scott, the keenly focused economic exploitation of the whaling fleets, and the objective intellectual excitement of the scientists. None was either able or willing to take a holistic view of the pristine wilderness into which they were intruding and claiming rights of access and resource use.

During the 1970s, perceptions and attitudes began to shift once more, driven by three main influences. First, environmentalists increasingly questioned the role of science and the scientists, hitherto the 'White Knights' of Antarctica. Evidence revealed that science can be intrusive, damaging, and possessed of its own inexorable tendency to grow. In a pristine, fragile environment such as Antarctica, *any* activity has a noticeable impact. With low rates of weathering and flora and fauna at the extremes of their environmental tolerance, disturbance is rapid, and recovery of land surface, vegetation and wildlife very slow. Furthermore, any pollution, for instance, sewage, rubbish and engine effluents, disperses or degrades extremely slowly, as in the case of undecomposed stores found recently in the base-camp huts of early explorers.

This issue of the impacts and hence ethics of scientific research has not subsided. Under the title 'The dump at the bottom of the world', a newspaper article in 1989 claimed:

> The biggest and dirtiest base in Antarctica is McMurdo – the power house of the American presence on the ice . . . the station, founded 30 years ago, houses as many as 1200 people at the summer peak and is the logistics centre for the South Pole station, dozens of field parties, and its own scientific programme. In a pristine and beautiful landscape it is an awful reminder of the throwaway society of the last three decades. The US Navy, which provides the hardware . . . made McMurdo into a rubbish dump. In a climate where nothing rots and there was no pollution this led to an eyesore. [The US] Congress is to vote soon on a $30 million clean-up programme.
>
> (*Guardian*, 20 February 1989)

The second shift in attitudes was in part an outcome of the results of scientific research: a growing interest in the mineral potential of Antarctica. This was energized especially by the OPEC-created global oil crisis of 1973. Multinational oil and mining companies enthusiastically devoured scientists' results and read into them unrealistically euphoric prospects. This in turn was taken up by national governments, especially those of the claimant countries, and the USA. The potential for economic gain refocused attention upon the issue of individual national sovereignty and the authority of individual nations to explore and, potentially, exploit mineral resources in Antarctica. The prospect of economic development caused the third shift in perceptions, this time by Third World countries, which increasingly saw Antarctica as dominated by an élite club of predominantly First World nations. For instance, in some debates in the United Nations in the early 1980s, 'Malaysia and some allied third world countries castigated the Treaty nations as an "Antarctic Club", out to filch world resources from the less developed states' (Davis 1992: 40).

Debate has increasingly crystallized, therefore, around campaigns by the scientific and environmentalist communities for international collaboration and stewardship, and pressures by economic interests for development rights and hence individual control. Antarctic Treaty members, and especially the governments of claimant countries, have tried to steer a compromise path, not renouncing individual claims and hence potential political and economic gains, while supporting the principles of conservation and 'the global commons' concept. For example, as long as 1972 the Second World Conference on National Parks proposed the designation of Antarctica as a 'World Park' under the jurisdiction of the United Nations. Subsequently New Zealand offered to renounce its sovereignty claims, but received little support as the development–exploitation ethic continued to hold sway, fed by the prospect of possible mineral wealth.

None the less, as global environmentalism gained ground during the 1980s, Antarctica increasingly became a symbol. As Mickleburgh proclaims so cogently:

> The test of Man's willingness to pull back from the destruction of the Antarctic wilderness is the test case also of his willingness to avert destruction globally. If we cannot succeed in Antarctica we have little chance of succeeding elsewhere.
>
> (Mickleburgh 1988: 7)

Throughout the 1980s the battle for economic development and hence individual national jurisdiction focused upon the issue of minerals exploitation. In 1988 the Antarctic Treaty System nations finally agreed the Convention on the Regulation of Antarctic Mineral Resource Activities (CRAMRA), which meant that minerals exploration would be prohibited without the unanimous consent of all AT members. Opposition from the scientific and environmentalist communities and from nations such as France and Australia, was strong and sustained. For instance, in order to counter CRAMRA, the designation of the whole continent as a 'World Wilderness Park' was proposed, but it quickly became ensnared in confusion over institutional arrangements. Some nations, such as Chile and Argentina, saw the World Park and other conservationist proposals as serious threats to their territorial claims.

At the same time, more realistic assessments were being made of the mineral potential and of the practicality of exploiting what there was: 'there is hardly any significant deposit of minerals in Antarctica warranting a commercial mining enterprise' (Blay and Green 1994: 24). In 1990, a US congressional report estimated that profitable mining was unlikely for at least the next thirty years.

The power of the grip of sovereignty and the potential of economic gain was once more exemplified by the reluctance of the Antarctic Treaty members to give up CRAMRA despite the strength of the opposition and the fading mineral prospects. Chile and Argentina, for example, have been vigorously pursuing policies of permanent settlement, including families, with housing, schools, etc., on the islands and peninsula nearest to their homelands. The aim is clearly to establish rights of occupancy and hence sovereignty.

From formal negotiations, once more a compromise has been reached: in March 1991 CRAMRA was abandoned and replaced by the Antarctic Mining

Prohibition Act (AMPA). This actually does not 'ban' exploration and extraction but sets down a fifty-year moratorium, i.e. leaves the door ajar should perceptions and prospects change. This has been incorporated in the more general framework of the Protocol on Environmental Protection to the Antarctic Treaty, known as the Madrid Protocol, signed in October 1991. The individual member states of the Antarctic Treaty have adopted this Protocol and are obligated to comply by its provisions.

The complex and confused situation where Antarctica is suspended between global stewardship and individual ownership is exemplified by how the international agreements are articulated. Individual claimant nations fulfil their obligations to these agreements through their own legal systems, thereby retaining their sovereignty claims while conforming with the international stewardship ethic. Blay and Green (1994) have highlighted the resulting uneasy tensions by an examination of Australia's approach. Australia has been a strong and consistent supporter of the 'global commons' idea, yet retains her claim to jurisdictional sovereignty of 42 per cent of Antarctica. The Australian Commonwealth government passes domestic laws which cover the Australian Antarctic Territory (AAT). For instance, in 1980 the Antarctic Treaty (Environmental Protection) Act (ATEPA) became law and was later absorbed into the 1992 Antarctic (Environmental Protection) Legislation Amendment Act (AEPLAA). This 'specifically implements the Madrid Protocol into Australian domestic law' (Blay and Green 1994: 24).

Both the ATEPA and AEPLAA laws apply throughout the AAT to all people – Australians and non-Australians – and to Australian nationals anywhere in Antarctica, a feature typical of legal authority and jurisdiction. However, countries such as the USA and Russia, both countries with a powerful scientific presence in Antarctica, although not claimant nations, do not acknowledge Australia's claim of sovereignty. So a US citizen in the AAT could claim immunity from Australian laws on the grounds that they have no acceptable legality, even though they were enacted to fulfil obligations to international treaties and agreements signed by the USA. Equally, an Australian in the claimed territory of another nation could claim similar immunity, although still falling under the remit of Australian law. The confusion is compounded by non-claimant Treaty nations which themselves enact laws in order to comply with Treaty and Protocol requirements. Thus, the US Antarctic Environmental Protection Protocol Bill, introduced to implement the Protocol, makes it unlawful for anyone 'to conduct an activity within Antarctica, including scientific research, expeditions, and logistical support to the US facilities and bases, in a manner inconsistent with the protocol' (Blay and Green 1994: 25). In all these issues, apart from the inevitable legal wrangling, there is the problem of *enforcement*. In blunt terms – 'there is no polar police force' (Blay and Green 1994: 29).

Perceptions of and strategies towards Antarctica among the international community thus seem to swing pendulum-wise according to prevailing philosophies and paradigms. Since the 1991 Madrid Protocol, the pendulum force seems to be moving back to the science–conservation paradigm, informed by the 'global commons' and 'public heritage' philosophy. A cluster of causes, such as the fading of economic prospects, the continuing vigour of the environmental movement, energized, no doubt, by the glow of the 1992 Rio Summit, the ending of the cold war and the tendency of USA and Russia to focus their attentions more upon domestic issues at this time, all have some explanatory power.

Furthermore, a fresh set of perceptions have arisen out of the increasing concerns over the environmental health of planet Earth: 'scientists have discovered that Antarctica is a sensitive barometer of mankind's use and abuse of the planet' (Hodgson 1990: 20). Thus conceived, Antarctica becomes a 'global laboratory' or control environment against which human impacts over the rest of the planet can be monitored and measured. In these terms it is in the interests of all nations to ensure the preservation of Antarctica's pristine and minimally polluted status. This means that one of the responsibilities of whoever has power and authority is to minimize the introduction of alien and exotic elements and to ensure the removal of any such intrusions. One small but sentimentally significant example of this was the removal of the last teams of huskie dogs from the continent in 1993. They were no longer needed for transportation, and as an exotic species they were identified as an unnecessary intrusion.

A second emerging role for Antarctica, or at least the continental fringes and surrounding oceans, is as a wildlife reserve for unique faunal assemblages and as a 'last refuge' for threatened species. For instance, during 1993/4, environmentalists, and some governments, alarmed at the prospects of the lifting of the global ban on commercial whaling, were campaigning for the establishment of an 'Antarctic Whale Sanctuary'. In May 1994 the campaign achieved its primary goal. The International Whaling Commission, meeting in Mexico, agreed to establish such a sanctuary which should 'protect 80% of the world's remaining whales from commercial hunting' (*Guardian*, 28 May 1994). In the early 1990s, therefore, there seemed to be an emerging consensus and the will for a non-intrusive policy, articulated by agreements giving genuine authority and control to international institutions. Yet should such a system be put in place, there would still remain the issue of enforcement. Even if all 'users' of the continent agree to a strict code of conduct, unless there is effective 'policing' and subsequent stringent sanctions, inappropriate behaviour and negative impacts will prove impossible to prevent. The problems and dangers can be illustrated by a consideration of tourism, the latest wave of human activity to impose itself on the Antarctic continent.

Tourism is a 'fashion' industry, fed by perceptions of excitement, status, image, etc., and among the most rapidly growing sectors of this huge industry are adventure travel and ecotourism. Thus, adventurous or status-seeking wealthy élites, sated with the Galapagos or the Himalayas, are seeking new frontiers and experiences, and the tourist industry is eager to satisfy them – where better than Antarctica? In 1989 barely 3,000 tourists visited Antarctica, and in that year too the first tourist group skied to the South Pole, paying around $70,000 each for the experience. By 1993, over 6,000 tourists arrived, spending an average of $9,000. As the Chilean chief of Antarctic planning has observed:

Every day it is easier to get to Antarctica. . . . On the continental ice plateau you can land ski-equipped aircraft almost anywhere. It is also possible to land large-wheeled transports on areas of permanently bare ice, such as those near the Vinson Massif. We are planning to establish a base there to give us a regular airway from Punta Arenas to the South Pole.

(Quoted in Hodgson 1990: 25).

Antarctica is decreasingly protected by its inaccessibility in terms of time, cost, distance or even comfort. At present the tourists travel and stay on cruise ships. Once they arrive on the continental edge they take daily trips ashore by inflatable Zodiacs. The three main shore attractions are wildlife congregations, scientific bases and historic sites such as explorers' huts and old whaling stations. Such activity-experiences are directly intrusive. For instance, the tourist season is December–February, the southern summer, when the attractive fauna, for example, penguins and seals, are breeding. Increasingly large and frequent groups of photograph-hungry tourists cause stress among the colonies. There is pressure from the tourist industry, too, to establish on-shore facilities such as lodges and even hotels with their inevitable infrastructure and effluents, and to develop old explorers' huts and derelict whaling stations as 'heritage sites'.

There is growing concern among the scientific and environmentalist communities over this creeping intrusion and its impacts. The dilemma is not only ethical – whether tourism is an appropriate activity in Antarctica – but also logistical and legalistic. Tourist activities fall within the remit of the Madrid Protocol and the ATS. Furthermore, in 1991, the operators who organize trips to Antarctica formed the International Association of Antarctic Tour Operators (IAATO) to act as the self-regulatory body. At present, then, there are organizational structures and codes of conduct in place. Tour operators and tourists to a large extent abide by them, but because the landing sites are varied and scattered, monitoring and enforcement are impractical. Fortunately, many of the accessible and attractive sites are close to scientific bases, where tourist behaviour and impact can be observed, but the scientists may not have the legal right to enforce control, and there is no overall institutional body of authority. (These issues are explored in some detail in a special edition of the *Annals of Tourism Research* 21(2), April 1994):

Rising current levels [of tourism] prompt the question of whether Antarctica's environment is adequately protected against existing and possible future levels of tourist activity. Members of IAATO have the opportunity to exert appropriate pressure and influence on most tourists travelling to Antarctica. . . . The comprehensive review of Antarctic tourism proposed by Treaty members provides a starting point for discussion of existing tourism policy in view of current levels and forms of tourist activity.

(Enzenbacher 1992: 21)

Antarctica, therefore, is a mirror to mankind's complex mixture of nobility and frailty. On the one hand there is a burgeoning acknowledgement that the 'global commons' and stewardship philosophy is the way ahead. There is an awareness, too, that this may be the last chance we have to prove to ourselves whether we possess the will to change our approach from 'it's mine' to 'it's ours'. Even then, would Antarctica be used as a sop to our consciences: 'Look at how we have "saved" Antarctica for future generations'? Then we could carry on as before in other parts of the planet. On the other hand there is a deeply embedded reluctance to relinquish power and prospects and so to abandon the individual ownership paradigm. Perhaps, too, there is an amalgam of fear and distrust – the 'I will if you will' stand-off at the national scale!

9   Justice and order in international relations: the global environment

James P. Barber and Anna K. Dickson

INTRODUCTION

Justice and order are central concerns of international relations. Yet they are elusive concepts, difficult to define and even more to realize. In this chapter we investigate their implications for the global environment by discussing two case studies. The cases have different focuses, but each contributes to an understanding of the relationship between international justice and order and the environment.

However, before turning to the case studies we examine the concepts of justice and order through the eyes of a scholar of international relations, Hedley Bull. The advantages of concentrating on a single scholar are that there is a consistency of interpretation; a common platform from which the issues raised in the case studies can be evaluated; and finally it enables judgements to be made by challenging or sustaining his conclusions.

Hedley Bull and the anarchical society

In his major work, *The Anarchical Society*, Hedley Bull expounded a view of international society which emphasized the centrality of the state (Bull 1977). When we speak of international order, he wrote, we normally refer to order between sovereign states. Although he recognized that other forms of order can exist, the state system has predominated since the eighteenth century. Within this system Bull identified three sets of rules. The first underlines the prominence of the state. 'The daily actions of states', he wrote,

> in arrogating to themselves the rights and competences of principal actors in world politics, and in combining with each other to this end, in resisting the claims of suprastate or substate groups to wrest these rights and competences from them – display this principle and provide evidence of its central role.
>
> (Bull 1977: 68)

The second set of rules relates to coexistence. This has two aspects: one concerns interaction between states, the other the internal affairs of the separate states, based on the principle 'that states will not intervene forcibly or dictatorially in one another's internal affairs' (Bull 1977: 70). The third set of rules is above mere coexistence. They are designed to facilitate co-operation and mutual dependence, and cover not only political and strategic concerns, but also social, economic and environmental ones.

While Bull recognized that most people put a high value on order, it is not necessarily the overriding goal. It can be and is challenged by other values, including justice. He identified five interpretations of justice which are found in international relations:

1 interstate justice, which underlines the sovereign equality of states, their right to self-determination and control of internal affairs;
2 individual justice, which concerns the rights and duties of individuals irrespective of the state in which they live;
3 cosmopolitan (or world) justice, which overrides the interests of separate states and benefits mankind as a whole;
4 reciprocal justice, whereby established rights are mutually respected;
5 distributive justice, which concerns equality and determining rights and duties on the basis of an assumed common good.

Environmental issues fall within the scope of cosmopolitan and distributive justice, but Bull concluded that an international order based on the state system fails to emphasize these forms of justice, and only gives selective and ambiguous respect to individual justice. He wrote that the compact between states which is expressed in their mutual recognition of sovereignty 'implies a conspiracy of silence entered into by governments about the rights and duties of respective citizens' (Bull 1977: 83).

The state system favours interstate and reciprocal justice, giving priority to state interests. In contrast, cosmopolitan and distributive justice emphasize what is good for humanity, irrespective of state governments, including a more equitable distribution of wealth and a common approach to environmental problems. Although such sentiments may be admirable, Bull concluded that they have a subordinate position in international politics. 'The world society or community whose common good they purport to define does not exist except as an idea or myth which may one day become powerful, but has not done so yet' (Bull 1977: 87). There are individuals and representatives of interest groups who claim to speak for planet Earth, but their views are less effective than those of representatives of states. In so far as the common interests of mankind are articulated and aggregated, they come from sovereign states. The result is that 'the common good' is seen through the prism of state interests. The reality is that 'universal ideologies that are espoused by states are notoriously subservient to their special interests', and any agreements which are reached come from bargaining and compromise rather than concern for mankind as a whole (Bull 1977: 86).

Equally, although the aim of distributive justice is to improve the material standards of disadvantaged individuals and groups, most aid and trade is channelled through states and both donor and receiver states act in their own interests and not necessarily those of groups or individuals. International organizations, like the United Nations, take heed of cosmopolitan and distributive justice, but not at the expense of the interests of their member states. Bull concluded that ideas of world justice can only be realized in the context of a world society which does not exist. 'Demands for world justice are therefore demands for the transformation of the system and society of states, and are inherently revolutionary' (Bull 1977: 88).

The obvious conclusion is that in terms of cosmopolitan and distributive justice the state system fails to achieve basic goals, including those concerned with the environment and economic justice. As a result the state system is described by its critics as an obstacle to solving problems of common concern such as pollution, depletion of the earth's resources and wealth redistribution. To achieve such ends would require global planning and unity. Bull recognized the dissatisfaction and concluded that: 'A world society or community characterised by a sense of the common interests and values of all mankind . . . may not exist, except in embryo, but it is widely held that it should exist' (Bull 1977: 289). Equally he recognized that international society is characterized by massive differences in economic and social conditions, and the state system slows down the redistribution of resources by imposing barriers against the movement of people and goods.

Yet, although Bull recognized these problems and criticisms, he defended the state system. He did so for four reasons. First, he claimed that environmental and economic problems lie deeper than any particular international structure. What inhibits a common global plan for economic justice and environmental action 'is not the existence of states but the fact of human disagreement and conflict in the ecological realm itself'. He concluded that: 'Human conflict has sources that are deeper than any particular form of political order' (Bull 1977: 294). In short, according to Bull, the fault lies in human nature and not the state system. Second, Bull argued that there is no evidence to show that another structure would be more successful. What is required, he argued, is a greater sense of human solidarity, and that cannot be solved by structures. Third, the contribution of the state system to achieving common ends is undervalued. If economic and environmental issues are to be handled effectively, a form of order is required, and the state system provides that. Also Bull claimed that separate states have often stood as bulwarks against even greater social and economic injustice. He noted that it is poor and weak states which have used sovereignty as a defence against powerful international agents gaining even greater control of resources. Finally, Bull argued that if action is required quickly, and it certainly is for the environment, there is no point in asserting that effective steps can be taken only by an organization (a world authority) that does not exist and has no chance of emerging in the foreseeable future. It is unhelpful to regard the state system as an obstacle rather than a means through which some action can be taken (even on individual, distributive and cosmopolitan justice). In short, instead of crying for the moon we should do the best we can with what exists.

POLITICAL ISSUES IN ENVIRONMENTAL MANAGEMENT

It is no longer possible to treat environmental issues and politics as separate areas. First, those who make decisions now have to take account of the global environmental implications of those decisions. Previously, environmental issues have been dealt with at a local or regional level. The current crisis, however, is characterized by its global nature: it affects everyone, and as such can only be managed through co-operation by all. Second, many ideas previously taken for granted about how the international system operates are being challenged by environmental change and the need to respond to it.

The management of the environment can be approached from many different angles.[1] One of the approaches used has been to link the environment with processes of development because it is recognized that since the Industrial Revolution, environmental problems have increased at a phenomenal rate. For example, increasing amounts of gases have been pumped into the atmosphere and this has thickened the greenhouse blanket around the earth, trapping in heat. As a result we are now experiencing the phenomenon of global warming: if current practices continue, it is estimated that the average global temperature will rise by one degree centigrade by the year 2025 and three degrees by the end of the twenty-first century (Rowlands 1992: 26). If this happens it will affect not only climatic change, but also levels of rainfall, tidal patterns, drought and desertification among other things. It is thus an issue of significance for everyone.

The Brundtland Report (1987) linked the theme of development to environmental deterioration, pointing out not only the problems caused by industrial economies but also that many developing countries were destroying the environment in their struggle for survival. The Brundtland Report was the antecedent for the June 1992 United Nations Conference on Environment and Development (UNCED) in Rio de Janeiro, Brazil. The conference brought together delegates from 178 states and 650 Non-Governmental Organizations (NGOs). UNCED arguably represents 'a microcosm of the international environmental debate, both in terms of actors and arguments, and reflects the basic North/South[2] diplomatic divide on this issue' (Thomas 1992).

Two major conventions were signed at UNCED: the first on climate change (global warming) and the second on biological diversity. They both represent a recognition by the participants that these issues are global problems.[3] The issue of global warming entered the international agenda in 1988 at a conference in Toronto on the changing atmosphere. The conference called for a 20 per cent reduction in CO_2 levels by the year 2005. At UNCED the atmosphere was recognized to be part of the 'Common Heritage of Mankind'.[4] Although it is difficult to determine exactly which gases are causing global warming and to what degree they need to be reduced, the processes of industrial and agricultural production are recognized to be causal factors.

If the atmosphere is part of the global commons, it follows that all states must contribute to preserving it. The actions of one or just a few states alone would not be effective in reducing harmful emissions. However, the USA rejected any regulatory regime, and many developing countries reject the restrictions on their industrial development (which the developed countries have already achieved), unless compensation through funding is given.

Also agreed upon at UNCED was the formation of a commission on sustainable development, previously introduced in the Brundtland Report. The concept of sustainable development is a fairly slippery one, broadly implying development whereby the environment is protected to such a degree that environmental capacities are maintained over time (Jacobs 1992).[5] What the agreement represents is a recognition that environmental issues are not unconnected to development issues. However, the formation of the commission is such that it can influence policy only by embarrassing governments into compliance: it has no sanctioning power. On the one hand the North wants the South to pursue economic development programmes which will not harm the global commons; on the other hand the South is concerned about the costs of not exploiting its resources. If the North wants the South to consider its environmental concerns, the North must consider the South's concern with development. The South's claims are being made partly on the basis of equity and justice and also in the belief that the environment presents a lever for the South to gain concessions from the North. More importantly, the formation of the commission represents a recognition of economic interdependence in the global economy but not of a global obligation to control the exploitation of resources in the interests of the whole. The Rio Declaration on the Environment and Development thus represents a compromise between the values of state sovereignty and cosmopolitan justice.

At UNCED the state was the primary actor in the negotiations, despite the presence of numerous NGOs, and the agreements reached are intergovernmental in scope because the state has the capacity to determine the limits of the possible for all other actors. However, the environment, and its preservation, is recognized to be an issue which is global in scope. One approach is to argue that a state system which protects sovereignty cannot also provide protection for the environment, which is a global rather than a national issue. The state may not therefore be the most appropriate level at which to address problems.

However, in the wake of growing nationalism, and the creation of new states anxious to preserve their sovereignty, it seems likely that the state will remain as the major actor in the international system. Thus environmental issues will continue to be managed by a state system and all its constraints. The question remains whether a consensus can be arrived at which is broadly regarded as just.

THE GULF WAR

On 2 August 1990 Iraqi forces invaded and occupied Kuwait, a small oil-rich country at the head of the Persian Gulf. A major reason for the action was the poor state of Iraq's economy following a long war with Iran.[6] One way to turn the economy around was to sustain a high price for oil (Iraq's main export); and persuade those Arab states which had helped to fund Iraq's war effort to write off the debt. Kuwait was a key player in both these respects – as a major oil producer, and a substantial creditor of the war debts. However, she refused to co-operate (Kuniholm 1993). Saddam Hussein, the Iraqi leader, accused Kuwait of undermining Iraq's economy: by demanding repayment of wartime loans, refusing to offer further support, and depressing the price of oil by flooding the market. 'War', said Hussein,

> is fought with soldiers and much harm is done by explosions and killing, but it is also done by economic means. Therefore we ask our brothers who do not mean to wage war; this is in fact a kind of war against us.
>
> (Karsh and Rautsi 1991: 206)

When Kuwait failed to respond, Iraq invaded her.

If the invasion had succeeded, not only would Iraq's immediate economic situation be improved, but, by its control of Kuwait's rich oilfields, Iraq would have had a powerful (even controlling) position in the world's oil markets. Shortly after the invasion, Hussein revived the claim that Kuwait was not an independent country at all, but rather an integral part of Iraq. On 8 August Hussein formally annexed Kuwait as his country's nineteenth province.

Iraq's invasion and its claims were immediately condemned by the vast majority of states across the globe. The invasion came shortly after the collapse of the cold war, when the international community of states was seeking a 'new world order', and, added to that, there was particular concern at renewed instability in one of the world's most volatile and economically important regions (Barber 1993). At the United Nations, of which Kuwait was a member, news of the invasion was met by anger and consternation. A series of resolutions were passed calling on Iraq to withdraw; imposing economic sanctions and an arms ban on her; and threatening to employ military force if she failed to comply with the UN demands. The initial hopes that these threats would lead to an Iraqi withdrawal were not fulfilled. Hussein rejected the UN resolutions. He declared Iraq's intention to remain permanently in Kuwait, and threatened to turn it into a graveyard and destroy its oilfields if there were any attempt to reverse the annexation (Karsh and Rautsi 1991: 222).

Despite such threats a UN force was assembled in the Persian Gulf and the surrounding states. The UN has no military contingents of its own, and so when it mobilizes a force it has to rely upon contributions from member states. In this case the response was enthusiastic and broad-based, and the force contained units from the United States and Arab, European and Asian countries. Japan and Germany contributed substantial funds. However, the major contribution and the military command were provided by the US. (The Soviet Union did not supply troops, but supported the steps taken.) The Americans were prepared to take the lead because they saw Iraq's action as a challenge to the new world order, in which they cast themselves as leader, and because they believed the US had vital interests in the region – including the supply of oil and Arab–Israeli relations.

Although a powerful UN force was assembled, an attack on Iraq could not be taken lightly. Under Hussein's dictatorial leadership Iraq had built up a powerful army, battle-hardened in its war with Iran and equipped with sophisticated weapons. It was also known that the Iraqis were ruthless in their methods. They had used chemical weapons and gas in attacks against the Iranians and in quelling dissident groups within their own borders, including the Kurds. Furthermore, it was known that Hussein was eager to develop nuclear weapons. Despite these dangers and uncertainties the UN gave Iraq a deadline to withdraw from Kuwait. When that expired, on the night of 16/17 January 1991, UN forces launched operation 'Desert Storm' through a series of air and missile attacks upon Iraq.

A fortnight after launching 'Desert Storm' President George Bush, in his State of the Union message, explained the reasons for the attack and appealed to the American people to stand firm and together. He said that the cost in lives could not yet be measured, 'but the cost of closing our eyes to aggression is beyond mankind's power to imagine'. He claimed that the US had accepted the burden of confronting the aggressor because only the US possessed the moral standing and the resources. 'What is at stake is more than one small country; it is a big idea; a new world order.' The UN members, he said, had been drawn together by a diversity of motives, but there were central themes which they all shared: to ensure peace and security, freedom and the rule of law. The US had not wanted war, but she had to face an aggressor. 'Our purpose in the Persian Gulf remains constant: to drive Iraq out of Kuwait, to restore Kuwait's legitimate government, and to ensure the stability and security of this vital region.' We must be sure, he continued, that control of the world's oil resources do not fall into the hands of an aggressor. He concluded that 'Our cause is just. Our cause is moral. Our cause is right' (*Keesings*, January 1991). In response Hussein called on his people to wage a holy war, a *jihad*, against Satan's servants, whom he identified as President Bush, Mrs Thatcher and the Zionists. 'The great duel, the mother of all battles, has begun between the victorious right and the evil that will certainly be defeated' (Karsh and Rautsi 1991: 245).

The war cost many lives and resulted in vast destruction of property and environmental damage. In preparing for war President Bush had warned Iraq that the US would not tolerate 'the use of chemical weapons, support for any kind of terrorist activity or the destruction of Kuwait's oil fields and installations' (Roberts 1993). The Allies stated that their air attacks were concentrated exclusively on military targets, and overall they were remarkably accurate. Among other damage the air strikes succeeded in wrecking Iraq's army command and communications systems, its nuclear research reactors and chemical weapons facilities. Later, when the land war started, the air forces took a great toll of tanks and armoured vehicles. However, the Allied air forces also attacked parts of Iraq's infra-structure, claiming that they were legitimate military targets. They included water- and energy-supplies, oil deposits and refineries, and transport and communications systems. As a result of these attacks the whole civilian population suffered, and inevitably some bombs strayed from their targets and civilians as well as military personnel were killed. By the end of the bombing there was both loss of life and a badly damaged country.

The destruction of facilities and environmental damage inflicted on Kuwait by the Iraqis was even greater. The initial invasion led to considerable loss of life and physical damage. As soon as the war started Iraq artillery set alight Khafji oil-storage depot in northern Saudi Arabia, and in Kuwait they fired oil installations, sending a pall of smoke across the country. Their aim was partly to impede air attacks, but more importantly, they wanted to demonstrate to the UN the devastating consequences of prolonged conflict. That message was rammed home when Iraq began pumping oil into the Persian Gulf from the Ahmadi base, causing a hugh oil-slick in the shallow, enclosed sea that forms the Gulf. Again there was a partial military explanation, to deter an amphibious landing, but again the main message was the high cost of waging war against Iraq. The Allies succeeded for a time in reducing the spillage by bombing the oil pressure controls, but then the air attacks added to the slick by hitting two Iraqi tankers. The overall result was an enormous oil spillage, much larger than any previous oil disaster, even those involving the largest tankers.[7]

The loss of human life and the physical destruction increased enormously when the Allies launched their land offensive on 24 February. The Allied forces achieved quick and complete success, and severely damaged the Iraqi army. While thousands of Iraqis were killed, many through air attacks on the fleeing armies, Allied loss of life was small. However, the Iraqis caused enormous physical and environmental damage. Although Hussein did not carry out his threat to use chemical weapons, he ordered the despoliation of Kuwait. Most of Kuwait's 900 oil wells were set on fire, so that they burnt away about 3 million barrels per day. 'In many areas of the country black clouds had completely blocked out the sun and noxious gases were making normal life impossible' (*Keesings*, March 1991: 38119). The fires were not finally extinguished until November 1991, long after the fighting was over.[8]

At the UN the damage that the Iraqis had inflicted in despoiling Kuwait was condemned as contrary to the rules of war. All wars cause environmental damage, but the degree depends on the scale of the war and on the technology employed, and judgements about the application of the rules depends on the victors. In this case there was broad agreement that Iraq had violated a number of international agreements, including Article 23(g) of the Hague Regulations of 1907; Article 147 of the 4th Geneva Convention of 1949; and the 1977 Environmental Convention. However, with Iraqi forces driven out of Kuwait and in full retreat the Allies concluded that their task of restoring Kuwait's sovereignty and regaining order in the region had been achieved. They did not drive on to Baghdad to overthrow Hussein or challenge Iraq's sovereignty.

INTERNATIONAL SUGAR TRADE

Although Bull is primarily concerned with order, discussions on justice and its meaning naturally give rise to questions of equality. The principle of distributive justice refers to the redistribution of (economic) resources in the light of considerations of a desired end-point (usually referred to as the common good). The ideas of proportionate and distributive justice on a global scale embody within them the notion that it would be unjust not to recognize existing inequalities in the international system. Consequent upon this, world justice, or a more just world order, would seek to recognize inequalities among states and redistribute economic resources accordingly.

This section explores the idea of distributive justice in the context of international commodity trade. More specifically it looks at the special arrangements for sugar provided by the Sugar Protocol of the Lomé Convention.

If we examine the nature of international trade, we find that the pattern of trade is such that some countries depend heavily on trade in primary commodities and others on industrial goods and services. It is generally assumed that developing countries are more dependent on commodity exports than developed economies.[9] Although developed market economies account for a significant percentage of the value of commodity trade, developing countries depend heavily on commodity exports to the extent that the earnings from these exports account for a large percentage of their foreign-exchange earnings. Furthermore, these economies are more vulnerable to changes in prices because of their tendency to export a narrow range of products.[10] Thus the developing countries have repeatedly called for changes in the nature of international trade which would stabilize commodity prices at a reasonable level and so facilitate greater growth and development.

The claim that the international trading system does not operate for the benefit of the developing countries led to demands for change in the international economic order. The demand for a new international economic order (NIEO)[11] was an attempt by the South to persuade the North to change the existing nature of world economic relationships. The calls for change were based on the principle of mutual self-interest and interdependence. That is, the North should help the South not on the grounds of equity, but on the basis that southern prosperity was in the North's interest because of the South's potential to provide expanding markets and key raw materials (Brandt Commission 1980). The good of the whole global community would be served by changes in the nature of the international economic order.

The Lomé Convention (1975) was negotiated when notions of distributive justice were prominent in the debate for a NIEO. Lomé created a special trade and aid regime between the EC and its former colonies and dependencies, known collectively as the ACP (African, Caribbean and Pacific) states. Lomé's objective was to expedite development in the ACP states. The supporters of Lomé saw it as a concrete manifestation of growing interdependence within an international system where the economic and social concerns of the South were addressed.

One important facility offered by the Lomé Convention was the Sugar Protocol. As the most pressing demands at the time concerned the issue of price stabilization in commodity trade and the provision of trade preferences in recognition of unequal starting-points, the Sugar Protocol became a corner-stone of the Lomé Convention. The Sugar Protocol provided an example of a special arrangement for trade in a commodity which is produced in both temperate and tropical climates: in the former from sugar-beet, and in the latter from sugar-cane.[12] According to the Protocol, the Community undertakes to purchase and import, duty-free, 1.3 million tonnes of sugar from the ACP states annually. Furthermore, ACP sugar is marketed in the Community at the same price as EC sugar.

As a result of the CAP support system, the price paid to EC farmers has tended to be higher than the world market price for sugar.[13] The Sugar Protocol thus guarantees ACP sugar exporters a preferential market in the EC at prices currently (and historically) above world market prices. This is an important guarantee for those ACP producers whose economies depend significantly on sugar. For example, 90 per cent of Caribbean sugar is exported to the UK. At the same time, other markets such as the USA have been lost because of the reduction of regional import quotas since 1974. This serves to increase the level of dependence on the EC market as well as the value of this market to the ACP.

However, while sugar is a major export of several ACP states, the EC as a whole can supply its own sugar market without imports. The EC exported 4.7 million tonnes of sugar to the world market in 1989 (Commission of the EC 1990). It has occasionally been argued that ACP sugar is surplus sugar within the EC market. As there would appear to be no natural gap in the EC for ACP sugar imports, the question of why the Protocol was created immediately arises. Was the Protocol part of an EC effort towards greater justice in nature of international trade, or did it serve particular national interests in the EC and the ACP?

The Sugar Protocol emerged out of a specific historical context: that of the special relationship between the UK and the Commonwealth, in particular the Caribbean, at the time when Britain was negotiating entry to the EC. The UK was anxious to preserve this special relationship for historical and developmental reasons, as well as to safeguard raw cane-sugar supplies for British cane re-fineries. Thus Britain made one of its clauses for entry that Commonwealth (sugar) interests would have to be protected. Britain traditionally imported cane sugar to meet a significant percentage of domestic requirements. This sugar was imported raw and refined by British transnational companies (TNCs). Cane-sugar imports thus supported not only Commonwealth producer interests, but also British TNCs.

In addition the debate was influenced by the success of the Organization of Petroleum Exporting Countries (OPEC) in gaining control of the world oil market and virtually holding the world to ransom in 1974. The perception of commodity power was heightened by world shortages of other commodities, including sugar. The EC was particularly vulnerable to these shortages because of its dependence on imported raw materials. Thus the EC was anxious to guarantee reliable supplies of raw materials, and the Sugar Protocol provided one means of doing so.

The Sugar Protocol has been described as a historical accident arising out of political considerations and special needs (Southgate 1985). However, since 1975, whereas the needs of the ACP sugar exporters for a market for their sugar has not changed, the needs and priorities of the EC have. With new technological developments, beet-sugar production in the EC has become highly efficient, increasing yields and quality in field and factory. Together with the encouragement given by the CAP, EC sugar production has increased from 8 million tonnes in 1968 to 14 million tonnes in 1989. At the same time demand for sugar has fallen to 10 million tonnes. This means there is a large disequilibrium in supply and demand within the Community, which necessarily threatens the commitment to import ACP sugar. In addition, recent developments in the Uruguay round of the GATT negotiations mean that prices in the Community will be lowered, and this will lower the value of the Protocol to the ACP.

It is now becoming clear that ACP sugar is of decreasing value to the EC. The renegotiations of Lomé have been increasingly difficult in the shadow of recession in the North in the early 1990s, and new priorities have emerged with the demise of centrally controlled markets in Eastern Europe. An examination of EC development policy reveals that it is neither globally consistent nor politically neutral. That the EC has particular development policies with particular developing countries is not evidence of support for the idea of the redistribution of wealth on the global scale towards a more just world order. Rather the charge has been levied at the EC that its notion of development co-operation has been very particular and hierarchical, favouring some developing countries over others. This is particularly relevant if one considers that the Indian subcontinent, arguably containing some of the poorest countries in the world, is not at all high up in the hierarchy of privilege (Grilli 1993).

CONCLUSIONS

Bull, in the introduction to *The Anarchical Society*, argues that the current system of states is inhospitable to the idea of justice on the global scale. This is because the principle of sovereignty is so enshrined in the essence of statehood that justice is deemed inapplicable across state boundaries. Furthermore, there is no means of enforcement of international justice. In addition the notions of cosmopolitan and distributive justice are contrary to the principle of reciprocal justice, upon which the interstate system with its alliances and pacts is based. Ideas of cosmopolitan and distributive justice thus play only a small role in the current system. Do the case studies presented confirm or refute Bull's theses with reference to environmental concerns?

Global Environmental Change (GEC), as exemplified in problems such as global warming or ozone depletion, demands an approach which is based on principles of international or cosmopolitan justice. It therefore presents a challenge to an international system governed by interstate justice. 'The global political system, based on the primacy of sovereign states has created conditions detrimental to environmental protection' (Thomas 1992: 3). This is because it had regarded the environment and its resources as expendable, unlimited and available for exploitation. As a result there had been very little international co-operation on the environment.

Some signs of concern and change were exemplified in UNCED. This was a milestone in the history of environmental negotiations. It linked together states from both North and South as well as numerous NGOs in the common pursuit of a more sustainable development. However, the UNCED resolutions are limited in scope because there was such disagreement over how far an international convention could intervene in the regulation of matters regarded as being essentially within the domestic jurisdiction of the state. In particular there were obvious differences in approach between the North and the South as well as between states and NGOs. For example, the North argued that forests were a global resource and should be protected by international treaties. The South argued that its forests were a national resource and should be used according to each state's particular needs for fuel, lumber or food. The solution was a non-binding agreement acceptable to all but largely unenforceable in an international system without sanctions.

The methods of decision-making in UNCED were also limited in scope. The ultimate decision to adopt a resolution rests with individual states. States consult or are lobbied by NGOs and by TNCs to create policies favourable to their interests. However, TNCs often act in areas outside of state jurisdiction, and in practice states have proved unreliable in supporting long-term environmental safeguards when faced with short-term economic costs.

The Gulf crisis and the Allies' reaction demonstrate the commitment to the maintenance of a state-centred world order, as well as the protection of national sovereignty (interstate justice) and the pursuit of national interest. Despite UN restrictions on the use of force, the reality was that the conflict presented a threat to international order and to the state system, in that a recognized sovereign state was invaded, and nearly eliminated, by another. The Gulf War revealed that many states were prepared to form a coalition to drive Saddam Hussein out and thus protect that order. Interestingly, the US-led action demonstrated that ostensibly, it was also necessary to create an alliance to pursue national interests. A unilateral decision would not have been regarded as legitimate in terms of international law. Thus although the state system underlines that rights of non-interference are valued, in this case most governments were prepared to co-operate to defend the state system and international order, despite the human suffering and physical damage that would be caused.

The Gulf War was significant because it affirmed that the Allies' major concerns were: (1) to free Kuwait; (2) to protect her territorial sovereignty; (3) to protect the international system; and (4) to promote their own national interests. They have not sought to depose Hussein or interfere with the internal sovereignty of Iraq. Important to our analysis is that war, however justified, has a human and environmental cost. The human and environmental costs of the Gulf War were great, but neither deterred the Allies' action. Hussein's threats of environmental damage did not divert the Allies from acting to restore order and pursue their national interests. Order was thus given precedence over environmental costs.

The Sugar Protocol of the Lomé Convention may serve to redistribute economic resources or the gains from economic activity. However, its particular historical circumstances would lead one to conclude that the Sugar Protocol was negotiated to serve the interests of particular member states rather than the notion of distributive justice. The EC has no global development policy as such; there is no desire to alter the structure of the world trading system to create a more just world order in keeping with NIEO objectives. Although in practice (though not in motivation) the desired end of redistribution of resources may be served by providing preferential markets and higher prices, this cannot be seen as the overriding objective. This conclusion would fit in with the thesis that ideas of distributive and global justice are only a small part of the international system.

On the whole Bull's position appears to be confirmed, but there are a number of examples of a growing recognition of the requirement to meet the needs of developing countries with special policies which recognize that all states are not equal. The GATT has since 1970 allowed for special treatment of developing countries within its ambit. The UN has endorsed the Right to Development (1986).[14] It finds enactment in the commitment of the North to give 0.7 per cent of GDP as aid, which was reinforced at UNCED. The Montreal Fund was created in 1990, largely as a result of the work of the UNEP, to help developing countries phase out the use of CFCs and other harmful compounds and switch to less harmful compounds (Hurrell and Kingsbury 1992: 199).

There is also a growing recognition of the need to respond to accelerating ecological interdependence. NGOs have played a significant role in the creation of public awareness and political pressure on governments, as well as in identifying risks and proposing measures to deal with them (WCED 1987). The UCED conference, as well as condemning Iraq's environmental destruction and violation of international environmental agreements, affirmed the principle of international justice and the aspiration towards a more just environment. The World Bank has also expanded its agenda to include a new Global Environmental Facility (GEF) which will supply concessional aid for the preservation of natural resources, and in particular the preservation of biological diversity, the protection of the atmosphere and the conservation of energy. The GEF will also provide information relevant to formulating other global conventions and financing arrangements in UNCED.

Thus the state system, with all its limitations (and there are many), does pay some respect to cosmopolitan and distributive justice. One of the major questions facing the globe in the next century will be whether the current system can facilitate sufficient co-operation to address the development and environmental challenge. International relations provides two broad approaches to this question. The first, like Bull, would argue that the state system can be used to achieve desired objectives because it facilitates a minimum amount of order upon which reforms can be imposed. Thus states can be urged to co-operate through international conventions or institutions. The second, a more radical approach, would argue that a state system which protects sovereignty cannot also provide a global approach to dealing with environmental issues. The current international system is, however, characterized by a tendency towards the creation, rather than the dissolution, of states. There are, nevertheless, some signs that the state system may rise to the challenge, but it is too early to guarantee that it will. A mixed picture is likely to persist. However, it is important to emphasize and concur with Bull that order may be a prerequisite for global justice.

NOTES

1 It is not assumed that the management of the environment is the only way of dealing with the current crisis. Rather, in seeking to understand the implications of the work of Bull, it is necessary to trace the steps which have already been taken, and these have primarily been attempts at problem solving.

2 The 'North/South' terminology is generally conterminous with 'developed' and 'developing countries', but is also used to refer to a political grouping in international negotiations.

3 The convention on climate change aims to stabilize greenhouse gas concentrations at a level which will prevent harmful interference with the climatic system. The biological-diversity convention is aimed at preserving the biological diversity of species.

4 That is, an asset the use of which is available to everybody and the misuse of which affects the availability or use of that asset for all other users and potential users.

5 Significantly, in the United National Environment Programme (UNEP) the concept has been clarified in the statement that it *does not imply in any way encroachment upon national sovereignty.*

6 It was estimated that Iraq had an accumulated debt of about $70 billion.

7 It was estimated that between 7 and 9 million barrels were released, affecting more than 400 kilometres of the Saudi and Kuwait coasts and causing great destruction of bird and sea life.

8 In addition to the oil fires the Iraqis had laid over 500,000 mines in Kuwait and left behind large quantities of unexploded bombs and shells (Roberts 1993: 13–19).

9 This is a general statement disproved by the Newly Industrialized Countries (NICs), Australia and Canada. However, more significant than the total of commodity exports would be the general mix of the economy, and the specific nature of markets.

10 The tendency for prices of primary products to vary more than those of manufactures has been the subject of numerous academic and governmental debates. For example, see Spraos 1980: 107–28. However, more important than actual price variations is the effect of market instability on export earnings of developing countries.

11 The NIEO was passed as a General Assembly resolution in 1974.

12 Although recent developments in the sugar sector mean that an end-product, a sweetener, can be produced from a variety of sources, including maize, potatoes, artichokes, and significantly through chemical processes, producing artificial sweeteners such as aspartame (Nutrasweet).

13 It is also argued that the quantity of sugar the EC exports on the world market contributes to lower world sugar prices.

14 The right to development is a duty not to hinder the development of other countries as well as to assist actively in their development. This does not imply non-discrimination in development needs. For example, the charge of corruption that has been levied against many governments is inconsistent with the Declaration.

Part IV
Interspecies issues

10 Other species and moral reason

David E. Cooper

I

Why should we care about our treatment of animals, plants, and the wider 'living world'? Appeals to 'narrow human purposes', like 'health and affluence' (Naess 1991: 28–9), provide only a limited answer. Time was when livestock, for example, had to be treated reasonably decently in order to give a profitable yield. With factory farming, that time is past. More generally, technological ingenuity has discovered ways of catering to 'narrow human purposes' which permit, or require, disregard for the good of other species of life. Even if some dire warnings about the catastrophic effects for human beings of environmental exploitation are well founded, 'sustainable development' is clearly compatible with far greater exploitation than many 'environmentally concerned' people would tolerate. The 'health and affluence' of our descendants are unlikely to suffer if Lake Coniston, say, is drained and turned into another 'Silicon Valley'.

For many people, as just implied, appeals to 'narrow' human interests anyway miss the point. We should care about animals and other forms of life 'for their own sake', or at any rate for the sake of human goods of a more elevated kind than economic ones. Perhaps the 'or' is misleading here, for 'human nature may be such that with increased maturity a *human* need increases to protect the richness and diversity of life for *its own sake*' (Naess 1991: 177). That remark hints at an argument for concerning ourselves with other species to which I shall return, but only after rejecting a very different, and more familiar, kind of argument.

My critical target is an approach in 'non-human' moral philosophy which deserves to be called the 'mainstream' one, for it is the dominant one in 'animal ethics' and prominent, at least, in 'environmental ethics'. Let me say at once that I am on the side of the angels, in accepting the broad conclusion of 'mainstream' thinkers that many of the ways in which we presently behave towards animals, plants, forests, wildernesses, and so on are wrong, or worse. (Factory farming, for example, seems to me to be genuinely evil, though in this chapter I shall have little to say about animals not 'in the wild'. The distinction between being 'in' and 'out' of the wild is not, of course, a sharp one.) But I shall argue that the 'mainstream' approach is misguided and that it may even obstruct the causes in support of which its proponents speak.

A clear statement of the approach is given by a writer certainly not on the side of the angels, a defender of animal experimentation. Referring to the well-known positions of Peter Singer and Tom Regan, he writes:

> Despite their differences . . . [they] extend beyond the species barrier basic ethical principles. This extension is demanded by the logic of universaliz-ability – to seek . . . the consistent application of the principle that cases should be treated similarly unless there is a relevant difference between them.
>
> (Vance 1992: 1716)

On the 'mainstream' approach, that is, moral concern for other species is de-manded by reason, in the specific sense of logical consistency. Only if the differences between human and non-human life were relevant to moral discrimin-ation would it be rational to confine concern to the former: but they are not, so those who do so confine their concern are guilty of a 'speciesist' arbitrariness and unreason akin to 'sexism' and 'racism'.

Some illustrations will help. Jeremy Bentham famously asked for the basis of a morally relevant line between humans and animals.

> Is it the faculty of reason, or, perhaps, the faculty of discourse? But a full-grown horse . . . is . . . a more rational, as well as a more conversable animal than an infant of a day . . . old. But suppose the case were otherwise, what would it avail? The question is not, Can they *reason*? nor, Can they *talk*? but, Can they *suffer*?
>
> (Bentham 1960: ch. 17, sec. 1)

The implicit argument here is that since the basis for moral consideration is the capacity for suffering – if it were not, babies would not be due such consideration – then it is illogical to confine it to human beings. This argument also illustrates a typical 'mainstream' strategy: to show that a certain feature, like speech, cannot be relevant to moral concern, since not all human beings possess it. Here is a more explicit statement of the approach:

> In arguing that animals do have rights . . . [f]irst we select . . . a right which we are confident that humans do have. Then we ask whether there is a relevant difference between humans and animals which would justify us in denying that right to animals. . . . If not, then the right . . . is [one] possessed by animals as well as by humans.
>
> (Rachels 1989: 123)

Here are some illustrations of the same approach, this time in 'environmental ethics'. 'What needs to be established', writes one commentator on certain arguments for 'valuing' nature, is that 'Nature generally, or at least living Nature, also possesses those features that serve to mark out Man as a locus of value' (Kleinig 1991: 76). Finally, it has been said that the 'normative force' of Aldo Leopold's 'land ethic' 'lies precisely in the realm of reason and cognition'. This is because 'we ought to feel . . . loyalty and respect toward the community' to which we belong, and so are rationally required to take these attitudes towards the whole 'biotic community' of which we, as well as plants and animals, are 'kin members' (Callicott 1992: 196).

Readers familiar with these authors will notice that the 'mainstream' approach cuts across different 'meta-ethical' approaches. Bentham is a utilitarian; Rachels a proponent of 'rights-based' ethics; Callicott of 'sentiment-based' ethics. But whatever the crucial determinant of moral concern – happiness, rights, sentiment – the argument is that it is irrational to restrict such concerns to human beings, since the differences between ourselves and some other species which would alone justify such a restriction simply do not exist. (*Which* species qualify for concern may, of course, be affected by one's preferred 'meta-ethics'. For a utilitarian, only sentient creatures qualify, whereas it is consistent with the other theories that plants and 'biotic communities' do so as well.)

Typically, the 'mainstream' approach is yoked to a certain image of moral progress, that of 'the expanding circle'. We can 'imagine the history of moral development as simply an ever-widening moral circle – widening as new classes of sufferers . . . are drawn into it' (Ryder 1992: 3). On one familiar scenario, those initially in a person's circle of moral concern are members of the immediate family; this then expands, step by step, to include male, then female, members of the community, human beings in general, animals, plants, 'biotic communities', and finally, perhaps, even lifeless rocks and planets. The development is a rational one since, according to those enamoured of this image, 'the move from one ethic to the next is accomplished . . . by finding a determinant of moral considerability in that ethic and showing that a rigorous application of it leads us to the next kind' (Elliot 1991: 291).

I shall return to the metaphor of 'the expanding circle' when I come to criticism of the approach to which it is yoked. Before that, I want to raise two questions: one about the popularity of the 'mainstream' approach, the other about its relation to the notion of justice. The entrenchment of the approach owes, in the first instance, to strategic considerations. Accusations of 'speciesism' and 'sentientism', levelled against the failures to extend moral concerns beyond human beings and animals respectively, are designed to suggest parallels with the 'racism' and 'sexism' which just about everyone will at least claim to condemn. They do so by suggesting that those attitudes share what is widely held to be the arbitrariness and inconsistency exhibited by the 'racist' and 'sexist', who dis-criminate upon irrelevant grounds. More importantly, perhaps, the 'mainstream' approach exemplifies the almost obsessive urge in recent moral thought to minimize the dependence of judgements and principles upon 'emotion' or any-thing deemed 'subjective'. Thus Peter Singer announces near the beginning of *Animal Liberation* that 'nowhere in this book . . . do I appeal to the reader's emotions where they cannot be supported by reasons' (Singer 1975: xi). It may be, as those of the 'moral sentiment' school would urge, that emotions, like sympathy and loyalty, are required for moral concern to begin at all; but, once it has begun, reason in the form of consistency dictates how far it ought to extend. The person who, in Callicott's words, does not feel loyalty to the 'biotic community' is guilty of inconsistency if they feel loyalty towards a human community.

Turning to my second question, discussing the rights and wrongs of our current treatment of other species is, at the same time, to discuss its justice, when this term is taken sufficiently broadly. For, so taken, the words 'just' and 'unjust' are virtual synonyms of 'right' and 'wrong', in which case, of course, one cannot support the claim that our treatment is wrong by saying that it is unjust. One merely restates it. For considerations of justice to play a critical role, the notion must be understood more narrowly. When this is done, 'mainstream' writers differ as to whether the vocabulary of justice is the right currency to use in condemning our behaviour towards other species. Those who think it appropriate to regard animals and, perhaps, plants as possessing rights are likely to be most happy with that vocabulary: for it is common practice to describe violations of rights as acts of injustices. But plenty of 'mainstream' writers do not think it appropriate: whether because they are utilitarians who share Bentham's view that talk of rights outside of a legal system is 'nonsense on stilts', or because they think that animals and plants do not satisfy certain criteria for genuinely possessing rights (they cannot *claim* rights, for example), or because the whole idea of moral rights is too closely connected with an ethical position they do not share, that of liberal individualism (see Clark 1987). The effect of rejecting 'rights talk' on such grounds is to reduce enthusiasm for criticizing our treatment of other species on grounds of justice.

In one respect, however, all proponents of the 'mainstream' approach will be better disposed towards the vocabulary of justice than someone who rejects that approach. Of all the virtues, justice is the one which seems most intimately connected with the exercise of consistency. Someone who is erratically benevolent can still be, on balance at least, a benevolent person. But a wages tribunal, say, which is not bothered by whether its decisions are consistent with one another does not display a concern for justice. By complaining that our treatment of other species is inconsistent with the moral commitments to human beings which we already accept, 'mainstream' writers emphasize a condition which, if not sufficient for invoking justice, at least makes the rhetoric of justice unsurprising.

II

Criticism of the 'mainstream' approach might begin by challenging the associated image of 'the expanding circle'. It would, of course, be historical nonsense to suppose that, in all societies, moral thought has changed and progressed according to a single pattern of expansion, such as the scenario sketched on p. 139. Clearly, any number of factors – religious, geographical, and so on – have influenced the order and manner in which different peoples have expanded, or contracted, their circles of moral concern. In some societies, for example, certain animals have been embraced within such a circle before certain human beings – perhaps the South American one described here by two Spanish explorers:

> Though the Indian women breed fowl . . . they never eat them . . . and conceive such a fondness for them, that they will not sell them. . . . [If] a stranger . . .

finds himself under the necessity of killing the fowl . . . his landlady shrieks, dissolves into tears, and wrings her hands, as if it had been an only son.

(Quoted in Serpell 1988: 49–50)

It will be replied that the image is not intended as historical depiction, but as a 'model' of rational moral change. Human beings are creatures of limited sympathy and limited rationality: they are neither entirely self-centred nor wholly altruistic by nature, and while they are capable of appreciating what is logically implied by their original moral commitments, they can do so, typically, only in a gradual, step-by-step manner. Consequently, the 'normal' pattern of moral progress, in abstraction from 'distorting' factors (like a religious belief which promotes the interests of certain totemic animals over those of some human beings), will be the one suggested by the 'expanding circle' image. It is more obviously consonant with caring about one's family to care about human strangers than about chickens: hence the 'normal' pattern will be for the former to enter the circle of moral concern ahead of the latter.

Even when construed as a 'model' rather than as historical description, the image is a poor one. For a start, there is no clear criterion of consistency which makes indifference to strangers more obviously inconsistent with caring about one's family than indifference to the animals that share the family hearth. Nor, therefore, of any clear reason to regard the pattern just mentioned as the 'normal' one. Second, the image or 'model' implies a peculiarly conservative conception of moral progress as, simply, the extension to a wider constituency of already-established principles. This is to ignore the kind of progress where principles are re-evaluated. When the Buddha preached that even the lowest caste were deserving of compassion, he was not urging his fellow nobles to apply their principles more widely, but to reject an ethic in which men were honoured and respected on the basis of status, military prowess, virility and the like.

Finally, the 'model' implies that moral progress always occurs through recognizing that some previously excluded group – women, other races, animals, or whatever – is similar, in all relevant respects, to a group already included in the circle of moral concern. But this is to ignore the possibility, to which I shall return later, that a species ought to engage our concern because of respects in which it significantly differs from ourselves. In the case of concern for non-sentient life, moreover, attempts to argue that this is required because of the similarities between plants, say, and ourselves can look badly strained. To the claim that each living thing is 'in many ways like ourselves, responding . . . to environmental circumstances and so pursuing the realization of its own good' (Taylor 1986: 154), a predictable reply is that plants do *not* engage in any such pursuit and so are not, in that respect at least, at all 'like ourselves'. A similar response might well greet Callicott's comparison of 'biotic communities' with social ones.

This mention of people who resist the call to 'respect' non-sentient life leads me towards my central criticism of the 'mainstream' approach. For I want to reach it by first arguing that its proponents badly misconstrue the position of those – let's call them 'speciesists' – who refuse to extend concern beyond the sphere of human, or at any rate animal, life. On the 'mainstream' approach, such people must be either ignorant, inconsistent or evil. Either they do not recognize the similarities between human and non-human life; or they do, but fail to understand the moral implications of this; or they succeed on both counts, but just don't care about doing what is right.

'Mainstream' writers often prime the reader to suppose that 'speciesists' must be irrational (assuming that they are not ignorant or evil) by parodying their position. They are portrayed as arguing for the restriction of moral concern to humans either by citing some single feature which distinguishes human life (such as speech) or by invoking the brute reminder '*Because* they are *humans*'. It is indeed easy to dismiss such arguments. How, as Bentham asked, could one possibly regard a feature like speech as drawing a moral 'line'? As for 'Because they are humans', this cannot be a genuine reason for, but only an expression of, the 'speciesist''s conviction. However, 'speciesists' worth their salt do not argue in these ways. 'Because they are humans' is not arguing, idiotically, that the mere property of being human marks humans out for special concern. Rather, it gestures towards the existence of a range of features, bound up with humanity, which does so mark them out. Sane 'speciesists', moreover, never pick on just one feature, but remind us of a whole range of features – rationality, self-regard, moral sense, aesthetic sense, freedom of the will, responsibility, long-term pur-posiveness, for example – which, they argue, are distinctive of human existence. They then invite us to share the conviction, self-evident to them, that moral principles are shaped to guide the intercourse of such distinctive creatures with one another, and so cannot be applicable, except in the most extenuated sense, to our dealings with animals, let alone plants.

Those MPs who not only voted against a bill to ban fox-hunting but regarded the debate as a frivolous waste of parliamentary time are not necessarily guilty of either ignorance or inconsistency. They know as much about foxes, their similar-ities to and differences from human beings, as their opponents. But theirs is not necessarily an irrational refusal to extend concern to foxes in virtue of what they admit are relevant similarities, but incredulity towards the idea that the simil-arities can count when weighed against the massive differences. To take a very different example, charges of ignorance and inconsistency are surely not the appropriate ones to level against the moral indifference to nature which, pre-sumably, is the corollary of the following attitude:

> I only live in the middle of nature because the physicians have told me [to]. . . . I love everything except nature, because nature seems to me uncanny and I have experienced its malignancy. . . . I avoid it. . . . I am a city person and merely put up with nature.
>
> (Bernhard 1992: 62)

For this author, clearly, there is nothing in nature as he experiences it to call forth the consideration which, one assumes, he feels obliged to display to his fellows.

Critics of those who are callous towards wildlife, or indifferent to the fate of forests, would often do better to charge them, not with ignorance or inconsistency, but with a distorted perception, a lack of sensibility and imagination, or a failure in appreciation of 'the good life'. Indeed, we can go further, and here I reach my main criticism. It is *incoherent* to suggest that the practices and attitudes of 'speciesists' could *per se* display inconsistency. This is not because, after all, they are being perfectly consistent, but because judgements of consistency and inconsistency are made against a background of general practices and attitudes. A particular action may be consistent or inconsistent with the general practice which informs this domain of action, just as my response to a particular case may be consistent or inconsistent with my stated attitude towards that class of cases. But, as 'setting the scene' for the particular actions and responses thus judged for their consistency, the general practices and attitudes cannot themselves be similarly judged.

It may well be, of course, that a person who participates in a general practice towards human beings, and shares the attitudes which accompany that practice, finds it natural, or even irresistible, to extend the practice and attitudes towards other species. But those who do not are not guilty – whatever else they may be guilty of – of inconsistency: for that would imply that we can identify criteria of consistency that transcend those which are implicit within a general practice or attitude. Perhaps if everyone found it natural, or irresistible, to extend benevolence to foxes or forests, we could say that it would inconsistent not to – on the grounds, urged by Wittgenstein, that in the final analysis there is no distinction between an action's being entailed by a practice and its being one which everyone engaged in that practice finds it natural to perform (Wittgenstein 1969: secs 200ff.). But, self-evidently, many people do not find it natural, let alone irresistible, to extend the principles which govern their treatment of human beings into the realm of non-human life. On the contrary, some of them find it incredible that they should be urged to do so.

'Mainstream' theorists will be ready with at least two replies to this. First, they will deploy the strategy mentioned on p. 138. *Whatever* distinctive features of human beings are cited in support of confining moral concern to people – such as rationality and moral sense – there are some 'marginal' humans who lack all these features, babies and the hopelessly senile, for instance. If, as most 'speciesists' admit, these people deserve moral concern, then it is surely irrational not to extend this concern to other creatures just because they too lack these features. 'Speciesists' sometimes reply that the cases are quite different: unlike animals or plants, babies and the senile deserve moral respect since they either will be or have been 'full' human beings. But a better reply is that a sense of obligation towards 'marginal' human beings is, at least for us moderns, a natural, almost irresistible 'spill-over' from our practices and attitudes towards 'full' human beings. This 'spill-over' is not required by considerations of consistency, unless by 'consistent' we simply mean 'natural'. We can imagine, or find in the annals of history, peoples who do not feel compelled to regard babies and the senile in the same moral light as 'full' human beings. Lack of logic is surely quite the wrong charge to level against such peoples, repulsive as they may be.

A second 'mainstream' objection to my position will be this: surely 'speciesism' is closely analogous to 'sexism' and 'racism', and these surely are paradigms of moral inconsistency. In fact, not all critics of 'speciesism' (in my sense) are fond of this analogy, pointing out, for example, that whereas knowledge of a person's race is generally irrelevant to their treatment, 'with an animal, to know the species is absolutely essential' (Midgley 1983: 98). But suppose the analogy is a good one: it will serve the 'mainstream' case only if the proper complaint against 'sexism' and 'racism' is one of inconsistency. It is absurd, however, to suppose that 'racists', say, have generally been hopelessly ignorant about the similarities and differences between races; or that they have seriously regarded 'Because they are black/white/yellow' as a *reason* for refusing to people the same consideration they show to those of their own race. Today's revulsion against 'racism' is not the result of our having learned the true facts about other peoples, or of a sudden improvement in our powers of ratiocination. Without pretending to explain this revulsion, we do better to think of it in terms of a shift in perception or sensibility. For most of us today, it is natural, or irresistible, to extend the moral regard which informs relations with people known to us to 'strangers'. But we should not suppose that people in other, earlier societies, for whom such an extension of their familiar practices and attitudes was thoroughly unnatural, were guilty of inconsistency. To do so is once again to pretend that there are criteria of moral consistency which transcend the general practices and attitudes which furnish the setting against which accusations of inconsistency make sense. My case, therefore, does not require abandonment of the comparison between 'speciesism' and 'racism': in neither instance, as I see it, are we confronted with unreason in the sense of inconsistency.

III

I have tried to be careful, as in the previous sentence, not to deny the role of reason in non-human ethics *tout court*, but to reject the 'mainstream' equation of moral unreason with inconsistency. This is important to stress, since my position is not to be confused with that of an author who claims that environmental ethics must be 'based on a feeling', and not 'rational thought', and can then urge us – surely disingenuously – to feel ourselves 'part of a whole of which no part may rationally be said to be more important than another' (Kheel 1989: 263). I say 'disingenuously', since it is hard to believe this author honestly thinks there is *no* reason to regard her son, say, as 'more important' than the lumps of mud which she washes, without a second thought, from his leg.

In this final section, then, I want to indicate some reasons for rejecting 'speciesism', for having moral regard for other species. I focus on reasons liable to be overlooked by an obsessive 'mainstream' search, in the hope of finding inconsistency in the 'speciesist' outlook, for similarities between other species and ourselves. Reasons for concern for other species fall, I suggest, into two main kinds: those to the effect that it is an ingredient in 'the good life', and those to the effect that it is required for the full exercise of the virtues. There is no sharp distinction between these kinds. Some people, indeed, following Aristotle, would equate 'the good life' with the exercise of the virtues. But this would require stretching the modern notion of a virtue so as to include, for example, appreciation of beauty, surely an aspect of 'the good life'.

How might it be argued that regard for other species of life is an ingredient in a good human life, one that is full and flourishing, rounded and satisfying? Consider, first, a cluster of related capacities which, it would be generally agreed, are conditions for such a life: imagination, openness, empathy. The life of someone who is unimaginative, closed-up, rigid, and unable to appreciate how things are for others is a stunted one. Now, it would be difficult, perhaps impossible, to show that everyone who is callous or indifferent towards non-human life *must* be lacking in the qualities of imaginativeness and the rest. But the presumption that they are is not unreasonable and, in particular cases, there is evidence for it. Men like Jim Corbett, who converted from killing tigers to protecting them, report their growing appreciation of how things must be *for* the tiger: an appreciation incompatible with a zest for shooting it. Another example: it is hard, reading the passage from Thomas Bernhard quoted above (p. 142), not to feel that there must be 'something wrong with him' in his inability to see beyond the 'malignancy' of nature. And indeed there was: the Austrian novelist's hatred of nature was of a piece with his extraordinary misanthropy ('A man approaches another only to destroy him' (Bernhard 1991: 246)), both exhibiting a monocular, closed vision of life. It is pertinent, too, to note that many of those who have treated animals appallingly have furnished themselves, ingenuously or otherwise, with theories that relieve them from imagining how things might be for the animals by denying that they have any 'inner' life or feelings. One thinks of seventeenth-century Cartesian vivisectionists, for whom animals were merely complicated machines, and many twentieth-century behaviourist experimenters, for whom there is nothing 'behind' the animals' behaviour (see Rollin 1989).

Consider, next, another aspect of 'the good life'. The lives of people who feel 'alienated' or 'cut off' from, 'strangers' to, large portions of the world about them are not full ones, not fully satisfying or, one suspects, happy. This is so whether the world in question is the social or the natural one. To feel 'at home' in the many contexts into which one is thrown is a condition of well-being. At its worst, 'alienation' from the natural is the 'unhappy consciousness' of which Hegel (1977: B.iv.B) spoke: the medievals' dichotomous sense of a soul 'shackled' to a body. Elsewhere I have suggested (Cooper 1993) that our recent sentiment towards wildlife and tragic sense of its gradual demise are not unrelated to that increasing 'rootlessness' which is a cliché – but none the worse for that – of twentieth-century literature. There is a sense in which we moderns – with our experience of ever greater mobility, of the dissolution of local communities, of bewildering technological change, of the atrophy of traditions, and of ironic distance from the conditions which momentarily prevail – no longer have environments: limited milieux, that is, in which we know our way about, smoothly and unreflectingly. Wild animals *in situ* do have these: that is why, perhaps, they can represent for us a kind of life, integrated with or 'at home' in its surroundings, that we have largely lost. As Rilke put it in his 'Eighth Elegy', 'whatever we do, we always have / the look of someone going away', unlike the animals 'who stay in the womb that bore them forever'. This may help explain why many of us are so anxious that there should continue to be these animals.

The thought that our well-being requires some 'identification' with nature is, of course, a familiar one in recent environmental literature, poetry as much as philosophy. Hence references to a 'biotic *community*' of which we are members: or, more hysterically, to Nature as a single Self in which we so-called 'individuals' are barely distinguishable ripples. It is a pity that some of those who rightly stress the importance of some sense of identity with non-human life suppose that it is bound to promote a benign attitude. In fact, many nineteenth-century followers of Darwin – though not Darwin himself – deduced from our immersion in the natural order that we are engaged in a 'no holds barred' struggle with other species for survival: one in which we, as the 'fittest', should feel no qualms about the species which go under.

That, of course, is a hubristic attitude, one of the several ancestors of today's stance of technological domination over nature. The antidote to this is not another dose of the message that we are 'one with' nature but a recognition that, for all our continuity with it, nature is also 'the Other' to the human world of culture. Unlike leather and paper, which belong to culture, the animals and trees from which they are made are not themselves 'equipment', 'resources' or 'standing reserve', as Heidegger (1977: 17ff.) put it. Appreciation of this is itself an ingredient in 'the good life': for otherwise life threatens to become answerable only to the hubristic imperative of a febrile chase after affluence, one which, in Heidegger's words again, 'drives out' other perspectives on our existence, including those which might give to a controlled desire for affluence its point.

Let me turn to the second kind of reason for concerning ourselves with other species. There are, it seems to me, generally acknowledged virtues whose exercise requires this. I focus on the cluster of virtues which include responsibility, care, kindness and solicitude. Environmental philosophers often invite us to consider, and condemn, the behaviour of the last person, indeed the last animal, on earth who decides to destroy its lakes and forests. That this is wrong, they argue, shows that nature has 'intrinsic' or 'inherent' value, since the destruction cannot, *ex hypothesi*, adversely affect human beings or other animals. But there is an alternative diagnosis:

> what makes the vandalism . . . so objectionable is the vandalizer's attitude – that is, that it is an act of vandalism – and not the fact that the resultant world would lack some good that it would have independently of there being any one to appreciate it.
>
> (Kleinig 1991: 89)

This, it seems to me, is right. *Wanton* destruction of anything, including things few could regard as 'intrinsically' valuable, is always disturbing: for it manifests a peculiarly nihilistic attitude, incompatible with a sense of responsibility. Responsible people have to destroy things, including living things, but not wantonly, for the sheer hell of it.

Responsibility, as in the case of so-called 'carers', often demands, of course, much more than a presumption in favour of the existence of things and a consequent circumspection in one's destructive activities. It demands kindness and care. There is a cynical view, honoured by the title 'contractarian ethics', according to which we are only bound to exercise these virtues because of an implicit 'agreement' with other people that they will reciprocate when we are in need. On that view, we cannot be bound to show kindness and care towards animals. But it is a bizarre view, since these virtues are most purely exercised when we have nothing to expect in return. It is precisely because animals are relatively helpless and incapable of reciprocating the solicitude we extend to them that, according to Kant, 'we can judge the heart of a man by his treatment of animals' (Kant 1963: 241). (Compare Milan Kundera: 'Mankind's . . . funda-mental test . . . consists of its attitude towards those who are at its mercy: animals' (Kundera 1986: 289).) The care I show towards my fellows is, in comparison, too compounded with prudential considerations to provide as clear a test of my 'heart'. Someone who needs to ask why kindness towards animals, and not just towards humans, should be shown already displays that they are lacking in this virtue: for a virtue, though it may need to be learned and practised, is a disposition that 'comes naturally', a matter, if you like, of the 'heart'. Incidentally, I do not think one needs, eccentrically, to regard plants and trees as sentient in order to suppose that kindness and solicitude can be shown towards them too.

I close with a couple of predictable objections to my approach in this section. First, the complaint will be made that it is 'anthropocentric', since the reasons I have suggested for concern for other species include an appeal to 'the good life' of human beings. But if an anthropocentric reason is one which invokes human interests 'narrowly defined', such as health and affluence, then the complaint does not apply. If, though, anthropocentric reasons are ones which engage with what matters to us, with our conception of how our lives should be led, then no doubt my approach has been anthropocentric – but that is no cause for complaint. Reasons for doing or feeling are reasons for us. To serve as such, they must be capable of motivating us; and to do that, they must engage with what we want. Claims about the 'inherent' value of nature, made in an anti-anthropocentric spirit, could never provide us with reasons to care about nature, unless it could also be shown that so caring is implied by, or answers to, the ways in which we care about our own lives.

Second, it will be charged that some, at least, of the reasons I have suggested are not, strictly, moral ones. It may be 'a good thing' to live without a sense of being 'cut off' from the natural world, but it is hardly a duty or obligation. My response is: so much the worse for the 'strict' sense of morality if it restricts discussion of our treatment of other species, and indeed of one another, to matters of duties and rights. I am not sure how prevalent, outside of philosophy depart-ments, this 'strict' sense is, but it is certainly a rather recent one. My own predilection, it should be clear, is for a traditional notion of moral reason – one going back, certainly, to the Greeks – in which the central questions are those of 'the good life' and the exercise of the virtues: questions all too liable to be ignored by 'stricter' approaches that elevate the right over the good. Given the intimate connection between the concept of justice and those of duty and rights, it will follow, of course, that for those who share this predilection, the vocabulary of justice is not the most felicitous one in which to express a concern for other species.

11 Animal farming and the environment[1,2]

Alan T. Durning and Holly B. Brough

INTRODUCTION

Rings of barren earth spread out from wells on the grasslands of the former Soviet Turkmenia. Heather and lilies wilt in the nature preserves of the southern Netherlands. Forests teeming with rare forms of plant and animal life explode in flame in Costa Rica. Water-tables fall and fossil fuels are wasted in the United States. Each of these cases of environmental decline issues from a single source: the global livestock industry.

Traditionally, farm animals have played an indispensable role in keeping agriculture on a sound ecological footing by returning nutrients to the soil as manure, providing draught power, and grazing fallow fields. But today, some methods of raising cattle, pigs and poultry have put these animals at odds with the environment.

During the past fifty years, livestock industries have surged in one country after another as soaring grain yields made feeding animals on corn and barley relatively inexpensive, and intensive, specialized meat, egg and dairy farms proliferated. In much of the world meat consumption is climbing steadily; domesticated animals now outnumber humans three to one.

The factory-style livestock industries, now firmly entrenched in industrial countries, have environmental side-effects that stretch along the production line – from growing the vast quantities of feed grain to disposing of the mountains of manure. In developing regions, meanwhile, most livestock continue to be raised as a sideline to crops. Yet complex economic and social forces lead to mismanagement of herds, causing extensive and sometimes irreversible degradation of drylands and destruction of forests. World-wide, larger livestock populations emit the potent greenhouse gas methane into the atmosphere, contributing to climate change. High levels of meat consumption and production cause human losses as well. Meat-rich diets contribute to the diseases of affluence – such as heart disease, stroke and certain types of cancer – which are leading causes of death in industrial countries. Furthermore, rising meat consumption among the fortunate in developing societies sometimes squeezes out food production for the poor and boosts imports of feed grains.

Livestock create an array of problems not because cows, pigs and chickens are hazards in themselves, but because human institutions have driven some forms of animal farming out of alignment with the ecosystems in which they operate. Many governments – including those of China, the European Community and the United States – subsidize ecologically harmful methods of growing feed crops and raising animals. In Africa, expanding croplands and misguided development plans have reduced herding peoples' traditional range. And in South Asia, national laws have undermined villages' customary systems of grazing management.

Reversing these trends will not be easy, as many of the driving forces – such as population growth, inequitable development strategies, and economies that fail to reflect environmental costs in resource prices – are far broader and deeper than the livestock sector. Still, animal agriculture's worst offences can be redressed. Doing so will require eliminating governments' favouritism towards the industry, taxing or regulating environmentally destructive practices, and restructuring development strategies. More importantly, it will call for a rethinking of meat's role in diet. If livestock are to live in balance with the environment again, First World consumers will have to eat less meat, while Third World citizens will need to keep their meat consumption low.

LIVESTOCK ECONOMY

Domesticated animals have played a prominent role in the human economy for thousands of years, providing food, fuel, fertilizer, transport and clothing. During most of this time, their presence was largely beneficial. But in this century, the numbers and impacts of livestock have swelled apace with human population and affluence. Since mid-century, human numbers have doubled to 5.4 billion, while the number of four-legged livestock has grown from 2.3 billion to 4 billion. At the same time, the fowl population has multiplied from about 3 billion to nearly 11 billion. There are now three times as many domestic animals as people.

The world's most populous countries, China and India, are also the livestock titans. But population figures fail to reflect an important difference between First World and Third World animals. First-World animals live much shorter lives: well-fed American steers and broiler chickens, for example, reach marketable weights in one-fourth to one-half the time of Chinese ones. Thus, at any given instant, China has more chickens than the United States, but during a year's time, the United States raises and slaughters three times as many. As a result, the herds and flocks of the rich countries produce 61 per cent of the world's meat, 55 per cent of the eggs and 72 per cent of the milk.

Yet animals provide things besides food. Cattle were originally domesticated as beasts of burden, and throughout Asia and Africa, 80–90 per cent of agricultural land is still ploughed with draught animals. In India, livestock carry about half of all goods to market. Manure is a precious fertilizer and fuel in developing countries, and is collected and traded widely. The Chinese refer to pigs as four-legged fertilizer factories, and for centuries they have gathered every trace of manure for use in their fields. In the Sahel, farmers allow nomadic herders, or 'pastoralists', to graze their herds on crop residues after the harvest in return for the deposited manure. Though goats in India are prized for their milk, the average dryland farmer earns more cash from the manure.

Livestock are also wise investments. On farms that raise animals with crops, livestock shield farmers' incomes from the vagaries of the market and the weather. Their milk and meat provide supplemental cash, and if a crop fails, animals can eat the unharvestable plants. When the nearest bank is miles away, cattle become savings accounts. A six-year study in Lesotho found that investing in cattle earned farms the equivalent of a 10 per cent interest rate, while a bank account lost 10 per cent because of inflation. Not surprisingly, farmers put their money in cattle rather than banks.

In countries such as Botswana, cattle are esteemed not just for monetary reasons, but as a yardstick of social prestige. 'A man's wealth is measured not by his land or by his house, but by the number of cattle that he has', according to one Bayei tribe member. Cattle comprise the dowries of women and occasionally the payment for a good traditional doctor, and villagers eagerly trade all other livestock for cattle. In India, Hinduism preaches a reverence for cows that, together with the animals' economic value to poor households, helps account for the world's largest cattle population.

Livestock largely define the lives of pastoralists, the 30–43 million herders scattered on the world's drylands. Pastoralists prize cattle for their milk as savings accounts, and as coins of the realm. A traditional proverb of the Masai people of East Africa runs, 'One heifer is worth a man's head.' Pastoralists generally migrate with their herds between wet- and dry-season range, a practice finely tuned to difficult environments.

The world's goats and sheep, often disparaged as lowly and environmentally destructive, are actually a critical link in the poor's struggle for survival. Gandhi, for example, dubbed the goat the 'poor man's cow'. From meagre rations, goats provide meat in more manageable quantities than cows, as well as milk, fibre, hides and manure. They are also readily traded for goods or cash. Their hardy bodies can withstand drought better than cattle, and their procreative powers allow herds to recover more quickly from dry periods. In many countries, the 'poor man's cow' is also the poor woman's source of income. Though traditions vary, men across Africa and Asia generally control and herd cattle and camels, while women are responsible for goats and poultry. Processing and selling the milk, cream or liquefied butter from both cattle and goats is also women's domain. In Bangladesh, women often look after the small animals of the rich to earn an equal share of the offspring – one of the few economic activities they control.

Still, at a global level, the primary goal of raising livestock is to produce meat, milk and eggs. Meat has always been popular among those able to afford it, and over the centuries that group has swelled. More than a billion people now consume at least a kilogram a week. Meat consumption per person around the world ranges from a high of 112 kilograms a year in the United States to a low of 2 kilograms in India. National meat-consumption figures generally reflect income levels, with rich countries eating more meat than poor ones. But culture, religion, national taste and natural resource endowments also play an important role in dietary habits. Muslim teachings proscribe pork, for example, so Muslim nations consume little, while Hindus generally shun red meat of any type. Island nations such as Japan opt for seafood, while land-rich developing nations such as Argentina eat large amounts of beef and mutton.

With the ascent of the meat-eating class world-wide, global meat production has soared, nearly quadrupling since 1950. In 1990, the world produced 170 million metric tons – 32 kilograms per person. Among meats, pork is the world leader, and China is pork's leading consumer. Chinese pigs, though scrawny by western standards, are numerous enough to yield 35 per cent of the world's pork. The European Community (EC), where pork consumption has long been high, accounts for another 20 per cent. The former Soviet Union and Eastern Europe have increased production dramatically in recent decades – to about 10 per cent of global output apiece – by importing western livestock feed.

Beef production – dominated by large countries such as the United States, the former Soviet Union and Argentina – has risen slowly since 1976, when health-conscious North Americans (and, to a lesser extent, Europeans) began to cut back on beef in favour of less expensive poultry. Economic turmoil in Brazil and Argentina has also slowed the rise.

Poultry is the fastest-growing part of the global meat market, and chicken the most popular type of fowl, accounting for 68 per cent of poultry meat world-wide. Forty years ago, chicken meat was a scarce and expensive by-product of egg production. But the advent of abundant feed grains, drugs to prevent poultry diseases, and improved breeds allowed American farmers to start raising chickens on a massive scale. American-style chicken farming, using large buildings with controlled temperature and lighting, passed quickly to Europe, Japan, the former Soviet Union, Taiwan, Brazil, the Middle East and other regions, and poultry consumption is expanding rapidly.

Aside from meat, the most lucrative livestock products are milk, eggs and wool. Indeed, in Europe and India, dairy products surpass beef in economic value. World milk production is centred in Europe, the Soviet Union and North America, which together account for 75 per cent of global output. The total world-wide output of dairy products has doubled since mid-century, just keeping pace with population growth. Among major dairy products, only cheese has followed meat on the steady path of climbing per-person consumption; cheese production world-wide has doubled since 1970. World butter and milk consumption, by contrast, has climbed fitfully. Countries such as the former Soviet Union and India have boosted output, and western nations concerned about their fat intake have cut back, switching from butter to margarine. Egg-consumption trends have run roughly parallel to those of milk. The world's most affluent consumers eat fewer eggs than they did a decade ago, partly through health concerns, while consumers in middle-income countries eat more.

The world market for wool, meanwhile, has scarcely grown for two decades because of the profusion of inexpensive synthetic textiles made mostly from petroleum by-products. Since sheep are raised more for wool than for meat, sheep populations have been nearly constant throughout that period.

The modern demand for meat can no longer be sustained by traditional livestock production systems, which integrated animals with crops. Outside of the world's grasslands, most ruminant (cud-chewing) animals such as cattle and sheep traditionally ate grass and crop wastes on farms. Pigs and fowl, which cannot digest grass, subsisted on crop wastes, kitchen scraps and whatever else they could find. In either case, domestic animals turned things that people could not eat into things people could.

To raise meat output, livestock producers have adopted new, intensive rearing techniques relying on grains and legumes to feed their animals. For example, farmers have moved virtually all of the pigs and poultry in industrial countries into gigantic indoor feeding facilities. There, they eat carefully measured rations of energy-rich grain and protein-rich soya-bean meal. Cattle everywhere still spend most of their lives dining outdoors on grass, although some beef producers supplement that roughage with grain in the months before slaughter.

Large areas of the world's cropland now produce grains for animals. Roughly 38 per cent of the world's grain – especially corn, barley, sorghum and oats – is fed to livestock, up from 35 per cent in 1960. Wealthy meat-consuming regions dedicate the largest shares of their grain to fattening livestock, while the poorest regions use the least grain as feed. In the United States, for example, animals account for 70 per cent of domestic grain use, while India and sub-Saharan Africa offer just 2 per cent of their cereal harvest to livestock.

The expansion of the livestock economy has been the most dramatic change in world agriculture in recent decades. World-wide the focus of livestock production has shifted from the multiple benefits of manure, draught power, milk and eggs towards meat production. Along the way, factory-style production facilities have sprung up in much of the world, capitalizing on grain surpluses, advanced production technologies and a growing global class of consumers rich enough to eat meat regularly. But abundance in the world's butcher shops has its costs – many of which are currently billed to the earth.

LIVESTOCK ECOLOGY

'An alien ecologist observing . . . earth might conclude that cattle is the dominant animal species in our biosphere', writes University of Georgia biologist David Hamilton Wright (1990). Cattle and other ruminant livestock such as sheep and goats graze one-half of the planet's total land area. Ruminants, along with pigs and poultry, also eat feed and fodder raised on one-fourth of the cropland. Ubiquitous and familiar, livestock exert a huge, and largely unrecognized, impact on the global environment.

For hundreds of years, and even today in many parts of the world, livestock rearing served as a critical counterpart to crop production in agriculture, keeping farms ecologically balanced. Growing hay, legumes and other fodder for farm animals provides an economic motivation for environmentally sound crop rotation. Pastures and fodder fields suffer less soil erosion and absorb more water than row-crop fields, and nitrogen-fixing fodder plants such as alfalfa also improve soil fertility. Livestock sometimes provide weeding services too. Sheep weeded American corn fields before the Second World War, and ducks and geese still control weeds on South-East Asian farms.

Ecological burdens result from both modern, intensive livestock production methods – such as chicken and pig feeding houses and beef feedlots – and extensive forms – such as ranching and pastoralism. The environmental effects of intensive livestock operations run from grain fields to manure piles. And unsustainable grazing and ranching patterns of impoverished and affluent regions alike sacrifice forests, drylands and wild species. Multiple forces have disturbed traditional pastoralists' ecologically sound livestock systems, leaving herders to crowd with their animals in areas where the land is quickly laid to waste.

The concentrated feeding facilities of the industrial and newly industrializing countries use vast quantities of grain and soy, along with the energy, water and agricultural chemicals that farmers use to grow these crops. Pork production absorbs more grain world-wide than any other meat industry, followed by poultry production. Together they account for at least two-thirds of feed-grain consumption. Dairy and beef cattle consume much of the remaining third.

The efficiency with which livestock industries turn feed into meat, milk and eggs varies among the different types of animals and different countries. The United States, one of the more efficient livestock producers, uses 6.9 kilograms of corn and soya to put one kilogram of pork on the table. Farmers in other countries, notably the former Soviet Union, are less efficient, and use more grain for each unit of meat, milk or eggs – twice as much in the case of chicken.

Other resources add to the livestock and feed industry's environmental tab, such as the fossil fuels used to supply feed grain. Including fuel for powering farm machinery and for manufacturing fertilizers and pesticides, feed grain turns out to be an energy-intensive product. US corn fields – producing mostly feed – alone consume about 40 per cent of the country's nitrogen fertilizer, along with more total herbicides and insecticides than any other crop.

Moreover, almost half of the energy used in American agriculture goes into the livestock sector, and producing the red meat and poultry eaten each year by a typical American uses the equivalent of 190 litres of gasoline. Feed-grain farming guzzles water, too. In California, now the United States' leading dairy state, livestock agriculture consumes nearly one-third of all irrigation water. The beef feedlot centre of the nation – Colorado, Kansas, Nebraska and the Texas panhandle – relies on crops raised with water pumped out of an underground water source called the Ogallala aquifer, portions of which have been severely depleted.

With half of the grain and hay fed to American beef cattle growing on irrigated land, water inputs for beef production mount. More than 3,000 litres of water are used to produce a kilogram of American beef. Water use for pork, poultry and dairy production in the United States is much lower, because those industries are generally concentrated in areas where grain fields need no irrigation. Still, the water used to supply each American with meat, milk and eggs each day probably matches a typical American's daily water use at home, about 380 litres.

Meat production in other wealthy countries rings up similar resource costs. Japanese beef-cattle producers typically feed their animals twice as much grain as American beef cattle consume, aiming to produce the butter-soft beef Japanese consumers covet. In New Zealand, by contrast, sheep and cattle are raised purely on grass, with the result that energy use per kilogram of mutton or beef is one-fourth the level in the United Kingdom.

With so much feed, water and energy going into livestock production, other things are bound to come out. The most distinctive is manure, a valuable organic fertilizer and soil-builder in modest quantities but a dangerous pollutant in excess. Recent history in Hungary – a major meat-exporting and meat-consuming country – exemplifies the transformation of manure from resource to hazardous waste product. From 1960 to 1986, as the number of animals slaughtered in the country doubled, the use of manure as a fertilizer fell by one-fifth. Farmers opted for easy-to-spread chemical fertilizers instead of trucking manure from centralized feeding facilities. In the United States as well, much manure is wasted. For example, factory-style pig-raising enterprises rarely make full use of more than one-sixth of the fertilizing value of manure. Breaking the nutrient loop that once connected crops and livestock has left agriculture with problems at each end: high fertilizer bills and high waste-disposal costs.

The millions of tons of animal waste that accumulate at modern production facilities can pollute rivers and groundwater if precautions are not taken. If they get into rivers or open bodies of water, nitrogen and phosphorus in manure over-fertilize algae, which grow rapidly, deplete oxygen supplies, and suffocate aquatic ecosystems. From the hundreds of algae-choked Italian lakes to the murky Chesapeake Bay, and from the oxygen-starved Baltic Sea to the polluted Adriatic Sea, animal wastes add to the nutrient loads from fertilizer run-off, human sewage and urban and industrial pollution.

In the Netherlands, the pork-producing centre of Western Europe, manure is a major ecological threat. Sprayed over the fields month after month, nitrate and phosphate have saturated surface layers of soil and contaminated water in many parts of the area, pushing freshwater ecosystems into decline. The EC now terms the Netherlands, Belgium and France 'manure-surplus' regions: they produce more manure than their land can absorb.

Manure nitrogen, mixed with nitrogen from artificial fertilizers, also percolates through the soil into underground water-tables as nitrates. These substances can cause nervous-system impairments, cancer and methaemoglobinaemia, or 'blue-baby' syndrome, a rare but deadly malady afflicting infants. Nitrate contamination is pervasive in Western Europe, from Spain to Denmark, and is apparently widespread in Eastern Europe as well. Manure nitrogen also escapes into the air as gaseous ammonia, a pollutant that causes acid rain and other forms of acid deposition. The ammonia that the livestock industry discharges into the air is the single largest source of acid deposited on Dutch soils – doing more damage than the country's cars or factories, according to the country's National Institute of Public Health and Environmental Protection. The problem is less severe in other parts of Europe, with ammonia emissions per hectare generally less than one-fourth the Dutch rate. Still, concentrated livestock production everywhere runs the risk of contaminating surrounding areas with acids.

Extensive livestock production, like modern intensive production, has environmental side-effects. Many of the world's rangelands, covering one-third of the earth's land surface, bear the scars of improper livestock management: proliferating weeds, depleted soils and eroded landscapes. In Africa, swelling human populations, shrinking rangeland, the collapse of traditional systems of range management and misdirected development policies have conspired to concentrate cattle around water resources and towns, degrading the land. Elsewhere, many arid rangelands suffer from overstocking and mismanagement, while ranching in the tropical regions of Latin America – fostered by subsidies and land speculation – depletes forests and soils.

Cattle play a prominent role in global desertification – the reduction of dryland's ecological productivity. The process, however, is far more complex and varied than the word 'desertification', conjuring images of sand-dunes swallowing the range, implies. Initially, cattle over-graze perennial grasses, allowing annual weeds and tougher shrubs to spread. This shift in species composition is the most prevalent form of range degradation. The new weeds anchor the topsoil poorly, and can leave it vulnerable to trampling hoofs and the erosive power of wind and rain. Without the cover of perennial grasses, fires that naturally control bushes lose their tinder, so shrubs expand unchecked. As the variety of plant species dwindles, wildlife species also vanish.

Under persistent grazing, the bare ground becomes impermeable to rainwater, which then courses off the surface, carrying away topsoil and scouring stream beds into deep gullies. Upstream, water-tables fall for lack of replenishment; downstream, flooding occurs more frequently and sediment clogs waterways, dams and estuaries. In drier climates wind sweeps away the destabilized soil. Although the environmental status of drier rangeland may defy simple quantification, there is little debate that degradation is occurring in environments where rainfall is more plentiful and regular. The perennial plants that flourish in these intermediate zones are easily disrupted by cattle; clay soils are easily compacted and rendered impervious to water; and rains often arrive in strong, sudden downpours, sluicing away soils destabilized by cattle. In addition, these areas can support crops, so farmers have crowded pastoralists and their herds on to smaller areas, accelerating degradation.

Pastoralists have been accused wrongly of overstocking cattle and destroying range because it was common land. But traditionally, they managed their herds to accommodate the unpredictable environment, expanding them during rainy years so that a few animals might survive when drought returned. Moreover, since pastoralists depend on marginal rangeland, they have developed systems to control its use. The Zaghawa of Niger, for instance, move their camels and sheep north to wet-season Saharan pastures in separate, parallel paths, leaving ungrazed strips for their return treks. More commonly, pastoralists restrict access to dry-season range to reserve these fodder supplies for when they are most needed.

In truth, pastoralists are victims, rather than culprits, of environmental degradation. Chief among the actual causes is human population growth both inside and outside of pastoral communities. This is obvious in the southern regions of the Sahel, where the number of people has more than doubled since 1960. Cropland has expanded by one-third, and in the southern Sudan, the cultivation of millet has extended 200 kilometres north of the margin of crop-sustaining soil. Much of this expansion has occurred at the expense of range formerly used by pastoralists. State farms and peasants have sowed crops in river valleys and around water sources previously used by pastoralists during the dry season, pushing herds on to drier lands.

Unfortunately, the well-intentioned development plans of governments and aid agencies often worsened environmental conditions. Starting in the fifties, for example, the World Bank and other organizations supported borehole, or deep-well, drilling in dry areas previously inaccessible to cattle. In Botswana, boreholes extended grazing land by two-and-a-half times. Lacking traditional mechanisms to control access to the wells, herders let their cattle strip the surrounding lands of vegetation and crush them to moonscapes. As a result, rings of windswept sand extend more than 10 kilometers from boreholes in the Kgalagadi district of Botswana. This process is not, of course, limited to Africa.

National governments, eager to control and tax pastoralists, have encouraged them to settle in farming communities, grazing reserves or group ranches. Pastoralists have brought their herds to these new homes, but at an environmental cost. One irrigation scheme in the Sudan, for instance, replaced critical dry-season range with tenant farms. Managers strongly urged herders to work there, but discouraged keeping livestock, considering them pests. Though herders need their animals to survive when wage labour is unavailable, they cannot spare the time to take the herds elsewhere during the dry season. As a result, animals stay on the sandy range year-round, suffering deprivation and degrading the land.

Group ranches established in Kenya in the mid-sixties and grazing reserved in Nigeria have suffered their own problems. Because the best soils were already farmed, these projects were generally located on poor land: many of Kenya's group ranches contained no dry-season pasture or permanent water sources. In both countries, herders had to move their animals beyond property lines to survive, adding pressure to a dwindling range already burdened by the herds of other pastoralists. Though the situation persists in Nigeria, President Daniel Arap Moi recently disbanded group ranches in Kenya.

Finally, as rangeland shrinks, some wealthy farmers and herders are fencing remaining land for private use. This 'land grab' is occurring around permanent water sources in southern Somalia. Although the Somalian government owns all rangeland, it allows private ownership of farmland. Herders with money and political clout are fencing land near water as 'farmland', but reserving most of it for dry-season grazing. Like group ranchers, they spread their herds on the overcrowded communal range for much of the year, accelerating land degradation.

Outside of Africa, rangeland deterioration is more often directly attributable to mismanagement and overstocking. Savannahs and open shrubland make up the bulk of rangelands in South America, but their acidic soils yield poor-quality forage ill-suited to heavy stocking rates. None the less, ranchers commonly overstock their land with cattle, leading to weed invasion and erosion. In the temperate rangelands of Argentina, Paraguay and Bolivia, the loss of plant cover has intensified surface evaporation and led to soil salinization.

Wealthy nations are not immune from the effects of over-grazing on rangeland. Spain and Portugal still bear the scars of pro-sheep land policies that began hundreds of years ago. The western United States is likewise left with a sad legacy: the great cattle boom of the last century annihilated native mixed-grass ecosystems. And unsustainable practices – including overstocking and grazing cattle for too long in the same place – continue on much of the 110-million-hectare area of public land the federal government leases to ranchers.

In Australia as in the western United States, the worst over-grazing occurred a century ago in uncontrolled cattle drives, but the damage remains and over-grazing continues. Sheep and cattle graze 60 per cent of Australia's land, and half of the area they graze is in the arid and semi-arid zone. On those dry plains, some 56 per cent of the area has suffered from a shift in vegetation; 13 per cent of it is severely degraded.

Damage to rangeland is only one measure of the destructiveness of current grazing patterns. Forests also suffer from livestock production, as branches are cut for fodder or entire stands are levelled to make way for pastures. The roster of impacts from forest clearing includes the loss of watershed protection, loss of plant and animal species, and on a larger scale, substantial contributions of the greenhouse gas carbon dioxide to the atmosphere.

In India, the loss of forest to cattle stems from the lack of grazing land. India is home to 196 million head of cattle – 15 per cent of the global herd – but its 12 million hectares of permanent pasture are vastly inadequate to the needs of these animals. By comparison, the cattle country of Uruguay has 13 million hectares for 10 million beasts. Moreover, India's common land, crucial to the animals of the poor, has shrunk by about one-fourth over the past forty years. State forests, roadsides, and fallow lands have to make up the fodder deficit, but most cows still go hungry. Meanwhile, the need for fodder increases pressure on forest. In the Himalayas, Nepal has lost perhaps half its forests during the past twenty years, partly to fodder collection, and much of what remains is degraded.

Latin America has suffered the most dramatic forest loss due to inappropriate livestock production. Since 1970, farmers and ranchers have converted more than 20 million hectares of the region's moist tropical forests to cattle pasture. In Brazil, Bolivia and Colombia, forests are cleared primarily for pasture, and only subsistence farming destroys more forest in Peru, Venezuela and Ecuador. In the Brazilian Amazon, for example, about 10 million hectares have been cleared for cattle, though recent estimates indicate a decline in annual forest loss. According to the UN Food and Agriculture Organization (FAO) (1976), Central America has lost more than one-third of its forests since the early sixties; land in pasture, meanwhile, has climbed by at least 50 per cent. In Honduras, from 1952 to 1974, pasture in the highlands expanded by two-and-a-half times, and nearly 70 per cent of deforested land in Panama and Costa Rica is now pasture.

Eradicating tree cover sets the wheels of land degradation in motion. Shallow, acidic and nutrient-poor, tropical soils rapidly lose critical phosphorus and other nutrients when the forest is converted to pasture. To compensate for the fertility decline, ranchers often stock newly cleared land at four times the standard rate of one cow per hectare, which accelerates erosion and the vegetation shift to annual weeds and shrubs. Stocking rates fall precipitously thereafter, and most pasture is abandoned within a decade for land newly carved from the forest.

Where forests recede before advancing ranches, so too does the diversity of life. The tropical forests, covering just 7 per cent of the earth's land area, contain perhaps half of the earth's species. A typical hectare in the Brazilian Amazon, for example, hosts 300–500 different plant species, plus mammals, birds, reptiles, and thousands of distinct types of insects and micro-organisms, many of them unknown to science.

Forest destruction for ranching also contributes to climate change. When living plants are cut down and burned, or when they decompose, they release carbon into the atmosphere as the greenhouse gas carbon dioxide. In the atmosphere, carbon dioxide traps the heat of the sun, warming the earth. Since 1970, the expansion of pastures into Latin American forests has released an estimated 1.4 billion tons of carbon to the atmosphere, more than the United States (the world's leading carbon emitter) released in 1990.

In addition, livestock are a source of the second-most important greenhouse gas, methane. Ruminant animals release perhaps 80 million tons of the gas each year in belches and flatulence, while animal wastes at feedlots and factory-style farms emit another 35 million tons. In such operations, waste is commonly stored in the oxygen-short environments of sewage lagoons and manure piles, where methane forms during decomposition. Manure that falls in the fields, by contrast, decomposes without releasing methane because oxygen is present. Livestock account for 15–20 per cent of global methane emissions – about 3 per cent of global warming from all gases.

From the most immediate impacts – nitrogen contamination and retreating grasses – to the most far-reaching – loss of species and climate change – current methods of rearing animals around the world take a large toll on nature. Overgrown and resource-intensive, animal agriculture is out of alignment with the earth's ecosystems.

TILL THE COWS COME HOME

A meat-fed world now appears to be a chimera. World grain production has grown more slowly than population since 1984, and farmers lack new methods for repeating the gains of the 'green revolution'. Supporting the world's current population of 5.4 billion people on an American-style diet would require two-

and-a-half times as much grain as the world's farmers produce for all purposes. A future world of 8–14 billion people eating the American ration of 220 grams of grain-fed meat a day can be nothing but a flight of fancy.

Of necessity, a sustainable livestock system would be significantly smaller than the present one. Rich countries should expect to reduce their meat consumption, while developing nations should slow the growth of their meat intake. A study by David Pimentel and his colleagues at Cornell University (1980) estimated the potential for producing meat, milk and eggs in the United States without using feed grain. Such a system, they concluded, would save enormously on natural resources, reducing energy inputs by 60 per cent, for example. However, it would produce no more than half as much animal protein as the present grain-based system.

Fostering a sustainable livestock industry will require reintegrating livestock with crops where such farming systems have disappeared and nourishing them where they survive. It will also require reorientating rangeland management towards maintaining functional ecosystems rather than maximizing beef production. In the long run, farms supporting their animals with locally available feed and fodder – and carefully using manure – could restore livestock to a more beneficial position in human societies. Yet achieving that goal will ultimately depend on fundamental changes both inside and outside the livestock sector.

Many of the environmental problems associated with livestock production – whether excessive resource consumption in the First World or forest loss and land degradation in the Third World – have deeper roots. Below the subsidies and biased policies are the more entrenched forces of land speculation, population growth, and resources priced too low to reflect their environmental costs. Changes in livestock-sector policies cannot alter these factors, but addressing them directly would dramatically transform the livestock economy.

As overall economic reforms advance in the former Soviet Union, for example, the efficiency of resource use in animal farming will undoubtedly improve. The country wastes 10–15 per cent of its feed grain simply by failing to supplement livestock rations with essential protein-rich soya-bean meal. Likewise, much Russian milk spoils on the way to market for lack of efficient food distribution. Freer markets should trim such waste.

World-wide, much larger benefits would come from adopting systems of environmental taxation. Comprehensive efforts to tax products on the basis of their ecological costs would make fossil fuels far more expensive, reflecting the impacts of fuel combustion on air quality and climate stability. As a result, feed farmers would have to pay more for synthetic fertilizers and pesticides – which require fossil fuels for their manufacture – encouraging them to make better use of manure as a fertilizer. Factory-style animal-feeding operations would have to pay more for grain, encouraging them to decentralize to tap cheaper fodder supplies. All told, the price of meat might double or triple if the full ecological costs – including fossil-fuel combustion, groundwater depletion, agricultural-chemical pollution and methane and ammonia emissions – were included in the bill.

Other changes outside of the livestock sector are equally critical. Where land ownership is ambiguous, as in the forests of Latin America, establishing secure property rights for tribal groups and settled peasants would strengthen their hand against real-estate speculators. Where human numbers are growing and range shrinking too rapidly for traditional land uses to survive, as among pastoralists in Africa, curbing population growth and providing alternative livelihoods for some pastoralists would alleviate pressures on the land. Where state forests are over-burdened by villagers gathering fodder and fuelwood, as in India and Nepal, returning control of the woodlands to local communities would help re-establish effective forest management.

If the ultimate success of livestock-production reform depends on actions outside of the livestock sector, internal change is also indispensable. In industrial countries, priority must be given to appropriate government programmes and regulations for controlling pollution from factory-style production. In the Third World, innovative approaches are sorely needed for restoring traditional, extensive production methods to environmental balance. Finally, citizens everywhere – fully informed about healthy eating – can help restore livestock production to sustainability by adjusting their diets.

On the pollution front, several European nations are already taking steps to curb the run-off of manure into bodies of water. In parts of Germany and Austria farmers must plough liquid manure into the soil within twenty-four hours of spreading it. Denmark limits the quantity of waste the nation's farmers can spread on their land. Similarly, the Dutch are combating acid rains from manure-generated ammonia by covering manure piles and installing ammonia traps in the vents of indoor animal farms.

Unfortunately, pollution-control regulations sometimes overemphasize technological measures, with counter-productive results. For example, US regulations controlling water pollution from feedlots have accelerated the concentration of the industry because the mandated control techniques are cheaper to use in large facilities. Concentrated livestock production makes the use of diverse local feed and fodder difficult, impedes the return of manure to the soil, and boosts the share of wastes that are stockpiled in methane-generating conditions such as heaps and lagoons.

Livestock policies in developing countries need to address land degradation first. In Africa, this will mean building on pastoralists' traditions that allowed them to track shifting fodder supplies. Access to land is the critical foundation. Though some traditional range has disappeared, existing dry-season areas can be fenced and pastoralist associations established to regulate their use. Sadly, since most rulers in Africa have farming roots, pastoralists' need for land security receives little attention. In fact, most African range is state property. Mauritania is an exception: it recently granted pastoralists grazing and water rights on their traditional range, though enforcement measures are not yet in place.

Where pastoralists have lost their reserve of dry-season range, alternatives must be found. One promising approach is to reinvigorate the declining practice of farmers allowing pastoralists' herds on to their fallow and harvested land. Another approach, pioneered by the International Livestock Centre for Africa

(ILCA) in Addis Ababa, Ethiopia, employs 'fodder banks'. When seasonal rains begin, herders plant leguminous trees in fenced areas of 1–4 hectares, and feed their cattle there in the dry season when range grass is sparse. In alternate years, crops can be planted to capitalize on the build-up of manure. Fodder banks work well when herders have money for the investment and secure land rights.

Where loss of range or crumbling management traditions now limit herder mobility, herds may need to be reduced. The difficulty is that while the total number of cattle may be destructive, each family often owns fewer animals than it needs to survive. Buying out their herds can further impoverish them. As alternatives, governments can improve markets so herders can easily sell – and buy back – livestock. To assure economic security outside of cattle, ILCA is examining strategies to help pastoralists to bank some of their cattle-derived income. Though fraught with logistical and cultural constraints, the concept is noteworthy for its attempt to work with, rather than against, pastoralists' logic. In addition, encouraging herders to return to mixed herds of animals can help spread their economic risks and use the range more efficiently.

In other parts of the Third World, stall-feeding holds promise. Farmers confine their animals in pens and gather grass and fodder from their farms or common land. The benefits are multiple: it saves on precious farmland, halts over-grazing, and makes manure easy to collect. CIPAV, a non-governmental organization in Cali, Colombia, is successfully using sugar-cane and leguminous shrubs to feed penned pigs and sheep.

Domestic animals can sometimes play positive roles in restoring degraded range. The Center for Holistic Resource Management in Albuquerque, New Mexico, is restoring rangeland by managing cattle to mimic the grazing patterns of vanished wildlife herds. Counter to traditional range-management practices, cattle are stocked at high densities, but kept moving – their hoofs creating pockets in the soil that improve water infiltration and seed germination. Going further, some projects are actually replacing cattle with wildlife. Where wildlife herds still roam, as on many of Africa's savannahs, selling wild game meat can often provide pastoralists with alternative livelihoods that are ecologically and economically sustainable.

In the end, restoring livestock production to its historical role as a boon to the environmental sustainability of agriculture will depend upon more than rewriting policies and rethinking development strategies. It will require dietary changes among the world's meat eaters. Soaring consumer demand for meat drove the expansion of the livestock industry, so kitchen-counter reforms may be the ultimate arbiter of success or failure in the effort to transform animal agriculture.

In the United States, personal choices to follow nutritional guidelines would bring wholesale changes to livestock production. Meat consumption would decline overall, with grain-fed meat intake declining most steeply. In 1982, the Iowa-based Council for Agricultural Science and Technology estimated that reducing American fat intake to the recommended maximum of 30 per cent of calories would cut national pork consumption 40 per cent, beef consumption 20 per cent and poultry consumption 10 per cent. Leaner, grass-fed beef and lamb from pastures would be in high demand, while corn and soya-bean demand would drop by one-fourth.

Government policies can play a supporting role in changing diets by providing advice on healthy eating. Most Americans, for example, were brought up hearing about a diet balanced between the 'four food groups': meat and fish, dairy products, fruits and vegetables, and grains. These categories, popularized decades ago by the US Department of Agriculture, are now antiquated. Recently the Department drafted a new 'food pyramid', which placed emphasis on grains, legumes, fruits and vegetables rather than animal goods. But the agency retracted the draft when livestock producers complained.

Likewise, the US beef-grading system favours grain-fed cattle by awarding higher ratings for higher fat content – which increases when animals eat grain. The government could substitute an actual measure of fat content for the vague terms 'select', 'choice' and 'prime' that currently adorn meat labels. Shoppers might think twice about picking up a portion of beef if instead of 'choice' the label read '30 per cent fat'.

Yet governments usually follow rather than lead, and personal choices among the informed can provide a springboard for broader changes in national policies. As happened with tobacco, health warnings about meat eating are multiplying, and awareness of the environmental effects of meat production is rising. Just as cigarettes lost their allure, meat is losing its social cachet in some countries. Food marketers in the United Kingdom estimate that 2 million people in that country are strict vegetarians.

More important, the number of people limiting meat in their diets is rising rapidly. An estimated 6 million people in the United Kingdom dine on meatless meals most of the time. Average red-meat consumption per person has fallen 14 per cent in the United States since 1976. And beef consumption per capita has declined across Europe, as well as in Australia and New Zealand, during the same period.

In addition to health concerns, many people are troubled by the realization that more than one-third of the world's grain goes to feeding animals, while eight in every hundred people go hungry. Although hunger is not a consequence of meat production – most of the world's estimated 630 million hungry people are so poor that they simply cannot afford to buy food – feed grain could be needed to fight hunger in the future. World grain production per capita has been declining since 1984. If farmers and family planners are unable to reverse this trend, the feed grain of the affluent will eventually be needed to nourish the hungry.

The global livestock industry, with its manifold supports and as many environmental repercussions, defies simple reform. Indeed, many potential revisions, such as ecological taxes, must come from outside the livestock sector. Yet change is possible. Livestock have been boons to the human enterprise for millennia, and with enough pressure for reform, animal agriculture's current transgressions will end. Personal habits, just as national policies, can shift dramatically when enough people say 'Enough!'. Once that happens, it won't be long till the cows – and pigs and chickens – come home.

NOTES

1 This chapter has been reduced by the editors from Durning and Brough 1991. Full references to the authors' sources and data may be found in the original version (eds).
2 The authors are grateful to David Pimental, Frank Baker, Layne Coppock, Gary Vocke, Susanna Hecht, Robert Chan and Garth Youngberg for their insights and constructive criticisms on an earlier draft of this chapter.

12 Barriers to fair treatment of non-human life

Andrew Johnson

Fair treatment of other species is not won by winning the arguments: to translate principles into practice involves surmounting several further barriers. First, ignorance must be overcome about what is really in the best interests of creatures which may be very different from us. What are their needs, and how can they be assessed? Second, innate or culturally ingrained prejudices about animals and their role in society may need to be radically revised. Third, and overlapping with the second, subconscious beliefs and desires that are inimical to justice have to be exposed and neutralized. Only when these three hurdles are passed, and principles fit with knowledge and feelings, can the necessary institutional reforms hope to succeed.

THE NEEDS OF OTHER SPECIES

Interspecies justice, however defined, soon encounters a problem that is present in only a minority of cases of human justice: since other species cannot talk, they are unable to tell us what their needs are. How, then, can we judge these needs? It is tempting to assume that scientific measurement could establish welfare needs, but things are not quite so simple. If I am frightened or in pain, the experience is essentially a subjective state of mind, albeit the result of physical stimuli and their physiological effects. It is often argued that scientific studies of animals (or of other people) can deal only with their observed behaviour and physiology, and say nothing about mental states. But this does not entail, and should not lead to, the further claims that since subjective experiences cannot be measured scientifically, they are of no consequence or perhaps do not even exist. Such a belief is obviously convenient in certain circumstances: it enabled seventeenth-century scientists to claim that the live animals they cut up were just like clocks, that 'the cries they emitted when struck were only the noise of a little spring that had been touched, but that the whole body was without feeling' (quoted in Singer 1975: 220). Few people nowadays would admit to holding precisely such a view, which makes nonsense of the whole idea of animal welfare; but thinly disguised variants of it are still commonplace, the dogma often masquerading as scientific scepticism (see Harrison 1991; Carruthers 1992).

Of course it is impossible to be *certain* that other animals experience pain in the way we do, but neither can we be sure that other *people* feel pain as we do, just because they use the same word (see Wittgenstein 1969: 281ff.); nor are we normally troubled by sceptical doubts as to whether a child who cannot yet talk can feel pain. The real question is, how similar or how different are other creatures from human beings? Only when we have answered this do scientific studies of animal physiology and behaviour gain moral significance.

To judge the needs of other animals, we must make the effort of imagining ourselves into their position. Such 'anthropomorphism' is anathema to psychologists of the Behaviourist school, who favour a mechanistic view of biological science, but without some such empathy there is no way we can hold that it is 'good' for an animal to survive, or to avoid pain. By imagining ourselves as geese or rabbits, and using our imagination to interpret their behaviour and their needs, we are merely extending to other species a practice we use all the time with our own.

The use of analogy between humans and other animals requires respect for interspecies differences, and should not be confused with a literal anthropomorphism in which all the actions and thoughts of people can be transferred to other species on a one-to-one basis. Although many animals react as humans do to pain, hunger, thirst or extremes of temperature, these are very general patterns with numerous exceptions. Nor do similar gestures and expressions necessarily reflect similar feelings: as the Cheshire Cat remarked, 'A dog growls when it is angry and wags its tail when it's pleased. Now *I* growl when I'm pleased and wag my tail when I'm angry' (Carroll 1866: ch. 6).

Sympathetic identification with the needs of other animals and perception of their relevant similarities and differences are fundamental to the determination of interspecies justice. This is not to claim that we could ever understand just what it would be like to *be*, say, a bat (see Nagel 1974); rather, that it is only possible to discuss justice towards bats in terms of what we *can* identify with, such as the needs to survive, to keep warm, to satisfy hunger, and to avoid pain. The 'five freedoms' proposed by the Farm Animal Welfare Council all involve needs of this sort:

> freedom from thirst, hunger or malnutrition;
> appropriate comfort and shelter;
> prevention, or rapid diagnosis and treatment, of injury and disease;
> freedom to display most normal patterns of behaviour;
> freedom from fear.
>
> (FAWC 1988)

MEASURING ANIMAL WELFARE

The practical assessment of animal welfare involves recognizing ways in which norms such as the 'five freedoms' are not being achieved. Just as a doctor assumes that a child with a broken bone or an ear infection is in pain, so obvious damage or sickness can sensibly be connected with suffering in other species.

It can reasonably be held that 'pain in animals is manifested by abnormal be-haviour which can be alleviated by analgesic procedures which relieve pain in humans' (RSPCA 1980). Abnormal behaviour or growth are the first symptoms of many illnesses, and the general welfare of domestic animals depends very much on the ability of their keepers to detect and interpret such signs. Unfortun-ately, it is sometimes claimed that normal rates of growth or production are *sufficient* indicators of welfare, which is quite untrue.

A controversial issue in farm-animal welfare is how far animals are harmed by being unable to behave 'naturally'. The Behaviourist school of animal psy-chologists – whose experiments mainly involved caged animals – tended to assume that welfare could be reduced to the avoidance of unpleasant stimuli. By this criterion, life in the battery house with plenty of food, water and warmth does not seem too bad. But fieldwork by ethologists has shown that many species have a complex repertoire of apparently instinctive behaviour patterns – nest building, for example – which they perform without being taught, given the appropriate stimulus. When battery hens go through the motions of nest building, though they have no straw, it can be claimed that their natural drives are frustrated and that they must therefore be suffering.

As well as being unable to fulfil some of their natural behaviour patterns, animals in captivity often perform sequences of action that are not observed in the wild. These 'stereotypies' include pacing back and forth, gnawing at cage bars, and repeated head 'weaving' movements. Such stereotypies, or an unusually drooping posture, indicate (by reference to analogous human behaviour patterns) extreme boredom, unhappiness or frustration. Physiological measurements of variables such as heart rate or blood cortisol levels can also be used as indicators of stress, though with the reservation that since we are a long way from a quantifiable biochemical index of human happiness or misery, measurements of physiological abnormalities in other species are partial evidence rather than definite proof of suffering (Broom 1988).

Another scientific approach to measuring welfare involves experiments in which animals are given choices of different environments – for example, hens have been allowed to choose between various types of housing, with the strengths of their preferences being assessed by putting food in the less favoured environ-ment, or making them run the gauntlet of unpleasant stimuli to reach the preferred area (Dawkins 1980: 89).

The question of what is 'normal' or 'natural' behaviour is not always easy to answer for domesticated animals, many of which would no longer be viable in the environments of their wild ancestors, and it presents even more difficulties with transgenic animals. It is conceivable that transgenic animals might be produced for which life in a factory farm would involve no frustration; however, given present funding priorities, it can be doubted whether the attempt will even be made.

A further issue, which science is peculiarly ill-equipped to deal with, is how far individual animals have their own particular needs. There are enormous differences in how different people react to solitude, institutionalization and various kinds of discomfort and deprivation, so why should one regime suit all cows, pigs or horses? The basis of modern intensive livestock production is that the beasts are all to be treated as interchangeable cogs in the machine, and the mass of scientific knowledge about animals tends to reinforce this view: variations between individuals are as much a nuisance to the zoologist looking for valid generalizations as to the farmer who wants standardized pigs to fit standardized crates.

Whatever the limitations of particular ways of finding out what is good or bad for other species, the methodological difficulties are mere niceties compared with the far more difficult issue of motivation: why should we care enough to make the effort to find out?

HUMANS, ANIMALS AND SOCIETY

Rationally, there may be arguments for some changes in relations between our species and others. But even if such arguments are based on natural emotions, they must contend with other innate or culturally determined prejudices, which can be difficult to overcome.

It is impossible to separate the roles of nature and nurture in establishing attitudes towards other species. According to Edward O. Wilson, the founder of sociobiology, we are *naturally* disposed to be interested in and attracted to other living creatures (1984). Though such attitudes are learned, they come easily to us. Wilson refers to this natural tendency to focus on life as 'biophilia', and hopes it will promote greater understanding and valuing of other organisms.

It has also been argued that evolution has predisposed us to hate or fear certain creatures such as snakes and spiders, a hypothesis that gains some support from experiments. Laboratory-reared rhesus monkeys will become afraid of snakes if shown a video of a wild-reared monkey showing fear of a snake, but seeing a 'doctored' video of a monkey apparently frightened of a flower does not make them afraid of flowers (Hinde 1991: 596). And if people are shown pictures of spiders at the same time as being given a mild electric shock, the fear thus conditioned is less easily extinguished than fear conditioned in the same way to pictures of, say, houses or flowers. However, recent experiments have apparently demonstrated similar extinction-resistant fears of guns and electric sockets, for which there could not possibly be any evolutionary basis (Davey 1994).

The case for 'biological preparedness' to like or dislike particular species is further confused by the wide range of cultural variations in attitudes. While people of European descent tend to fear spiders, they are eaten as a delicacy in many parts of the world, they are frequently kept as pets by children in the Brazilian forest, and in east Bengal they are traditionally collected to release at weddings as a symbol of good luck (Davey 1994). Nor is the snake universally reviled: though it can be argued that its widespread and powerful symbolic status – whether for good or evil, health or sickness, creation or death – is evidence of a special degree of importance which may indeed be genetically determined (Willis 1990).

Whatever the origins of our views, we certainly regard different animals in very different lights. Certain species have traditionally been feared, as direct threats to human life or as pests which harm our economic interests, and consequently have been hated and persecuted, often quite disproportionately. Others have been regarded as prey, and of these some, such as pigs and sheep, have been successfully domesticated. Food animals are primarily valued as an economic resource, and concern for their welfare has tended to stop at the level needed to ensure their satisfactory growth for breeding or slaughter. This is equally true for other 'useful' animals – wool and fur providers, pest hunters, or beasts of burden. For the majority of modern town-dwellers, however, all the above categories of involvement with other species are quite remote – though they may still consume the end-products of hunting and farming. Most people in industrialized countries encounter and value animals as pets, or as objects of aesthetic pleasure in nature parks, at the garden bird table, or on television. From this secure and comfortable view-point, wild animals are no longer to be feared, and the curious ambivalence of our relationship with domesticated animals is increasingly sanitized and concealed.

It is too easy for us to forget that our enlightened attitudes may be something of a luxury. To country-dwellers, mink and foxes are still 'vicious killers' whose predations are regarded practically as crimes, in a way that recalls the medieval practice of trying and sentencing animal malefactors in court cases. When a sow and her six piglets were tried in 1457 for killing a child, the sow was sentenced to death by hanging, but her offspring were excused on the grounds of their tender years and the bad example shown by their mother. According to James Serpell (1988: 161), this kind of retributive justice was thought necessary, both to set an example and to restore the community's moral equilibrium. The criminalization of predators and pests may be functionally justifiable in the context of subsistence farming, and doubtless has a long history, but it sits uneasily with our current perceptions of nature as fragile and threatened, rather than robust and threatening.

Traditional attitudes towards prey or livestock are more complex. On the one hand, sympathy seems out of place, since the relationship is intended to end with the animal's death and consumption; but on the other, successful hunting and husbandry require a degree of sympathetic understanding which conflicts with the killer instinct. In *The Golden Bough*, Frazer (1922: 684) describes how Finnish hunters used to try to convince the bear they had just killed that it had met its death by accident, and how their bards composed funeral orations in which they begged its spirit to take favourable reports of them to the other bears. It would be pleasant if such conduct were evidence of natural human respect for animals' lives, but the behaviour of primitive hunters does not all support such a thesis. Yi-Fu Tuan (1984: 89–90) reflects on the innocent callousness of a Gikwe bushman roasting alive his infant son's tortoise, and describes an ingeniously cruel Inuit trap consisting of a sharpened whalebone tied into a U shape, covered with fat and left to freeze. The thongs are cut, and the frozen bait put out for foxes and wolves. When it is swallowed, the fat melts and the whalebone springs open, impaling the prey from within.

It is difficult to say how far the detachment from animal suffering common in many cultures derives from deliberate policy and how far it is genuinely unreflective, but the extent of cultural differences is quite clear. Not only do the Italians shoot larks, the Koreans eat dogs, and the English hunt foxes, but the general level of sensitivity seems to vary enormously between, say, India and China. The variety of attitudes within a single culture may be almost as great. In 1908 Westermarck observed that 'At present there is among ourselves no topic of moral concern which presents a greater variety of opinion than the question how far the lower animals may be justly sacrificed for the benefit of man' (1908, vol. 2: 514). This is almost equally true today; for while there has been a certain convergence towards greater sensitivity among the refined urban class, and increasing marginalization of activities such as hunting, attitudes towards farmers and others whose work involves animals have become more polarized. Society as a whole, through its tacit condoning of the status quo, now suffers from a kind of schizophrenia about the exploitation of animals.

How far our treatment of other species is actually improving has been studied by historians and sociologists. In his seminal study *Man and the Natural World*, Keith Thomas (1983) chronicled changing attitudes in England from 1500 to 1800, and the more recent history of animal-welfare organizations and animal-protection legislation seems to confirm the idea of progress towards more humane standards of behaviour. But while cruelty may be on the wane, the same period has witnessed tremendous dislocation and destruction of wild species through the impact of expanding human activities on their habitats.

Stephen Kellert has questioned whether public interest in wildlife and animal-related issues really has increased. In an extensive survey of articles in American local newspapers since 1900, Kellert and his colleagues found that the number of animal-related articles had not increased significantly over the period. At all dates, the bulk of the articles emphasized the material and practical value of animals, and less than 5 per cent of the total were primarily concerned with moral questions of their right and wrong treatment. The research indicated a decline in articles emphasizing dislike or fear of animals, and an increase in those expressing emotional detachment from other species; and in general, attitudes towards animals tended to become more positive as the century progressed (Kellert and Westervelt 1982).

Prevailing social views, as measured in such surveys, or expressed through morals and legislation, are not necessarily consistent, any more than those of individuals, and the protection afforded particular species may seem a matter of pragmatism as much as principle. When a pet-shop owner was fined over £1,000 for keeping a bird of prey in cramped conditions, an animal-welfare magazine commented, with only slight exaggeration:

> It was said that an eagle owl did not have enough room in the cage to spread its wings. The cage width was 75% of the bird's wingspan.
>   Had it been a chicken, of course, Mr —— could really have packed it in. A 30 inch wingspan chicken can be put in 4 inches of cage width.
>   Then he would not have been fined, he would have been given a subsidy.
>
> (*AgScene*, no. 74 (1984))

Quite apart from the different economic roles of chickens and eagle owls, etc., perceptions of their relative values depend very much on their different aesthetic and symbolic attributes. In a survey of British children aged from 4 to 14, the ten best-liked animals were all mammals with humanoid features (although no birds reached the top ten, the two most popular were the penguin, which walks like a person, and the parrot, which talks) (Morris 1977: 262–3). There is ample evidence to support the view that pet animals are very often perceived and treated as if they were children, in both western and non-western societies. Furthermore, many varieties of dog in particular have apparently been bred to emphasize child-like features of appearance and behaviour.

Animals have many more symbolic roles than that of kin substitute. The study of animal symbolism is a major part of anthropology, and the interpretations given to animal symbols are a continuing source of controversy in that discipline. However, it seems certain that preconceptions about animals will be coloured by their symbolic roles, and may not always be fair. To give just one example, the eagle has proud and lordly associations despite the fact that it is largely a robber and scavenger. (Morris (1977: 262–3) notes that an attempt to substitute the rattlesnake as the American emblem, because it gives fair warning to an enemy, never provokes a fight, but is fearless in self-defence, was a miserable failure despite all evidence of the snake's worthier nature.)

One point from anthropology which needs to be considered is the extent to which animal symbolism is a metaphor for thinking about and understanding human society. Lévi-Strauss, famously, made the point that animals 'are good to think', and this has sometimes led to the misguided belief that the classifications and symbolic significance which societies apply to the natural world are no more than projections of essentially human concerns. From this it is a short step to the claim that animals are 'only important because they can tell us something about ourselves' (Tester 1991: 42), or that 'animal rights is only marginally concerned with animals. More importantly, it is part of a social project to classify and define humanity' (Tester 1991: 48). If this were actually true, it would obviously undermine the whole project of extending justice to other animals, but it seems far more reasonable to believe, with Mary Douglas (1990: 33), that this kind of mirroring is a two-way process, which only works because animal categories are defined in patterns already used as categories of human social relations. In his recent book *Picturing the Beast*, Steve Baker (1993) gives an interesting account of animal symbolism in the contemporary media, without falling into the trap of assuming that animals are *only* important symbols. In fact, his final chapter on 'Strategic images for animal rights' specifically considers how the constructive use of representations could change society to the advantage of animals.

PSYCHOLOGICAL BARRIERS TO INTERSPECIES JUSTICE

Even if it is possible to overcome culturally induced prejudices and take due account of conflicts of interest, actually achieving fair dealing with other species can be impeded by a whole range of psychological obstacles.

Most directly, a crucial question is, how far is cruelty enjoyable? For a minority of psychopaths, there is obviously pleasure in the pain of other people or animals, and cruelty to animals often goes together with cruelty to other humans (Serpell 1988: 85). But is this *schadenfreude* confined to psychopaths, or is it present to some extent in everyone? Yi-Fu Tuan (1984: 7–8) argues that 'power in itself is good', and that we are conditioned by society to repress our natural pleasure in domination and destruction. Even love is devouring:

> What we love we wish to incorporate, literally and figuratively. In a moment of exuberance, Chekhov exclaimed, 'What a luxurious thing Nature is! I could just take her and eat her up . . .'
>
> (Tuan 1984: 9)

Hunters also claim to love their quarry, and it is striking how many conservationists and wildlife photographers of the older generation were killers in their youth. Such love is of a grossly defective kind, in its lack of sympathy for the object of affection, but examples such as these might encourage us to reflect on whether there is not some kind of continuum between the psychopath's morbid obsession and an equally rare love free from any taint of selfishness.

This theme has been developed by Erich Fromm (1974: 346–7), who points out that indifference can be as destructive as hatred, and that the impersonal and distant machinery of modern warfare has caused as much pain and death as hot-blooded hand-to-hand fighting. It may thus be questioned how far the trend Kellert observed away from dislike of animals towards emotional detachment is necessarily a good thing for the beasts in modern farms or laboratories. What difference does it make *to the animals* if they suffer at the hands of jolly peasants indulging in traditional rituals, or in a mechanized slaughterhouse operated mechanically by impassive and uncaring workers? In the latter case, the 'system' is supposed to minimize suffering, but indifference remains only a limited advance on cruelty. Since far more animal suffering is the result of disease and neglect than of deliberate cruelty, it is vitally important how far people are held to have a positive duty of care for animals in their charge rather than merely a negative duty not to abuse them.

The words we use to describe animals play a subtle but important role in conditioning the way we perceive them. Factory farming developed through the application of industrial methods of production to livestock husbandry, and its proponents apply mechanical terminology to animals with apparent relish. If challenged, they will claim that describing cows as machines for making milk out of grass is only a metaphor, and quite without import for the animals' welfare, but this kind of linguistic mud has a habit of sticking. Euphemisms are frequently employed to conceal the unpleasanter aspects of our dealings with animals. 'Service' or 'covering' describe the act of copulation; and 'in-hand service', where the female animal is caged or tethered and forced to submit, is remarkably different in emotional overtones from the word 'rape', which we should use in a human context. Farmed fish, absurdly, are 'harvested' rather than 'slaughtered'; and in America, slaughterhouses are described as 'meat factories'. Even dining on 'pork' or 'beef' seem somehow less offensive than eating 'pig' or 'cow'. And we frequently refer to an animal as 'it', while always using 'he' or 'she' for humans.

The technical language used by laboratory scientists who experiment on animals may also serve as a euphemistic device to enable them to think of the animals as objects rather than as sentient living creatures. Mary Phillips claims that, contrary to all reason, researchers actually categorize and perceive laboratory animals as different creatures from domestic ones:

> The majority of them had pets at home, with whom they seemed capable of empathizing enormously. But their pets were individuals whom they knew by name, and whom they would *never* use in an experiment. Laboratory animals were (usually) nameless, de-individualized creatures, whose sole purpose in life was to serve in a scientific experiment. Researchers continually made distinctions between lab animals and pets, on the one hand, and lab and wild animals on the other.
>
> (Phillips 1993: 76–7)

The individuality of pet animals makes them seem much more important than their laboratory cousins, which are thought of as mere representatives of a type. But 'the rat' as a species has no prior existence independent of the actual rats to which it refers; rather, the universal is 'a common and confused image of many things' (Abelard 1929: 240). And just as our affection for other people is not simply based on what they have in common – that they breathe air, walk upright, and so on – so feelings towards other animals are surely coloured by the fact that they are individuals with their own particular traits.

More people would be far more horrified at the idea of eating dogs or cats, whom they have encountered as individuals, than sheep or chickens, which to the untutored eye all look much alike. This seems to be the basis of Raymond Frey's assertion that the value of chickens' lives is 'exceedingly minimal':

> This [belief] is the case, I think, with the overwhelming majority of us. For chickens are mass-produced in their billions, rarely achieving any individuality in our eyes, are not noted for their behavioural, let alone intellectual affinities to ourselves, are rarely, if at all considered to be self-conscious, are rarely contemplated for inclusion in the class of persons, and in general, lead us to believe that, for most purposes, one is pretty much as good as another.
>
> (Frey 1983: 109)

This sort of argument could equally be applied to Negro slaves or starving Somalians, but to do so would be thought distasteful. This is presumably because our knowledge of individual people leads us to believe that what appears from a distance as a seething mass of indistinguishable faces is actually an aggregation cf distinct human beings similar in many ways to ourselves. Closer acquaintance would reveal that they have personal loves and needs, and are loved and needed, much as we are ourselves. To say that one hen is the same as any other 'for most purposes' actually means 'for eating by humans'. To anyone who has kept or observed a small flock of poultry, it soon becomes disturbingly apparent that they are different from each other, not just from their own point of view, but from that of a reasonably sensitive observer.

There are plenty of arguments for eating hens or sheep, but it is not fair to claim that we are entitled to do so because they are not in any sense individuals. However, as Stephen Clark has pointed out, it is a highly convenient attitude.

> We passers-by cannot distinguish, or do not trouble to distinguish, one calf from the next, and therefore assume that they are but mass-produced examples of a type, that only the ongoing life of the species is worthy of any respect at all, not this poor clone. We speak of the Cow, the Pig, the Fox, and somehow persuade ourselves thereby that we do not damage when we kill a cow, a pig, a fox. Of animals we are superstitiously Platonic: it is the Idea that is real to us, not the individual suffering entities.
>
> (Clark 1977: 63)

From an early age, many people have deeply ingrained feelings of dislike or fear of certain animals. Adverse reactions to snakes and spiders are by far the most common phobias of this sort, and it has been suggested that they are associated with more general feelings of disgust at dirty or slimy things of animal origin, which may have evolved as a protection against disease (Davey 1994). Exaggerated mythologies often develop around animals that are believed to be dangerous – frequently out of all proportion to the damage actually caused by such species – and they are spoken of in terms such as 'filthy, disreputable, gluttonous, sly, ruthless, evil, cowardly, bloodthirsty and savage' (Serpell 1988: 160). Typically, the wolf has been seen as the Devil incarnate, 'red tongued, sulphur breathed and yellow eyed' (Lopez 1978, cited by Serpell 1988: 160).

In the ancient world, animal sacrifices were very widespread, and in nearly every case the performance involved a ritual of blame-shifting. The animal was made to appear a willing victim, and the priests took elaborate precautions to cleanse themselves of guilt. For example, in ancient Babylon, the head priest would whisper in the ear of the sacrificial victim, 'This deed was done by all the gods; I did not do it' (Burket 1983, cited by Serpell 1988: 167–8). Purification is a central purpose of animal sacrifices, the sins of the community being transferred to a spotless animal victim to appease the gods. Campaigners against vivisection argue that the animals 'slaughtered on the altar of science' have, beyond the purely practical purpose averred by their killers, a primitive symbolic significance similar to that of the scapegoat which carried away the sins of the Israelites.

Superstitions about cleanliness count for more than animal welfare among the traditionalist faithful of a number of religions, who insist on having their meat slaughtered by traditional ritual methods. Despite recommendations by the Farm Animal Welfare Council and the RSPCA that pre-slaughter stunning be made obligatory, many Jews and Muslims still take advantage of the exemption from this requirement allowed them under the 1974 Slaughterhouse Act.

Anyone who is a vegetarian, or whose child is a vegetarian, will be aware of the considerable pressures exerted by friends, relatives and society at large to abandon such freakish ideas and conform to decent norms of behaviour. This kind of pressure can be an obstacle to reform, and while in the case just given the majority of people are members of the conformist party, similar social forces can also act within smaller groups. Thus, hare coursers, badger baiters or dog-fight fans are all members of close-knit peer groups from which they can break free only at a price in conviviality and the esteem of their fellows.

Even worse, the partakers in unsavoury activities often show particular zeal for luring their acquaintances into complicity in the guilty act. Cruel and pointless acts demanded of members of a group may also serve to act as initiation rites and to cement group solidarity for other purposes. Examples include the 'blooding' of young huntsmen, or the bizarre parties Aristotle Onassis was reputed to throw abroad his Antarctic whaling ship:

> As he sipped hot toddies with his guests, the gunners made use of their grenade harpoons with a terrible diligence. A broad cloak of blood extended over the surface of the sea. . . . The men were invited to try their skill with the harpoon gun. 'I think he simply wanted them to feel the blood on their hands and share the guilt.' . . .
>
> (Evans 1986: 112)

A common reaction to moral problems is simply to deny their existence, a policy made easier if the evidence can be concealed. So in 1881, when the London Zoological Society discovered to their chagrin that some of the public were beginning to object to their displays of large snakes consuming live ducks, rabbits, and occasionally even goats, their reaction was not to feed the pythons a humanely killed diet, but to replace the flamboyant spectacle by extreme secrecy at feeding times (Salt 1921: 164).

A similar response may be discerned when proud inventors fail to get the public adulation they feel they deserve. Like naughty boys, the creators of the latest in anti-personnel weapons or dry-sow stalls react to adverse criticism, not by changing their ways, but by skulking into private laboratories or windowless barns. Behind closed doors there are no unwelcome critics to question the refinement of techniques for blowing people up, or the economic marvels of twenty-four-hour confinement in tubular steel cages.

The paradox in our society is that such people, whom the public cannot bear to look at directly, are often funded and supported by the same public, with very few dissenting voices. For the majority, it seems, out of sight really *is* out of mind, and when people are challenged about this, a typical reply is, 'Please don't tell me about it: I'd rather not hear.' But is it really an option to choose ignorance in this way?

Although there is no way that what is once known can be deliberately un-learned, for we have little conscious control over what we forget, prudence soon teaches us that there are some things we would sooner not find out. While this need not be morally wrong, it is often the fear of being put in a moral quandary which persuades us to turn a deaf ear or a blind eye. It would not be a better world if wildlife were still being massacred, the environment still polluted, wars still waged and babies battered, only we knew nothing about it. We might *feel* it was a better world if we could live in such a selfish fantasy-state, but such delusions will certainly not help put things right. The small things we *can* do can only be recognized if we are prepared to look at the problems.

Quite innocent enthusiasms for one particular kind of moral good too easily lead to overriding or ignoring other competing or incompatible goods.'Rights' are particularly prone to take over in this way, and the legitimate right to enjoy property can soon extend to the unchecked right of an animal's keeper to abuse, injure or dispose of his charge as he could an inanimate object. A subtler variant of this kind of folly is shown by those for whom all activities beyond their favourite concerns are reprehensible luxuries. So it may be thought wicked to give your pet food and affection because somewhere in the world there is a person who needs food and affection more. But nobody is wholly altruistic, including those who make such criticisms, and there is no evidence to suggest that in general people who love animals love humans any the less for it.

Sometimes there are real conflicts of interest, more substantial than mere questions of priority, between the needs of different individual animals or different species in wildlife management, or even between the needs of individuals and the long-term benefit of their own species. Such conflict, starkly portrayed by Baird Callicott (1980) in his article 'Animal liberation: a triangular affair', have led to polarization between animal-rights activists and environmentalists, particularly in the United States. Callicott argues in favour of hunting game for food, and culling surplus population in the interests of long-term ecological balance, whereas most supporters of animal rights object to hunting and would favour the immediate needs of individual animals over long-term 'management' policies. While there have been many attempts to reconcile the two camps, and re-emphasize their common ground, important differences in perspective are likely to resist definitive resolution.

INSTITUTIONAL BARRIERS TO INTERSPECIES JUSTICE

In a democracy, legislation and its enforcement depend, in the end, upon public opinion. Since animals do not have votes, progress towards a just environment for them presupposes progress in the human public consciousness, away from the view of animals as merely useful objects. This may occur as part of a more general trend away from narrowly instrumental values; it may be influenced by the philosophical debates referred to in chapter 10; or it may reflect advances in knowledge about the lives of other species, perhaps through exposure to animals in zoos or to wildlife programmes on television.

Even if there were broad consensus on the idea of interspecies justice, vested interests can prevent legal reforms reaching the statute-book, or lobby for favourable interpretations of the law in actual court judgements. Furthermore, ensuring compliance with the letter and spirit of laws to protect other species requires an adequate system of inspection and enforcement.

It is impossible to describe briefly the complex web of political lobbying that connects with the passage or blocking of new measures to protect other species, but excellent accounts of the political process are given in Richard Ryder's *Animal Revolution* (1989) and Robert Garner's *Animals, Politics and Morality* (1993). Some aspects of farm-animal legislation are discussed in more detail in my *Factory Farming* (1991). The effectiveness of legislation depends largely on the way it is framed. For example, the 1972 German Animal Protection Act contained a clause insisting that animals must be given accommodation that takes account of their natural behaviour, beyond the need to avoid pain, suffering or injury. But attempts to use this legislation against battery-egg producers were unsuccessful, partly because the defence could invariably produce expert scientific or veterinary witnesses ready to testify that life in the battery cage did not involve any hardship for the chickens. Courts tended to the view that if established experts could not agree on the suffering caused by such confinement, it was unreasonable for such a widely used and formerly acceptable system suddenly to be ruled cruel. After a number of conflicting verdicts, and much lobbying by egg producers, the 1972 Act was amended to include more detailed regulations specifically allowing battery cages subject to certain minimum standards.

The Codes of Practice recommended for farm animals in the United Kingdom have also been shown to carry little weight in courts of law, where expert witnesses are always available to argue both for and against the status quo. On the whole, such progress as has been made towards the reform of intensive livestock farming, both in the United Kingdom and overseas, has been through the introduction of detailed regulations setting minimum standards or forbidding certain practices (Johnson 1991: 211–13).

Even with legislation in place, its enforcement requires adequate arrangements for the detection and prosecution of offenders. In the United Kingdom, the RSPCA often work with police to investigate cases of cruelty and uncover dog-fighting or badger-baiting rings. Farms and slaughterhouses are visited by inspectors from the Ministry of Agriculture and local authorities; and premises registered for scientific experiments on animals are inspected by the Home Office. But animal-welfare groups point out that there are too few inspectors, that they usually give advance warning of their visits, and that prosecutions initiated by government-appointed inspectors are extremely rare (Garner 1993: 132–3).

Attention is often diverted from issues of interspecies justice by more pressing concerns, of which money must be the most universal. When businessmen have to choose between better standards of animal welfare and larger profits, the financial bottom line usually wins the day. As farming becomes more competitive, high standards of stock handling that do not produce cash dividends are perceived as a luxury few can afford. More efficient markets will thus tend to force welfare standards down towards the minimum legally acceptable or enforceable level. Levels of care for pet and laboratory animals are probably more resistant to economic pressures, as funds available are more likely to be reflected in the number of animals kept rather than the degree of comfort they are afforded.

The effects of economic development on wild species are almost inevitably bad. Even where wild animals or plants are not simply regarded as a resource to be exploited, it is notoriously difficult to express concern for their interests in terms that have any impact on the appropriation of habitat for farming or industrial development projects. These tend to be evaluated in terms of their costs and benefits for certain sections of the human population, and if wildlife gets a look in at all, it is often only in terms of the assumed willingness of interested people to pay for its preservation, or to accept financial compensation for its destruction. The morality of this approach has been widely questioned (for example, Peterson and Peterson 1993), as well as the practicality of making 'non-market' valuations (for example, Common *et al.* 1993).

Environmental economists tend to counter their critics by claiming that while there are difficulties in making 'correct' valuations of species and habitats, some figures must be put on them in order to rank rival projects in a competitive order and so make a rational choice of the best available option. A compromise which is sometimes adopted is to allow conventional economic appraisal subject to side-constraints such as the obligation to avoid extinction of any endangered species. This method, particularly in the USA, has led to the catapulting to fame of such obscure species as the northern spotted owl and the Tellico river snail darter, as their rights to escape extinction were asserted in confrontations with developers (Clark 1993; Kellert 1986). However, it can be objected that treating such side-constraints as absolute can quickly lead to all options being closed off without leaving any way to achieve a decision.

It has been proposed that valuation for conservation can be better represented using a 'pluralistic' approach, in which different *kinds* of values (aesthetic, recreational, wildlife, cultural, heritage, etc.) are acknowledged, but not assumed to be commensurate with each other. This gives a multidimensional framework for thinking about the issues involved, but emphasizes the need for judgement which cannot simply be made by adding up scores using a simple numerical formula (Rothenberg 1992). This sounds more like traditional politics, but such ideas are directly opposed to those of most economists, who are vehemently against them.

The most important contemporary aspect of interspecies justice is the increasingly global forum in which the debate must be held. The vast majority of species are highly vulnerable to the effects of international trade and politics, even if they are not actually traded as commodities themselves.

At the relatively local level, British farmers have quite justifiably argued that they should not have to fund expensive improvements in livestock welfare if their produce is expected to compete with that of other European countries where standards are lower; and when European laws are introduced to supersede those current in the various countries of the European Union, there is inevitably a levelling downwards of the better national regulations towards the lowest common denominator. Even when individual countries do promote better standards, the effect of the trade is that production simply shifts elsewhere. For example, in the year that the United Kingdom announced a ban on veal crates, exports of British calves to Europe rose by 81 per cent, and imports of Dutch veal more than doubled (*AgScene*, nos 91, 93 (1988)). Long-distance road haulage of British livestock to slaughter on the Continent has increased dramatically, and the pleas of animal-welfare organizations for better transport regulations and more effective enforcement measures have been largely ignored.

At the global level, free trade in animal produce allows countries with bad welfare and environmental records to compete on even terms with those with stricter standards. GATT rules prohibit barriers to trade tariffs or bans on products judged ethically unacceptable by the importing country, and threaten those already in place, such as the European import ban on seal pelts and American measures to encourage 'dolphin-friendly' tuna fishing. The CITES convention on trade in endangered species also risks contravening GATT regulations (Lang and Hines 1993: 65–7).

International trade in other commodities can also threaten global interspecies justice, as capital is moved to areas where goods can be produced most cheaply, often partly because of lax environmental regulations. Multinational companies will also be tempted to locate their animal-research establishments in countries with less stringent controls. The remedy for these problems is not necessarily a reduction in trade, but an improvement of internationally agreed standards of environmental and species protection, to which free trade can be tied using realistic inspection and enforcement procedures.

LEARNING TO UNDERSTAND

The welfare of other species can be comprehended only through the combination of scientific knowledge with a more subjective sympathetic understanding. This sympathy itself cannot be unreflective: our natural and learned attitudes to other species are psychologically complex, and need to be subject to rational moral scrutiny if they are to be more than mere prejudices. Finally, knowledge of other cultures, and of the potential conflicts within them between politics, economics and ethics, will require a further effort of understanding if there is to be any chance of development towards ethical harmony on a scale sufficient to meet the often global issues involved in interspecies justice. If such harmony can be more than mere compromise at a comfortable common level, then we may hope for political progress towards more just environments, for humans and other species.

Bibliography

Abelard, P. (1929) *Glosses on Porphyry*, in R. McKeon (ed.) *Selections from Mediaeval Philosophers*, vol. 1, New York.

Abernethy, V. (1979) *Population Pressure and Cultural Adjustment*, New York, London: Human Sciences Press.

Alger, C. F. (1988) 'Perceiving, analysing and coping with the local–global nexus', *International Social Science Journal* 117, The Local–Global Nexus: 322–40.

Allan, W. (1965) *The African Husbandman*, Edinburgh: Oliver and Boyd.

Allen, J. C. and Barnes, D. F. (1989) 'The causes of deforestation in developing countries', *Annals of the Association of American Geographers* 75 (2): 163–84.

Almond, B. (1987) *Moral Concerns*, New Jersey: Humanities.

Almond, B. and Hill, D. (eds) (1991) *Applied Philosophy: Morals and Metaphysics in Contemporary Debate*, London: Routledge.

Aristotle (1976) *Ethics*, trans. J. A. K. Thomson, Harmondsworth: Penguin.

Attenborough, D. (1979) *Life on Earth*, London: BBC/Collins.

Attfield, R. (1991) *The Ethics of Environmental Concern*, Athens, Ga.: University of Georgia.

Attfield, R. and Wilkins, B. (eds) (1992) *International Justice and the Third World*, London: Routledge.

Baker, S. (1993) *Picturing the Beast: Animals, Identity and Representation*, Manchester: Manchester University Press.

Barber, J. P. (1993) 'The search for international order and justice', *The World Today* 49 (7): 158–64.

Barry, B. (1991) *Liberty and Justice: Essays in Political Theory 2*, Oxford: Clarendon Press.

Bauman, Z. (1993) *Postmodern Ethics*, Oxford: Blackwell.

Bayles, M. D. (1980) *Morality and Population Policy*, Alabama: University of Alabama Press.

Beaujeu-Garnier, J. (1966) *Geography of Population*, London: Longman.

Bellamy, D. and Quayle, B. (1986) *Turning the Tide*, London: Collins.

Bentham, J. (1960) *The Principles of Morals and Legislation*, Oxford: Blackwell.

Berlin, I. (1990) *The Crooked Timber of Humanity*, London: Fontana.

Bernhard, T. (1991) *Correction*, London: Vintage.

—— (1992) *Wittgenstein's Nephew*, London: Vintage.

Bilsborrow, R. E. (1992) 'Population, development and deforestation: some recent evidence', United Nations Expert Group Meeting on Population, Environment and Development, New York, 20–4 January 1992.

Biraben, J. N. (1979 'Essai sur l'évolution du nombre des hommes', *Population* 34 (1): 12–19.

Birch, C. (1988) 'Eight fallacies of the modern world and five axioms for a postmodern worldview', *Perspectives in Biology and Medicine* 32: 12–30.

Blay, S. and Green, J. (1994) 'The practicalities of domestic legislation to prohibit mining in Antarctica', *Polar Record* 30 (172): 23–32.

Boserup, E. (1985) 'Economic and demographic interrelationships in sub-Saharan Africa', *Population and Development Review* 11 (3): 383–98.

Brandt Commission (1980) *North–South: A Program for Survival*, London: Pan Books.

Broady, P. (1991) 'Antarctica: more than ice and penguins', in S. J. Mayers (ed.), *Antarctica: The Scientists' Case for a World Park*, London: Greenpeace, 4–9.

Brooks, H. (1992) 'Sustainability and technology', in IIASA, *Science and Sustainability: Selected Papers on IIASA's 20th Anniversary*, Vienna: IIASA.

Broom, D. M. (1988) 'The scientific assessment of animal welfare', *Applied Animal Behaviour Science* 20: 5–19.

Bull, H. (1977) *The Anarchical Society*, London: Macmillan.

Bunyard, P. (1991) 'Antarctica: the ethics of conservation', in S. J. Mayers, *Antarctica: The Scientists' Case for a World Park*, London: Greenpeace, 17–19.

Burke, E. (1955) *Reflections on the Revolution in France*, Chicago: University of Chicago.

Burket, W. (1983) *Homo Necans*, trans. P. Bing, Berkeley: University of California Press.

Caldwell, J. C. (1975) *The Sahelian Drought and its Demographic Implications*, Overseas Liaison Committee, American Council on Education, OLC Paper no. 8, December 1975.

—— (1991) 'The soft underbelly of development: demographic transition in conditions of limited economic change', Proceedings of the World Bank, Annual Conference on Development Economics, Washington, D.C.: The World Bank, 207–74.

Callicott, J. Baird (1980) 'Animal liberation: a triangular affair', *Environmental Ethics* 2: 311–38.

—— (1992) 'Can a theory of moral sentiments support a genuinely normative environmental ethic?', *Inquiry* 35: 183–98.

Carroll, L. (C. L. Dodgson) (1866) *Alice in Wonderland*, London.

Carruthers, P. (1992) *The Animals Issue*, Cambridge: Cambridge University Press.

Carson, R. (1962) *Silent Spring*, Boston, Mass.: Houghton Mifflin.

Clark, M. E. (1993) 'Tasks for future ecologists', *Environmental Values* 1: 35–46.

Clark, S. R. L. (1977) *The Moral Status of Animals,* Oxford: Clarendon Press.

—— (1987) 'Animals, ecosystems and the Liberal ethic', *The Monist* 79: 114–33.

Clarke, J. I. (1965) *Population Geography*, Oxford: Pergamon.

—— (1976) 'Population and scale: some general considerations', in L. A. Kosinski and J. W. Webb (eds) *Population at Microscale*, Auckland: New Zealand Geographical Society.

—— (1989) 'A quarter of a millennium of world population movements, 1789–2039s', *Espace, Populations, Sociétés* 3: 295–304.

—— (1993) 'Education, population, environment and sustained development', *International Review of Education* 39 (1–2): 41–9.

Clarke, J. I., Curson, P., Kayastha, S. L. and Nag, P. (eds) (1989) *Population and Disaster*, Oxford: Basil Blackwell.

Clarke, J. I. and Rhind, D. W. (1992) *Population Data and Global Environmental Change*, ISSC/UNESCO Series, 5.

Club du Sahel/CILSS (1981) *The Sahel Drought and Development Programme 1975–1979*, Paris, September 1981.

Commission of the EC (1990) *The Agricultural Situation in the Community*, 1989 Report, Brussels: EC.

Common, M. S., Blamey, R. K. and Norton, T. W. (1993) 'Sustainability and environmental valuation', *Environmental Values* 2: 299–334.

Commoner, B. (1988) 'Rapid population growth and environmental stress', in *Consequences of Rapid Population Growth in Developing Countries*, UN Expert Group Meeting, New York.

—— (1990) *Making Peace with the Planet*, New York: Pantheon.

—— (1991) 'Rapid population growth and environmental stress', in *Consequences of Rapid Population Growth in Developing Countries*, London: Taylor and Francis.

—— (1992) 'Population, development and the environment: trends and key issues in the developed countries'. United Nations Expert Group Meeting on Population, Environment and Development, New York, 20–4 January.

Cooper, D. E. (1993) 'Human sentiment and the future of wildlife', *Environmental Values* 2: 335–46.

Countryside Commission (1993) 'Golf courses in the countryside', Countryside Commission, Manchester, CCP 438.

Davey, G. C. L. (1994) 'The "disgusting" spider: the role of disease and illness in the perpetuation of fear of spiders', *Society and Animals* 2.

Davis, B. W. (1992) 'Antarctica as a global protected area: perceptions and reality', *Australian Geographer* 23 (1): 39–43.

Davis, K. and Bernstam, M. S. (eds) (1990) *Resources, Environment and Population: Present Knowledge, Future Options*, New York: The Population Council. A supplement to vol. 16 of *Population and Development Review*.

Dawkins, M. S. (1980) *Animal Suffering*, Oxford: Oxford University Press.

Demeny, P. (1989a) 'Demography and the limits to growth', Population Council Research Division, WP1989, no. 2.

—— (1989b) 'World population growth and prospects', Population Council Research Division, WP1989, no. 4.

Douglas, M. (1990) 'The pangolin revisited: a new approach to animal symbolism', in R. Willis (ed.) *Signifying Animals*, London: Unwin Hyman, 25–42.

Durning, A. T. and Brough, H. B. (1991) *Taking Stock: Animal Farming and the Environment*, Worldwatch Paper 103, Washington, D.C.: Worldwatch Institute.

Ehrlich, P. R. (1990) 'The population explosion', *The Amicus Journal*, winter, 22–9.

Ehrlich, P. R. and Ehrlich, A. H. (1990) *The Population Explosion*, New York: Simon Schuster.

Ehrlich, P. R. and Roughgarden, J. (1987) *The Science of Ecology*, New York: Macmillan.

Elliot, R. (1991) 'Environmental ethics', in P. Singer (ed.) *A Companion to Ethics*, Oxford: Blackwell.

Elsworth, S. (1990) *A Dictionary of the Environment*, London: Paladin, Grafton Books.

Enzenbacher, D. E. (1992) 'Tourists in Antarctica: numbers and trends', *Polar Record* 28 (164): 17–22.

Evans, P. (1986) *Ari: The Life and Times of Aristotle Socrates Onassis*, London: Jonathan Cape.

Falkenmark, M. (1990) 'Global water issues confronting humanity', *Journal of Peace Research* 27: 177–91.

FAO (1977) *Production Yearbook 1976*, Rome.

—— (1991) Forest Resources Assessment 1990 Project, 'Second interim report on the state of tropical forest'. Tenth World Forestry Congress, Paris, September 1991.

FAWC (Farm Animal Welfare Council) (1988) *Report on Priorities in Animal Welfare Research and Development*, Surbiton: FAWC.

Feinberg, J. (1973) *Social Philosophy*, Englewood Cliffs: Prentice Hall.

Flew, A. G. N. (1991) 'The concept, and conceptions, of justice', in B. Almond and D. Hill (eds) *Applied Philosophy: Morals and Metaphysics in Contemporary Debate*, London: Routledge.

Frazer, J. G. (1922) *The Golden Bough* (abridged edition), London: Macmillan.

Frey, R. G. (1983) *Rights, Killing and Suffering*, Oxford: Blackwell.

Friberg, M. and Hettne, B. (1988) 'Local mobilization and world system politics', *International Social Science Journal* 117, The Local–Global Nexus: 341–60.

Fromm, E. (1974) *The Anatomy of Human Destructiveness*, London: Jonathan Cape.

Gallopin, G. C. (1991) 'Human dimensions of global changes: linking the global and local processes', *International Social Science Journal* 130, Global Environmental Change: Concepts, Data, Methods, Modelling, Co-operation with Natural Sciences: 707–18.

Garner, R. (1993) *Animals, Politics and Morality*, Manchester: Manchester University Press.

Gauthier, D. (1986) *Morals by Agreement*, Oxford: Clarendon Press.

Gellner, E. (1988) *Plough, Sword and Book: The Structure of Human History*, London: Collins Harvill.

George, P. (1959) *Questions de géographie de la population*, Paris: PUF.

Goudie, A. (1984) *The Nature of the Environment*, Oxford: Basil Blackwell.

—— (1993) 'Environmental uncertainty', *Geography* 78 (2): 137–41.

Goudsblom, J. (1989) 'Human history and long-term social processes: towards a synthesis of chronology and "phaseology"', in J. Goudsblom, E. L. Jones and S. Mennel (eds) *Human History and Social Processes*, Exeter: University of Exeter Press, 11–26.

Gould, S. J. (1989) *Wonderful Life: The Burgess Shale and the Nature of History*, London: Hutchinson.

Gower, B. (1992) 'What do we owe future generations?', in D. E. Cooper and J. A. Palmer (eds) *The Environment in Question: Ethics and Global Issues*, London: Routledge, 1–12.

Grainger, A. (1986) *Desertification: How People Make Deserts, How People Can Stop, and Why They Don't*, London: Earthscan.

Grilli, E. (1993) *The European Community and the Developing Countries*, Cambridge: Cambridge University Press.

Gutman, A. (1980) *Liberal Equality*, Cambridge: Cambridge University Press.

Hardin, G. (1968) 'The tragedy of the commons', *Science* 162: 1243–48.

—— (1972) 'Exploring new ethics for survival: the voyage of the spaceship Beagle', New York: Viking.

—— (1974) 'Living on a lifeboat', *BioScience* 24: 561–8.

—— (1979) 'Lifeboat ethics: the case against helping the poor', in J. Rachels (ed.) *Moral Problems*, New York: Harper and Row.

—— (1989) 'There is no global population problem', *The Humanist* 49: 11–14.

Harrison, P. (1991) 'Do animals feel pain?', *Philosophy* 66: 25–40.

Hayek, F. A. (1960) *The Constitution of Liberty*, London: Routledge.

Hegel, G. W. F. (1977) *The Phenomenology of Spirit*, Oxford: Oxford University Press.

Heidegger, M. (1977) *The Question Concerning Technology and Other Essays*, New York: Harper and Row.

Hernandez, B. E. (1991) 'To bear or not to bear: reproductive freedom as an international human right', *Brooklyn Journal of International Law* 309.

Higgens, G. M. and Kassam, A. K. (1985) *Potential Population-Supporting Capacities of Lands in the Developing World*, Rome: FAO Technical Report no. INT/75/P13.

Hinde, R. A. (1991) 'A biologist looks at anthropology', *Man* 26: 583–608.

Hirsch, F. (1976) *Social Limits to Growth*, London: Routledge and Kegan Paul.

Hodgson, B. (1990) 'Antarctica: a land of isolation no more', *National Geographic Magazine* 177 (4): 2–51.

Hollis, M. (1987) *The Cunning of Reason*, Cambridge: Cambridge University Press.

Hume, D. (1985) *A Treatise of Human Nature*, Harmondsworth: Penguin.

Hurrell, A. and Kingsbury, B. (eds) (1992) *The International Politics of the Environment*, Oxford: Clarendon Press.

Illich, I. (1971) *Deschooling Society*, London: Calder and Boyars.

—— (1976) *Limits to Medicine*, London: Calder and Boyars.

IUCN (1980) *World Conservation Strategy*, Paris: IUCN/UNP.

Jacobs, M. (1992) *The Green Economy*, London: Pluto Press.

Jacobson, H. K. and Price, M. F. (1990) *A Framework for Research on the Human Dimensions of Global Environmental Change*, ISSC/UNESCO Series: 3.

Jaiswal, P. L. (ed.) (1977) *Desertification and its Control*, New Delhi: Model Press.

Jantsch, E. (1980) *The Self Organizing Universe*, Oxford: Pergamon.

Johnson, A. (1991) *Factory Farming*, Oxford: Blackwell.

Kamenka, E. (ed.) (1979) *Justice*, London: Edward Arnold.

Kanoh, T. (1992) 'Toward dematerialization and decarbonization', in IIASA, *Science and Sustainability: Selected Papers on IIASA's 20th Anniversary*, Vienna: IIASA.

Kant, I. (1948) *The Moral Law*, London: Hutchinson.

—— (1963) *Lectures on Ethics*, New York: Harper and Row.

Karsh, E. and Rautsi, I. (1991) *Saddam Hussein: A Political Biography*, New York: The Free Press.

Kates, R. W. (1988) 'Theories of nature, society and technology', in E. Baark and U. Severin (eds) *Man, Nature and Technology: Essays on the Role of Ideological Perceptions*, London: Macmillan, 7–36.

Kellert, S. R. (1986) 'Social and perceptual factors in the preservation of animal species', in B. Norton (ed.) *The Preservation of Species*, Princeton: Princeton University Press, 50–73.

Kellert, S. R. and Westervelt, M. O. (1982) 'Historical trends in American animal use and perception', in *Transactions of the 47th North American Wildlife and Natural Resources Conference*, Washington, D.C.: Wildlife Management Institute, 649–64.

Keesing (1991) *Keesing's Contemporary Activities: Weekly Diary of Important World Events*, Bristol: Keesings Publications.

Keyfitz, N. (1992) 'Completing the worldwide demographic transition: the relevance of past experience', *Ambio* 21 (1): 26–30.

Kheel, M. (1989) 'Nature and feminist sensitivity', in T. Regan and P. Singer (eds) *Animal Rights and Human Obligations*, Englewood Cliffs: Prentice Hall.

Kleinig, J. (1991) *Valuing Life*, Princeton: Princeton University Press.

Krieger, M. H. (1970) 'Six propositions on the poor and pollution', *Policy Sciences* 1: 311–24.

Kundera, M. (1986) *The Unbearable Lightness of Being*, London: Faber and Faber.

Kuniholm, B. R. (1993) 'The US experience in the Persian Gulf', in R. F. Helms II and R. H. Dorff (eds) *The Persian Gulf Crisis*, Westpoint: Praeger.

Lang, T. and Hines, C. (1993) *The New Protectionism: Protecting the Future Against Free Trade*, London: Earthscan.

Le Grand, J. (1991) 'Equity as an economic objective', in B. Almond and D. Hill (eds) *Applied Philosophy: Morals and Metaphysics in Contemporary Debate*, London: Routledge.

Lemonick, M. D. (1990) 'Antarctica', *Time* 135 (3), 15 January: 32–8.

Leopold, A. (1949) *A Sand County Almanac*, New York: Oxford University Press.

Little, P. D. and Horowitz, M. M. with Endre Nyerges, A. (eds) (1987) *Lands at Risk in the Third World: Local Level Perspectives*, Boulder: Westview Press.

Livi-Bacci, M. (1992) *A Concise History of World Population*, Oxford: Blackwell.

Locke, J. (1963) *Two Treatises of Government*, Cambridge: Cambridge University Press.

Lopez, B. (1978) *Of Wolves and Men*, New York: Charles Scribner's Sons.

Luhmann, N. (1988) *Ecological Communication*, Cambridge: Polity Press.

McCloskey, H. J. (1983) *Ecological Ethics and Politics*, New Jersey: Rowan and Littlefield.

McCormick, J. (1989) *Global Environmental Movement: Reclaiming Paradise*, London: Bellhaven.

MacIntyre, A. (1988) *Whose Justice? Whose Rationality?*, Notre Dame, Indiana: University of Notre Dame Press.

—— (1990) *Three Rival Versions of Moral Enquiry: Encyclopaedia, Genealogy, and Tradition*, London: Duckworth.

McMichael, A. J. (1993) *Planetary Overload, Global Environmental Change and the Health of the Human Species*, Cambridge: Cambridge University Press.

McQueen, J. (1983) *The Franklin: Not Just a River*, Harmondsworth: Penguin.

Maier, J. (1991) 'Making ecologists see red', *Time*, 16 September: 60–1.

Malthus, T. (1970) *An Essay on the Principle of Population and a Summary View of the Principle of Population*, Harmondsworth: Penguin.

Mauron, Alex (1993) 'Genetics and intergenerational concerns', *Societas Ethica* Conference, Sicily.

Mayers, S. J. (ed.) (1991) *Antarctica: The Scientists' Case for a World Park*, London: Greenpeace.

Meadows, D. H. *et al.* (1972) *The Limits of Growth*, London: Pan.

Mickleburgh, E. (1988) *Beyond the Frozen Sea: Visions of Antarctica*, London: Bodley Head.

Midgley, M. (1983) *Animals and Why they Matter*, Harmondsworth: Penguin.

Mill, J. S. (1954) *Utilitarianism*, London: Dent.

Morowitz, H. J. (1991) 'Balancing species preservation and economic considerations', *Science* 253: 752–4.

Morris, D. (1977) *Manwatching*, London: Jonathan Cape.

Myers, K. (1971) 'The rabbit in Australia', in P. J. den Boer and G. R. Gradwell, *Dynamics of Populations*, Proceedings of the Advanced Study Institute on the Dynamics of Numbers in Populations (Oosterbeek), Wageningen, 478–506.

Myers, N. (1992) 'Population environment linkages: discontinuities ahead?', United Nations Expert Group Meeting on Population, Environment and Development, New York, 20–4 January 1992.

Naess, A. (1991) *Ecology, Community and Lifestyle*, Cambridge: Cambridge University Press.

Nagel, T. (1974) 'What is it like to be a bat?', *Philosophical Review* 83: 435–50.

National Academy of Sciences (1992) Report of the Committee on Population, National Research Council, 5–6 December 1991.

Nozick, R. (1975) *Anarchy, State and Utopia*, Oxford: Blackwell.

Nussbaum, M. (1990) *Love's Knowledge: Essays on Philosophy and Literature*, Oxford: Oxford University Press.

Odum, H. T. and Odum, H. C. (1976) *Energy Basis for Man and Nature*, New York: McGraw-Hill.

OECD (1991) *The State of the Environment*, Paris: OECD.

O'Neill, O. (1993) 'Justice, gender, and international boundaries', in M. Nussbaum and A. Sen (eds) *The Quality of Life*, Oxford: Clarendon Press.

Ophuls, W. and Boyan, A. S. (1992) *Ecology and the Politics of Scarcity Revisited: The Unraveling of the American Dream*, New York: W. H. Freeman and Company.

Parsons, J. (1994) 'Population, environment and policy relations: an historical overview', in B. Zaba and J. I. Clarke (eds) *Environment and Population Change*, Liège: Ordina.

Passmore, J. (1979) 'Civil justice and its rivals', in E. Kamenka (ed.) *Justice*, London: Edward Arnold.

—— (1980) *Man's Responsibility for Nature: Ecological Problems and the Western Tradition*, London: Duckworth.

Paulino, L. A. (1986) 'Food in the Third World: past trends and projections to 2000', International Food Policy Research Institute, Washington, D.C.

Pence, G. (1991) 'Virtue theory', in P. Singer (ed.) *A Companion to Ethics*, Oxford: Blackwell.

Peters, K. E. (1987) 'Humanity in nature: conserving yet creating', *Zygon* 24: 469–85.

Peterson, M. J. and Peterson, T. R. (1993) 'A rhetorical critique of "nonmarket" valuations', *Environmental Values* 2: 47–65.

Phillips, M. T. (1993) 'Savages, drunks and lab animals: the researcher's perception of pain', *Society and Animals*, 1: 61–81.

Pimental, D. *et al.* (1980) 'The potential for grass-fed livestock: resource constraints', *Science*, 22 February.

Pirages, D. C. (1977) *The Sustainable Society*, New York: Praeger.

Plato (1974) *The Republic*, Harmondsworth: Penguin.

Primoratz, I. (1989) *Justifying Legal Punishments*, Atlantic Highlands: Humanities Press.

Prigogine, I. and Stengers, I. (1984) *Order out of Chaos: Man's New Dialogue with Nature*, London: Flamingo Books.

Prosser, R. F. (1992) 'The ethics of tourism', in D. E. Cooper and J. A. Palmer (eds) *The Environment in Question: Ethics and Global Issues*, London: Routledge, 37–50.

Rachels, J. (1989) 'Why animals have a right to liberty', in T. Regan and P. Singer (eds) *Animal Rights and Human Obligations*.

Rawls, J. (1972) *A Theory of Justice*, Oxford: Oxford University Press.

—— (1981) 'Justice as reciprocity', in C. L. Reid (ed.) *Choice and Action*, New York: Macmillan.

—— (1985) 'Justice as fairness: political not metaphysical', *Philosophy and Public Affairs* 14: 223–51.

Raz, J. (1986) *The Morality of Freedom*, Oxford: Clarendon Press.

Redclift, M. (1993) 'Sustainable development: needs, values, rights', *Environmental Values* 2: 3–20.

Regan, T. (1983) *The Case for Animal Rights*, Berkeley: University of California Press.

Regan, T. and Singer, P. (eds) (1989) *Animal Rights and Human Obligations*, Englewood Cliffs: Prentice Hall.

Ricca, S. (1989) 'International migration in Africa: legal and administrative aspects', Geneva: ILO.

Richmond, A. H. (1993) 'Environmental refugees and reactive migration: a human dimension of global change', unpublished paper presented at IUSSP Congress at Montreal, August.

Ricklefs, R. E. (1990) *Ecology*, New York: W. H. Freeman and Co.

Riley, E. D. and van Liere, K. D. (1978) 'The new environmental paradigm: a proposed measuring instrument and preliminary results', *Journal of Environmental Education* 9: 10–19.

Roberts, A. (1993) 'The Gulf War and the environment', *The Oxford International Review* IV (3): 13–19.

Rollin, B. (1989) *The Unheeded Cry*, Oxford: Oxford University Press.

Rothenberg, D. (1992) 'Individual or community? Two approaches to ecophilosophy in practice', *Environmental Values* 1: 123–32.

Rowlands, I. (1992) 'The international politics of environment and development: the post UNCED agenda', *Millennium* 21 (2), summer 1992: 209–24.

RSPCA (Royal Society for the Prevention of Cruelty to Animals) (1980) *Pain and Suffering in Experimental Animals in the United Kingdom*, Horsham: RSPCA.

Ryan, A. (ed.) (1993) *Justice*, Oxford Readings in Politics and Government, Oxford: Oxford University Press.

Rybakovsky, L. (1992) 'Catastrophe in the Chernobyl atomic power station: demographic aspects'. UN Expert Group Meeting on Population, Environment and Development, New York, 20–4 January.

Ryder, R. D. (1989) *Animal Revolution: Changing Attitudes Towards Speciesism*, Oxford: Blackwell.

—— (1992) *Painism: Ethics, Animal Rights and Environmentalism*, Cardiff: University of Wales College of Cardiff.

Sagoff, M. (1988) *The Economy of the Earth: Philosophy, Law, and the Environment*, Cambridge: Cambridge University Press.

Salt, H. (1921) *70 Years Among Savages*, London: Allen and Unwin.

Schatzki, T. R. (1993) 'Theory at bay: Foucault, Lyotard and the politics of the local', in J. P. Jones, W. Natter and T. R. Schatzki (eds) *Postmodern Contentions: Epochs, Politics, Space*, New York and London: Guildford Press, 39–64.

Serpell, J. (1988) *In the Company of Animals: A Study of Human–Animal Relationships*, Oxford: Blackwell.

Shaw, R. P. (1989) 'Rapid population growth and environmental degradation: ultimate versus proximate factors', *Environmental Conservation* 16: 199–208.

Shepard, P. (1982) *Nature and Madness*, San Francisco: Sierra Club Books.

Shoard, M. (1987) *This Land is Our Land*, London: Paladin/Grafton.

Simmons, I. G. (1992) 'Roses and yew-trees', *Global Environmental Change*, 2: 329–6.

—— (1993) *Interpreting Nature: Cultural Constructions of the Environment*, London: Routledge.

Singer, P. (1975) *Animal Liberation*, New York: Avon.

—— (1993) *Practical Ethics*, Cambridge: Cambridge University Press.

Skillen, A. (1991) 'Welfare state versus welfare society?', in B. Almond and D. Hill (eds) *Applied Philosophy: Morals and Metaphysics in Contemporary Debate*, London: Routledge.

Southgate, J. (1985) *The Commonwealth Sugar Agreement*, London: C. Czarnikow Ltd.

Spraos, J. (1980) 'The statistical debate on the net barrier terms of trade between primary commodities and manufactures', *Economic Journal* 90: 107–28.

Stern, P. C., Young, O. R. and Druckman, D. (1992) *Global Environmental Change: Understanding the Human Dimensions*, Washington, D.C.: National Academy Press.

Taylor, P. W. (1986) *Respect for Nature: A Theory of Environmental Ethics*, Princeton: Princeton University Press.

Teitelbaum, M. S. and Winter, J. M. (eds) (1988) *Population and Resources in Western Intellectual Traditions*, New York: The Population Council, A Supplement to vol. 14 of *Population and Development Review*.

Tester, K. (1991) *Animals and Society: The Humanity of Animal Rights*, London: Routledge.

Tetrault, M. (1992) 'Environment and development: the crucial decade', *Development*, CIDA, spring.

Thiam, B. (1992) 'The demographic consequences of environmental degradation: impact on migratory flows and on the spatial redistribution of the population', United Nations Expert Group Meeting on Population, Environment and Development, New York, 20–4 January.

Thomas, C. (1992) *The Environment in International Relations*, London: RIIA.

Thomas, K. (1983) *Man and the Natural World: Changing Attitudes in England 1500–1800*, Harmondsworth: Penguin.

—— (1992) Introduction to C. C. W. Taylor (ed.) *Ethics and the Environment*, Oxford: Corpus Christi College.

Thompson, J. (1992) *Justice and the World Order: A Philosophical Inquiry*, London: Routledge.

Tolba, M. K. (1982) 'The United Nations Conference on Desertification: a review', *Mazingira* 6 (1): 14–23.

Treumann, R. A. (1991) 'Global problems, globalization, and predictability', *World Futures* 31: 47–53.

Tuan, Yi-Fu (1984) *Dominance and Affection: The Making of Pets*, New Haven: Yale University Press.

UNCOD (1977) *Proceedings of the United Nations Conference on Desertification*, Nairobi, 1977.

UNFPA (1991) *Populations, Resources and the Environment: The Critical Challenges*, New York, p. 154.

United Nations (1988) *World Population Prospects*, New York: United Nations.

—— (1990) *World Population Prospects*, New York: United Nations.

United Nations Population Division (1991) *Long-Range World Population Projections*, ST/ESA/SER.A/125.

US Government (1991) *Selected Major International Environmental Issues: A Briefing Book*, Report prepared for the Committee on Foreign Affairs, US House of Representatives.

US Office of Technology Assessment (1990) *International Policy Dimensions of Global Warming: US Influence and Regional Trends*, Washington, D.C.

US Supreme Court (1972) *Eisenstadt* v. *Baird*, 405, U.S. 438.

Vance, R. P. (1992) 'An introduction to the philosophical presuppositions of the Animal Liberation/Rights Movement', *Journal of the American Medical Association* 268: 1715–19.

Wallerstein, I. (1974) *The Modern World System*, New York: Academic Press.

Walzer, M. (1977) *Just and Unjust Wars*, New York: Basic Books.

—— (1983) *Spheres of Justice*, New York: Basic Books.

WCED (1987) World Commission on Environment and Development, *Our Common Future*, Oxford: Oxford University Press.

Weiss, E. B. (1989) *In Fairness to Future Generations: International Law, Common Patrimony, and Intergenerational Equity*, New York: United Nations.

Westermarck, E. (1908) *The Origin and Development of the Moral Ideas*, London: Macmillan.

Willis, R. (1990) 'The meaning of the snake', in R. Willis (ed.) *Signifying Animals*, London: Unwin Hyman, 246–52.

Wilson, E. O. (1984) *Biophilia*, Cambridge, Mass.: Harvard University Press.

—— (1989) 'Threats to biodiversity', *Scientific American* 261 (3): 60–6.

Wilson, E. O. (ed.) (1988) *Biodiversity*, Washington, D.C.: National Academy Press.

Wittgenstein, L. (1969) *Philosophical Investigations*, London: Macmillan.

World Bank, *World Population Prospects 1989–1990 Edition: Short and Long-term Estimates*, by R. A. Bulatao, E. Bos, P. W. Stephens and M. T. Vu, Baltimore and London: Johns Hopkins University Press.

Wright, D. H. (1990) 'Human impacts on energy flows through natural ecosystems, and implications for species endangerment', *Ambio*, July.

Zaba, B. and Clarke, J. I. (eds) (1994) *Environment and Population Change*, Liège: Ordina.

Zaba, B. and Scoones, I. (1994) 'Is carrying capacity a useful concept to apply to human populations?', in B. Zaba and J. I. Clarke (eds) *Environment and Population Change*, Liège: Ordina.

Index